ALSO BY VANCE H. TRIMBLE

THE UNCERTAIN MIRACLE
The History of Hyperbaric Medicine
(1974)

SCRIPPS-HOWARD HANDBOOK
Methods, Policies and People (Ed.)
(1981)

REAGAN, A Biography
Mosaic Press Classic Miniature Edition
(1982)

HEROES, PLAIN FOLKS, and SKUNKS
Autobiography of "Happy" Chandler
(1989)

FAITH IN MY STAR
Sayings of E. W. Scripps (Ed.)
(1989)

SAM WALTON
Biography of Founder of Wal-Mart
(1990)

THE ASTONISHING MR. SCRIPPS
Biography of America's Famous Penny Press Publisher
(1992)

OVERNIGHT SUCCESS
Biography of Fed Ex Founder Fred Smith
(1993)

AN EMPIRE UNDONE
Biography of "Whiz Kid" Chris Whittle
(1995)

Alice & J.F.B.

Vance H. Trimble

ALICE & J.F.B.

THE HUNDRED-YEAR SAGA
OF TWO SEMINOLE CHIEFS

Market Tech Books
Poets of America Press

Published by Market Tech Books/Poets of America Press, a division of Market Tech Associates, Inc. 1304 Hilltop Avenue, Wilmington, DE 19809 First Edition, 2006

Manufactured in the United States of America by Thomson-Shore, Inc., Dexter, Michigan

Library of Congress Cataloging-in-Publication Data

Trimble, Vance H.- 1st ed.
Alice & J.F.B.: The hundred-year saga of two Seminole chiefs
p cm.
1. Davis, Alice Brown-biography 2. Brown, John F.-biography
3. Chiefs-Seminoles 4. Indians-Seminoles

ISBN 0-9705399-4-0 (alk. paper)
I. Title

Jacket painting "Seminole Woman Day-dreaming" and title page sketch by Dolores Cary
Book design by Richard Ellwanger and Vance Trimble
Contributing photographer: Jacklyn Patterson
Production consultants: Patsy Willcox and Emmy Ezzell

Remembering jejune days as cub
reporter on the *Wewoka Times-Democrat*
and my lucky discovery in Wewoka High
journalism class of my marvelous sweetheart
of a lifetime, Elzene (1912-1999)

CONTENTS

Acknowledgements

Diligent research led me fortunately to three little-known or obscure collections of personal information about the Davis and Brown families that give this book its close-up flavor of the intimacy of their lives.

These are the Garrard Ardeneum in McAlester, Oklahoma, established by Alice Brown Davis's granddaughter, the late Aleece Locke Garrard; the private collection assembled by Alice's great grandson, Eugene C. Aldridge II, with the enormous help of his wife Martha, and maintained in their home at Richardson, Texas; and at the SEMINOLE NATION MUSEUM in Wewoka, Oklahoma, several hundred Brown and Davis family papers, photographs and artifacts not all of which have yet been removed from random cardboard boxes and properly sorted and catalogued.

Most valuable resource is the Garrard Ardeneum. Aleece, a person of merit and wealth, began the Ardeneum collection with intention of writing a biography of her grandmother to validate the latter's fame and accomplishments. It grew into an extensive and important repository of family data. The material encompasses not only the Browns and Davises, but Aleece's Choctaw ancestors and their exciting adventures on the Indian frontier.

The Ardeneum occupies two residential buildings in McAlester maintained by a charitable foundation set up by Mrs. Garrard. The documents, books, and photographs have been masterfully arranged in archival boxes by Francine Locke Bray of Indianapolis, who is a Locke descendant. She was enormously helpful in guiding my research in the Ardeneum, as well as elsewhere, and knows perhaps more than any other person about these families. Not normally open to the public, the Ardeneum is, however, accessible to scholars.

Gene and Martha Aldridge have for fifteen or twenty years valiantly researched family history and genealogy, starting with Dr. Brown's life. They gathered a ton of information. Martha is an accomplished and indefatigable genealogist, and could put her finger on nearly every twist and turn in this scenario. I conferred with them at their home in Richardson on the outskirts of Dallas. They graciously made available everything they had collected—tribe rolls, census reports, birth and death records, newspaper clippings, photographs, books, magazines, journals, and family memoirs. We spent hours discussing the ups and downs of their investigations, their notes and recollections of conversations within the family in which Dr. Brown and Lucy described dramatic events that illuminated their early years. These oral memoirs, passed down through several generations, make possible factual recreation of dramatic episodes that enliven the story telling. I am deeply indebted to the Aldridges for friendship and assistance.

The popular and well-run SEMINOLE NATION MUSEUM is by far the tribe's best historical resource. It was established by the citizens of Wewoka, and is not an official function of the Seminole Nation. It displays outstanding exhibits that attract thousands of visitors annually. As with civic efforts in many small towns, the SEMINOLE NATION MUSEUM has budget constraints that have not permitted sorting the Brown letters, photographs and artifacts in their storage; that would be a mission of worth for some philanthropist. Richard Ellwanger, the executive director, threw wide the museum doors and co-operated with great generosity and offered cogent guidance and counsel. The same is true of his associate Lewis Johnson.

In this book's notes and bibliography, material from the Garrard Ardeneum is identified as "Brown-Locke-Davis Family Papers"; information provided by Gene and Martha Aldridge is labeled "Aldridge Files"; and data found in the SEMINOLE NATION MUSEUM is labeled as "Brown-Davis Family Miscellany."

An easily accessible gold mine of Indian and Oklahoma history, covering many exciting eras and a wide range of personalities and episodes, is available in the Oklahoma Historical Society's *Chronicles of Oklahoma*. Reading a hundred or so of these enlightening articles vastly broadened my knowledge of the frontier times. While a bit tedious, it proved valuable to dig into newspaper files from Indian Territory and Oklahoma Territory.

I owe much to the diligence and intellect of Josh Clough, a young graduate assistant at Western History Collections at the University of Oklahoma. Sleuthing in musty Government records, Josh unearthed reams of material giving fresh insight into these families, in particular correcting serious errors in previously published accounts of Dr. Brown's military experiences.

At the Oklahoma Historical Society I received generous help from William Welge, director of the research division. The Konawa Genealogy Society of the Kennedy Library, Inc. of Seminole County at Konawa, Oklahoma has a large data bank on Seminole Indians. It was not only opened to me but its creator, Dr. Arthur M. Kennedy, and three charming operatives, Barbara C. Jones, Anita Hancock Rannels, and June Nichols Neal, graciously pursued every clue that showed promise.

For helpful information or advice I also thank Glenn Sharpe of Wewoka, a grandson of Seminole Chief Chili Fish; Judy Dotson of Tulsa, Oklahoma and Lufkin, Texas; Dr, Clara Reekie, former curator of The Five Civilized Tribes Museum at Muskogee, Oklahoma; Shirley Pettengill of Park Hill, Oklahoma; Carolyn Trimble, librarian, Wewoka Public Library; Margaret Kymes of Muskogee, Oklahoma; Mary Ann Norman, Wewoka High School librarian; Kay Carter, associate director, Waring Historical Library, Medical University of South Carolina, Charleston; William M. Straight, M. D., Miami, Florida; Bonnie Crawford, former librarian, Public Library at Okemah, Oklahoma; Susan Allison Miller of Arizona State University, Tempe, Arizona, and Joycette Griffis of Arlington, Texas, and Gerald Eugene Davis of Chico, California, the last-named three being direct descendants of the Brown family.

For advice and counsel I am much indebted to noted historical scholars and archivists: Dr. Daniel Littlefield, Jr., of the University of Arkansas at North Little Rock, Arkansas; Don DeWitt, curator, the Western History Collections at the University of Oklahoma, Norman; and Dr. Patricia Wickman of the Florida Seminoles, Hollywood, Florida.

In the late stages of this work, when a personal handicap intervened, John Laakman of the Veterans Administration Medical Center in Oklahoma City was a savior. He shepherded me into the VA impaired vision program and supplied devices and medical help that permitted me to complete paginating the manuscript on the computer. John is kind and dedicated.

Others who made major contributions to this book include Dolores Cary, the award-winning sculptor who created the bronze statues for Elzene's *Singing Tower* in Oakwood Cemetery in her Surrey Hills studio at Yukon, Oklahoma. She granted use of her intriguing oil portrait "Seminole Woman Day-dreaming," an apt depiction of aspiring females in Indian Territory days, as the dust cover illustration and also painted the title page sketch.

Creating the electronic graphics and text files for the printer was an extraordinary personal accomplishment of Richard Ellwanger's artistic and entrepreneurial skills. He also co-designed the book.

With diligent care, Tara Sheffield, a Wewoka high school cheerleader and my writer apprentice, copy-read the computer pagination.

Friends at the University of Oklahoma Press graciously responded to our plea for technical manufacturing guidance. Emmy Ezzell, assistant director/production manager, and Patsy Willcox, who retired as production manager at the end of 2005, helped us conquer the jungle of intricacies to successfully convert computer manuscript and graphics into a hardcover book. Patsy and Emmy are peerless in their field. They also enlisted their University Press colleagues who did the tricky conversion of footnotes to end notes, namely: Alice Stanton, managing editor; Steven Baker, assistant managing editor; and Jennifer Abercrombie, editorial assistant.

And, finally, a Mount Vesuvius effusion of my deepest love for our daughter Carol Ann, who has never failed to support and enhance her daddy's endeavors, and who is the publisher of this book through her communications company in Delaware.

Foreword

Of sixty thousand Indians from five tribes uprooted in the 1830's from their Southern homes by the Government and cruelly herded into America's western wilderness, nothing historically significant should have been anticipated from one unknown girl among the Seminole émigrés. Yet *Kúnu Hvt'kē* (White Skunk) was a child of destiny.

Out of the Florida Everglades, this naïve teenager brought an astounding legacy. It was that in the new land, two of her half-white half-Indian children, a son and a daughter, would each rise to become Principal Chief of the Seminole Nation.

Her story is an enthralling narrative of romance and adventure in the combative Indian country upheaval. The pioneer saga resonates in the present as an exceptionally personal day-to-day close-up of long ago triumph and heartbreak. *Kúnu Hvt'kē's* legacy was to exert influence on her tribe for a long period; it spanned much of eight decades, from Lincoln to F.D.R.

The oddest quirks of Fate guided her footsteps. Especially in the chance meeting during a blizzard with Dr. John Frippo Brown, the twenty-years-older Army surgeon who wooed and won her. Their happy marriage produced eight children, the foremost being John Frippo Brown Jr. and Alice. Alice would go down in history as the first female Indian chief in the West.

This is an extended biography that encompasses the lives of the entire family, a story largely ignored by historians and here recounted fully for the first time. Both John F. Junior and Alice were as Destiny-driven as their mother. Close examination of their human needs and limitations reveals their inner feelings—accomplishments, admiration, aggression, anger and affections. And is the more honest, candid and compelling precisely because of such inquisitiveness. Their lives are in marked contrast. Chief John F. Brown was highly regarded for his Christianity, literary knowledge, financial skill, courage, vision, and leadership. Chief Alice Brown Davis, equally loyal to her people, was energetic, intelligent, and ultra compassionate, but bogged down and haunted by endless tragedy in her own household.

This saga runs through the years of interminable oppression of the Seminoles and other tribes by the Presidents and the Congresses, the Civil War, the deadly outrages of whiskey and outlaws, controversy and struggle over statehood for Oklahoma, the oil boom that spawned illiterate Indian millionaires, and finally the Great "dust bowl" Depression.

Writing this book took three years of steady research, but the endeavor fortunately brought to light much fresh data. Hard digging uncovered a new trove of this family's correspondence, memoirs, oral histories, and "lost" diaries. This fascinating material was enhanced by interviews with living Brown descendants tracked down across the country.

Newspapers, journals, magazines and books of their time, and since, have perpetuated many errors of fact regarding them. In the main those are here corrected. This book goes beyond the prism of legend and folklore, and presents in accurate and vivid detail the entire cast of characters created by the legacy of *Kúnu Hvt'kē* and reveals the two chiefs as ardent and mettlesome stalwarts of our long ago times.

Vance Trimble
January 9, 2006
at Wewoka

Alice & J.F.B.

1

Red Threads of Destiny

ON A MUGGY morning in late June 1836, John Frippo Brown, M.D., pensive and uncertain, arrived in the port of New Orleans on a schooner from Charleston, South Carolina. At age thirty-six, Dr. Brown was ripping apart his old life. Abruptly, he had abandoned his splendid practice as physician to wealthy aristocrats in Charleston. He had come to Louisiana to plunge into dangerous adventure as a contract surgeon for the United States Army.

He and fellow passengers coming on deck found the waterfront jangling with bustle and tumult. Close by clustered Mississippi River steamboats, most with red paddlewheels and decks bordered by ornate white filigree. Two or three stern-wheelers maneuvered near the schooner, their eighty-foot tall stacks belching raven plumes. Hoarse steamboat whistles set ears atingle.

Dr. Brown could hear and feel a hum, the alacritous vigor of the Crescent City. The atmosphere of New Orleans touched all senses. The nose detected quaint and exotic smells, dominated by the moist aroma of coffee roasting in not-too-distant commercial ovens. On shore rose mournful strains of a throaty chorus from slave-gangs struggling and sweating to load or unload cotton bales. In busy times, sailors told the passengers, 50,000 bales might lie on the wharves. On a boom, New Orleans now verged on becoming the third largest city in America.

Dr. Brown directed porters to carry his trunk ashore. Then he picked up his black satchel, and briskly followed down the gangplank. To Louisiana he had come to deliberately distance himself from his past, bringing only his skill as a healer. He had been successful, admired, and prosperous in South Carolina's most demanding metropolis. Something changed him, something drastic and sudden. Exactly what, he did never explain.

Near the wharf, Dr. Brown hailed a carriage.

"Fort Pike," he told the driver. "First, take me through the *Vieux Carré*." [1]

Travelers returning to Charleston had intrigued him with lusty tales of vigorous and exotic Creole life in the French Quarter. He must visit Royal Street, with its Old World ambiance of cafes, hotels, banks, and resplendent shops. Perhaps he would chance to see Bernard de Marigny, the quixotic Creole millionaire known to spend more money, offend more people and fight more duels than anyone in New Orleans.

When his carriage turned off Rampart Street into *Rue d'Amour* (Love Street), Dr. Brown may have thought of his own shattered home life, some tragedy involving his young wife Mary and the inexplicable death, at about five or six, of their curly haired blue-eyed little daughter Clara. In some major way, he had become a disappointment to his family. His brothers Robert and James and sisters Martha and Isabella were treating him virtually as an outcast. [2] It is not clear to this day what went wrong.

The *Scottish* Browns of Charleston occupied upper class prominence as merchants, planters and professionals. Martha had married a Shackelford who owned a 1,000-acre plantation and eighty-five slaves. John Frippo's parents were immigrants from Paisley on The Clyde, Scotland. Their utmost ambition had been that he go back across the Atlantic to the distinguished University of Edinburgh for his medical education. Instead, he had chosen the just-opened Medical College of South Carolina. His extensive course ran from 1827 through 1829. His preceptor was the esteemed Dr. Francis Yonge Porcher, only thrity-nine, but affable and renowned for his knowledge of anatomy. [3]

Not unlike the fashionable gallants he now saw sauntering the languid streets of the *Vieux Carré*, the physician from Charleston was himself well-turned out. Thick-chested, he was reasonably tall, ruddy-cheeked, with a serious mien, unblinking deep-set azure eyes. Habitually he would sit erect in a carriage, perhaps smoothing the black velvet collar of his stylish linen coat. In questioning the driver, his tone would be quick, firm. He had rather thin lips, teeth with an alabaster gleam, a narrow handsome nose. His fingers were long and tapered, obviously strong. [4]

At Fort Pike, a corporal escorted Dr. Brown along the promenade. The sultry breeze stirred Spanish moss dripping from a line of fat oaks. He was led under the mouths of thirteen cannon jutting from arched brick casemates, and into the office of the commandant, Major J. Mountfort.

Their meeting was formal, stiff, and brisk, Dr. Brown would later recall. [5] Major Mountfort's curt manner came as no surprise. Back in Charleston, Dr. Brown became aware that the United States Army set extremely rigid standards for physicians entering its Medical Department. Of twenty-two candidates for commissions as Army Surgeon recently examined in New York, only five were accepted. Short of career military surgeons, the Army recruited citizen physicians, who were available, qualified and willing to accept temporary duty. With a license from a respected medical university, Dr. Brown faced no challenge on competency.

However, the Fort Pike commandant promptly raised one critical question. Did his visitor possess complete surgical instruments, specifically saws and knives for amputation, lancets, probes? Pointedly, Major Mountfort said Dr. Brown was required to furnish his own instruments. "Otherwise the Government must provide them—at your expense." [6]

Knowing this stipulation, Dr. Brown was not fazed. He lifted his black satchel onto the major's desk and opened it for inspection, nodding affirmatively.

The major seated his visitor at a desk, on which were paper and pen. At the commandant's dictation, Dr. Brown wrote this employment agreement:

This contract entered into this 22nd day of June 1836 at Fort Pike, New Orleans, between Major J. Mountfort and Dr. John

5

F. Brown of Charleston, South Carolina. Witnesseth that for the consideration hereafter mentioned the said Dr. John F. Brown promises and agrees to perform the duties of an assistant surgeon, agreeably to the Army Regulations at Fort Pike. And the said Major J. Mountfort promises and agrees on behalf of the United States to pay, or cause to be paid, to the said Dr. John F. Brown the sum of one hundred dollars for each and every month, or at that rate, he shall continue to perform the services above stated, which shall be his full compensation and in lieu of all allowances and emoluments whatever. This contract to continue in force during the pleasure of the parties.

John Frippo Brown, M. D. signed. So did the major, and affixed his seal. His adjutant folded the document and later shoved it into the dispatch pouch going to the Surgeon General in Washington City.

Outwardly, this Fort Pike contract appears to signal no more than a hasty interlude of adventure for the South Carolinian. It became much, much more. Not even Dr. Brown on that June day could have remotely foreseen how temporarily committing his medical skill to the military would dramatically alter his entire future, and eventually affect in a major way the course of Indian history on the western frontier. Certainly, he would have been astounded at this juncture to know that one of his sons and one daughter, both yet to be born, were destined to become Indian tribal chiefs.

ON THIS SAME JUNE DAY, a thousand miles away in the treacherous Everglades of Florida, the moccasin-clad feet of a frightened Seminole girl were madly trampling her own and Dr. Brown's red threads of destiny.

The Indian girl was running for her life. In pursuit came a dozen or so United States Army mounted troopers. They rode hard but their horses' erratic gait over the swampy terrain wrecked their aim, sending most rifle shots harmlessly wild.

Of this slender maiden, Dr. Brown knew nothing. At this moment, not even that she existed; nor of her dangerous plight; certainly not the slightest inkling that eschatology entwined them. *Man's Fate is born from the womb of time.* The Charleston physician, having

6

read the ancient philosophers, was a believer in Lachesis. *We can do nothing, can know nothing.* He readily accepted *ipse dixit*, that the red thread of destiny is unbreakable. *Our life skein is preordained.*

The Indian girl kept running. A bullet whistled dangerously close. Fleeing with her were ten or fifteen other Seminole women and children. Out gathering berries, they were startled when the soldiers rode into view. Assuredly they were keenly aware that the Government had re-opened its off-and-on campaign to conquer all the Seminoles in Florida, intending to forcibly remove all survivors from their ancient homeland and herd them out to the untamed frontier west of the Mississippi River. [7] The berry-pickers had been surprised because the Army's renewed assault on the Seminoles had started mainly in the north, not near the secluded camps these natives inhabited around Lake Okeechobee.

The Indians raced toward their nearest protection, the rampant saw grass. By plunging into this four-foot high foliage, they could hide—and escape. They knew secret trails through the swamp; the soldiers did not. Almost certainly, the Indians would lose blood from cuts and scrapes inflicted by the cruel teeth of the saw grass, but wasn't that better than taking a bullet?

In childhood, John Frippo Brown had been only obliquely aware of what was called "the Indian problem." He recalled listening to agitated conversation by his South Carolina elders about slave escapes. Plantation owners expressed outrage that the runaways were welcomed in Florida by the Seminole tribe, which gave the Negroes safe haven.

As he grew up, he realized the President and Congress considered this complex issue larger, and more drastic and urgent than merely a question of slave havens in Florida. The Indians simply were in the way of civilization. For centuries they occupied and controlled vast domains along the East coast. The natives tied up thousands of square miles of lush and fertile land primarily to assure themselves enormous territory for nomadic hunting and fishing. The growth of the new nation was thwarted by such an obstacle. The solution decided on by the powers in Washington was to uproot all the Indian tribes in four states—Alabama, Georgia, Tennessee, and Florida—and move them out. That would open land into which white settlers could come, and would tame the wilderness, and push the American frontier westward. The government would write treaties and would compensate the tribes, financially and otherwise, for their lost homelands, and then take the Indians west and resettle them on the virgin plains beyond the Mississippi and Arkansas Rivers. This tactic would likewise put to good use at least the fringes of the 800,000 square miles that doubled the size of the United States when President Thomas Jefferson doled out $15 million for the fortunate Louisiana Purchase.

The Indian tribes, not unexpectedly, declined to surrender their homes, their traditions, and the land that held the bones of their ancestors, and provided their sustenance. They would not hear of moving. When negotiations broke down, the Government turned bellicose. The tribes must submit to eviction, or be exterminated! That stalemate led in Florida to decades of conflict and battle, much of the most crucial warfare pushed in the 1830s under President Andrew Jackson. Eventually the federal government would conquer the Seminoles, but at the cost of the lives of 1,500 United States soldiers, and loss of $30,000,000 in property.

American generals found this war much different from normal combat. The elusive Seminole warriors rarely stood and fought. Their better understanding of the quirkiness of the Florida terrain augmented their cunning and trickery. They could suddenly emerge and massacre a hundred soldiers before a sentry uttered a warning cry. The continuing warfare was vicious. Government troops and envoys, traders, slave-hunters, and many settlers were killed. Scalps were taken. Few Indians were caught or killed. But the bulk of the oppressed tribe, about 5,000 Seminoles and their Negro slaves, were hammered back into the Everglades where they long eluded capture.

President Jackson's administration had persuaded some tribes—Creeks, Chickasaw, Choctaw, finally some of the Cherokees—to move. But this migration to the western frontier was achieved by Washington's devious and false promises, as well as bribes, and numerous pitched battles, massacres, assassinations, and scalping. Neither the white nor red men were happy with the resultant situation.

The Seminoles resisted, and refused to be bought off. Their chiefs vowed to defend their homeland to the death, and were doing so.

Caught up in all of this as a hapless victim, the running Indian girl was a blurry will-o-the-wisp. Slender, agile and growing tall, she at this time is fourteen or fifteen, and comely. She is full blood Seminole. Her hair is exceptionally dark, brushed to a radiant gleam, parted in the middle, and braided to hang down her back. She has wide brown eyes that dominate her roundish face. They open like windows to reveal in their depths an intelligent alertness, the flash of courage and daring, and latent wisdom beyond her years. Her name is *Kúnu Hvt'kē* which translates in English to White Skunk.

Eventually her tribe was to be captured, stripped of all possessions—ponies, cattle, hogs, farming tools. Left weak, battered and tattered, impoverished, these Indians would be rounded up and marched to Fort Brooke at Tampa Bay on Florida's west coast, and locked up under guard. Finally the captive Seminole families would be callously herded like so much livestock and forced to make the long, anguishing, and deadly water and land journey to Indian Territory.

Even though Dr. Brown was not yet aware that White Skunk existed, the red threads of their destinies were slowly and inexorably moving toward each other. Fate would bring them face to face out on the raw new Indian frontier during a once-in-a-million medical emergency triggered by a raging blizzard.

IN HIS QUARTERS at Fort Pike, Dr. Brown would go to his desk, light the lamp, sit down, and reach for a fresh quill pen. From a copious paper stack he would take a clean sheet. Writing was his frequent nightly ritual. [8]

During the daytime he was busy doctoring the 100-man Marine Corps battalion assigned to him. Every week or so he found time to venture into New Orleans' cosmopolitan scene. He dined in the majestic St. Charles hotel, attended both *grande* and *comique* operas at the Théâtre d'Orleans.

An avid reader, he scoured bookstalls for Charles Dickens and other contemporary authors. He kept an eye out for books by Balzac, Hawthorne, Thomas Carlyle, Alfred Lord Tennyson, Victor Hugo and Stendhal.

But he chiefly was interested in medical journals and books. He had stacks of them in his room at Fort Pike, the pages dog-eared. He was reading like mad—and taking every opportunity to write just as furiously.

One night he closely examined the nib of his pen. It was made from a goose feather. He dipped it in the silver ink well. He thought a moment and then, centering the words at the top of the page, he wrote:

Phthisis Pulmonalts

Dr. Brown was in the early stages of writing a book on medicine. [9] In fact, it probably would spread into two volumes. He estimated his manuscript could run as much as a thousand pages. He intended this work to cover current procedures known in both Europe and the United States. He kept up with new techniques by regularly reading the latest medical journals. And his own experience had been wide-ranging. He would utilize that. (Many years later he would sit and go over these very pages with his children. His hand-written manuscript would survive to be bequeathed to his great grandchildren, and they in 2003 would donate a copy to the Oklahoma Historical Society.)

After considering the best opening for his treatise on tuberculosis of the lung (*phthisis pulmonalis*), he wrote:

> This is a subject upon which I enter with very little satisfaction. Confessedly there is no disease involved in such obscurity and no one in which our art so often fails as in ulcers of the lungs.
>
> An ulcerated state of the lungs constitutes the worst form of pulmonary consumption, and its cure rendered tedious if not impossible from the parenchymatous from the constant exposure of the ulcer to the air, and by the motion of the lungs, constantly tearing the parts asunder.
>
> But we know that wounds of the lungs often do heal, hence it follows that obstacles to the cure proceed in a great measure from the altered and morbid action of these organs. But I believe the great mortality of the disease is owing partly to our own inattention. [10]

Here he seemed to pause and think through how he wanted to continue. He wrote a series of side notes. He expressed his own opinion that tuberculosis frequently is triggered by "sedentary occupations, particularly by those requiring bent positions of the body, by exposure to heat, the inhalation of acrid and irritating particles, playing on wind instruments, the forcible employment of the voice, as in preaching, debauchery, the suppression of any of the ordinary evacuations, as the menses or hoemorrhoids." [11]

Physicians of his time were testing many vapours as inhalants to cure consumption. He intended to write about and evaluate experiments with sulphuric ether, tolu, turpentine, tobacco, and tar baked over a fire. None seemed successful. However, he read of an extremely startling treatment undertaken by one of his medical "heroes," Dr. Philip Syng Physick of Philadelphia, the world-famous "father of American surgery."

Dr. Physick had required one of his T.B. patients to inhale the vapour of unwashed sheep wool. [12] That worked for Dr. Physick—but one time only. "It is so unpleasant and so often failed, that it is no more used," Dr. Brown wrote. Another tuberculosis sufferer was forced to live with cows. "Absurd as this may seem, two or three cases are said to be cured by it."

Another experiment doubtless had him wagging his head in wonderment, as he wrote:

> Among other projects for the cure of this disease it has been recommended to dig a hole in the earth and place the patient in it with his head out. This I saw tried when I was in Edinburgh, but so far from proving useful, it uniformly aggravated the disease by inducing catarrh. [13]

In the 1830s physicians did not yet have the ubiquitous stethoscope. Nor laboratory microscopes. Clinical thermometers were rare. The Army had only about 20 in its entire Medical Department. To diagnose fever, doctors customarily felt to see whether the patient's skin was moist or dry. They also examined tongue, eyes, ears, and checked on the bowels.

His research for his "Theraputics" book gave John Frippo Brown hints of a coming sea change in medical practice. But likewise strongly reinforced his belief that physicians of his day were eminently correct in establishing as their essential and primary treatment—bleeding the patient!

From his first days as a medical student, he recognized the efficacy of venesection, also called phlebotomy. Blood-letting, he knew, had for centuries—before the time of Hippocrates—been considered a tried and true remedy for certain illnesses. Specifically for fevers, inflammations, a variety of disease conditions. Ironically, it was also at times resorted to for hemorrhage. Over the years the procedure became controversial, and fell in and out of favor.

But the celebrated physicians he personally knew, such as Dr. Physick, relied heavily on venesection in a variety of situations. Whatever Dr. Physick undertook was acceptable to Dr. Brown. While still a medical school student, he had managed, through Charleston colleagues, to meet the famous University of Pennsylvania surgeon. Dr. Brown kept track of Dr. Physick's successful career, could understand why he had VIP clients, wealth, fame.

The Philadelphia surgeon was also willing to take personal risks. Dr. Physick was stricken in 1793 with yellow fever. At the same time his colleague, Dr. Benjamin Rush, "the father of American psychiatry," fell ill with the same disease. Daringly and courageously, they decided to bleed each other. They did and, survived. [14]

Not every move by Dr. Physick produced medical magic. He was called to Washington in June 1833 to treat President Andrew Jackson. The President had started bleeding in the lungs, believed the aftermath of two bullets taken in old duels. Dr. Physick considered the situation and decided to try venesection. It was not the ailing President's lucky day; he got no relief.

One year later, Dr. Physick operated successfully on Chief Justice John Marshall, then in his seventies, who suffered a gall bladder attack. The surgeon removed 1,000 gallstones. Another of his VIP patients was the charming White House hostess, Dolley Payne Todd Madison, wife of the fourth President.

Physicians made up their own guidelines on how much blood to draw. Dr. Brown's limits ranged anywhere from six ounces to one and one-half pounds of blood. For many an evening, his quill pen illuminated wide-ranging facets of bloodletting. He wrote about the necessary lancets and cups, the best places to find a vein (wrists) or artery (forehead). He described situations to be avoided, as well as detailing successful procedures.

Writing his book proved no easy task. He could heft the stack of pages he had produced, and mentally catalog subjects yet to be covered. With luck the manuscript would be finished, he calculated, in perhaps two years.

Before beginning the evening's labor by lamplight, he would often take a break to compose his thoughts, as he later recalled to his family. [15] That gave him opportunity to sharpen a feather into a new quill pen, or twiddle with an old one. At times he would ponder this new life that stretched out before him, uncertain and unknowable. Conversely, in dreams his thoughts surely wandered back to Charleston, and the agonizing past. If memories of the heartbreak involving Mary and little Clara left him shaken, from his subconscious might have emerged a maxim he had read years ago and often quoted as essential truth—man was but a mere speck on the axle of the universe.

AFTER TWELVE MONTHS at New Orleans, Dr. Brown catapulted himself into the intensifying Indian war in Florida by accepting a new contract to go to Fort Brooke at Tampa Bay. [16] He arrived just as Colonel Zachary Taylor took command of the Florida campaign against the Seminoles, succeeding General Thomas Jesup, who had both failed to win the war and worn himself out.[17] Taylor, fifty-three, had thirty-one distinguished years in the Army that included the War of 1812 and Indian fighting. "General Jessup's [sic] instructions left Taylor free to plan his own campaign, but carried one explicit order: to destroy or capture the Seminole Indians." [18]

By December, Taylor had his force of 1,100 mounted soldiers ready for action. The Seminoles reportedly were gathering for a final stand near Lake Okeechobee. Their leaders, Wild Cat (*Coacoochee)* and Sam Jones (*Arpeika)*, were known as fierce fighters. On December 19, 1837, Taylor marched out to attack the Indians at Okeechobee. With the troops went mule-drawn Army ambulances and Dr. Brown and two other assistant surgeons.

John Frippo Brown was on the verge of seeing in one hour's time more bloody wounds than he had encountered in all his years of Charleston practice. [19]

As Taylor advanced, Wild Cat and Sam Jones fell back, avoiding a battle, luring the U.S. troops into the difficult swampy, forested regions. On Christmas morning, the Seminoles hid in dense timber, being split in three groups and well protected. Taylor's men would be forced to advance through a swamp with saw grass four or five feet tall. "Here, on a battleground selected by wiliest of the Seminole leaders and between forces vastly unequal in their firing power, the hardest battle of the Seminole War was fought." [20]

Taylor left horses and baggage under guard and sent his men ahead on foot into the saw grass. They were met by a blast of destructive gunfire. The first volley killed Colonel Gentry; in confusion, troops fell back; twenty-three other soldiers quickly fell. Lieutenant Colonel Thompson moved up five companies of the Sixth Infantry trying to encircle the hidden Indians. They were stymied by the swamp, and held up. Thompson fell, mortally wounded; one company had but four men not hit by Indian bullets.

Though it was later learned that Wild Cat and Sam Jones had a mere four hundred warriors, the fierce firefight would rage for three hours.

In a reasonably well-protected cabbage-tree hummock, Dr. Brown had set up his field aid station. Stretcher-bearers stumbled in with dead and wounded. First arrival was a soldier who suffered a hatchet blow that took off one ear, and half his face; one eyeball dangled. Not much could be done, as Dr. Brown recalled in later years. The wounded man screamed a few minutes, moaned, gasped, and lapsed into eternal silence. [21]

Then came two infantrymen from the Sixth whose chests had been pierced by musket balls. They could hardly breathe, coughed violently, and spit blood. Each was given thirty or forty drops of laudanum, and their gaping wounds dressed; but their chance of survival was nil.

A trooper from the Fourth was hit by a ball that fractured his upper right arm. He was a luckier casualty—he would live. Dr. Brown had the rifleman's clothing cut away, and his arm washed. Two stewards applied a tourniquet below the right shoulder, and stretched out the wounded arm and held it steady.

There was going to be pain—a lot. Use of anesthesia was still a few years away. Surgeons could only rely on oral morphine and laudanum, rum and whiskey to partially knock out their patient. Still worse, they yet didn't know to use antiseptics.

With a razor-sharp knife, Dr. Brown severed the skin and muscles to the bone, took from his kit a saw, and using his thumb as a guide quickly cut the humerus. He tied off the blood vessels, checked to ascertain there was no excess bleeding. Then the wound was closed, over a wad of lint, with adhesive straps.

Dr. Brown's table dripped blood for several hours. One hundred twelve soldiers were wounded, and twenty-six killed. The Indians escaped, leaving dead only nine Seminoles and one Negro.

In those times, before the advent of ether and chloroform, the chest and abdomen were considered off limits to surgeons. However, these battlefield physicians did believe that when a soldier was shot, any musket ball must be removed, if at all possible. Often that meant using a scalpel to murderously widen a wound so the surgeon could insert his thumb and forefinger—without surgical gloves—to extract the lead pellet.

During the Florida campaigns, one weary surgeon walked into the officers' mess tent. As he greeted the commander, he fumbled in his pocket. He slammed his fist down on the table and musket balls rolled out. "General, here's nineteen. Not a bad morning's work!" [22]

THE FLORIDA WARS brought a dozen or more Seminoles into prominence as cunning and dangerous fighters. Among the foremost was the handsome half-blood named Osceola, about thirty, slender, five-ten, with a strong yen for finery. He was fluent, as well as eloquent, in the white man's tongue, being the son of an Englishman. Though not a chief, he was a respected leader with a loyal following.

About a year before Dr. Brown came to Florida, Osceola and a small warrior band committed numerous murders. Just outside Fort King, his band hid in the woods waiting until the prominent Government Indian agent Wiley Thompson came out for a stroll. They riddled him with fourteen bullets, and put two shots in the lieutenant with him. Then they rushed to the sutler's house, killed him, and two clerks. The dead were scalped. There was no doubt it was Osceola's work; friendly Indians inside Fort King recognized his distinctive war whoop.

Months later when the Seminoles agreed to undertake negotiations for peace. Osceola, coming under a white flag, met at Fort Peyton with General Joseph Hernandez. Suspecting Osceola was merely spying, the Army ignored the truce, sprang a trap and took prisoner all the Indians. Along with a few sub chiefs, the captives included Osceola's two wives and two of his children. Initially, all were locked up at St. Augustine. Later, for safekeeping, the prisoners were transferred by ship to South Carolina's Fort Moultrie on Sullivan Island in Charleston harbor.

In that military prison occurred one of the most bizarre episodes in the war against the Florida Seminoles.

George Catlin, the celebrated painter, was putting on canvas hundreds of vistas and personalities that would become world-famous. When Catlin learned that Osceola was at Fort Moultrie, he went there and the notorious prisoner posed for his portrait. The Seminole leader was seriously ill and weak from a long siege of malaria. He was, in fact, dying, and knew it. However, he sat several days for the artist, decked out in full regalia with rifle, knife and feathered headdress. [23] Less than a week after the painting was finished, on January 29, 1838, Osceola died.

Dr. Frederick Weedon had, as military physician at the fort, been attending the prisoner. He insisted that he would personally prepare the Indian's body for burial, and took charge. For reasons never explained, the physician worked in secret, and alone closed the coffin lid. Osceola was buried on the fort grounds.

The reason for Dr. Weedon's secrecy was not disclosed at that time. Years later in the window of his drugstore in St. Augustine a large glass specimen jar was put on display.

It contained Osceola's head! [24]

A BELLYACHE suffered by General Winfield Scott was obliquely responsible for ending at the end of a single year Dr. Brown's stay at Fort Brooke. In early June 1838, Scott was visiting the Florida fort to discuss the Indian removal when he suffered a stomach cramp. Dr. Brown was summoned to treat him.

Whatever therapy Dr. Brown used gave relief, and apparently impressed Scott. Because of his attention to detail and a penchant for gaudy uniforms, Scott was known as "Old Fuss and Feathers." He was, however, highly regarded for his military skill.

In their sickroom conversation, General Scott revealed that he had just been designated by President Martin Van Buren to handle removal of the Cherokees. That would require him to assemble troops, set up several new forts, arrange transportation for the Indians, and also engage physicians to care for the tribal emigrants and his soldiers.

General Scott offered the physician employment as the contract Army assistant surgeon for one of his battalions. [25]

A change of scenery and the challenge of travel to the Western frontier appealed to Dr. Brown. He accepted General Scott's offer,[26] and prepared to ride horseback into the middle of Tennessee. On Wednesday, June 22, 1838, he arrived at Fort Cass on the Chickamauga River, near the present town of Charleston, Tennessee.

At first glimpse Fort Cass stunned him. He instantly realized he had made a very bad mistake. By no stretch of the imagination could this be called a legitimate United States Army fort; notwithstanding that it bore the name of Secretary of War Lewis Cass. It was nothing more than a miserable jerrybuilt stockade. To his eye it looked as though a bunch of rustics had been hired to cut trees, dig holes, and stand the logs upright to form the walls, and do little else. Describing Fort Cass later, he recalled: "Not fit for cattle. Certainly not for humans." [27]

Into Fort Cass and a half-dozen other rickety stockades, General Scott was ruthlessly herding at least 16,000 Cherokee Indians. They were being rounded up from four states—Georgia, Tennessee, North Carolina, and Alabama. Dr. Brown was astonished to witness such blatant military brutality. The Indian warriors, women, and children had been captured, many at bayonet point, and some shot if they resisted.

As the Cherokees were marched off to General Scott's stockades, their homes were left unprotected. Lawless whites surged in and plundered with impunity. Vandals stole the Indian horses, cattle, pigs, poultry—and crops and smokehouse provisions. Cherokee Chief John Ross protested and fought in the courts to try to stop the forced removal. At every turn, he and his allies were defeated. The state of Georgia seized his fine mansion and 800-acre plantation, to be given as a prize in a lottery open to white settlers.

Terribly disillusioned, Dr. Brown agonized over whether he wanted to remain a military physician. If he did, he rationalized that he could not alone change the United States Army system. He'd just have to make the best of his bargain.

After long soul-searching, and continuing doubts, he decided to fulfill the contract he made with General Scott. In consequence he was fated to become a front row spectator, and active player, in what are often termed the most pathetic episodes in American Indian history.

His duties took him directly into the day-by-day heartlessness of the infamous Cherokees' Trail of Tears, which reached its cruel zenith in the winter of 1838-39. The forced Indian removal was a series of events, not a sudden, one-time journey or march.

In all about 60,000 Indians would be rounded up—Cherokee, Creek, Seminole, Chickasaw, and Choctaw full bloods, along with their Negro slaves and freedmen, and the many half bloods of all tribes. And from their familiar homes and farms and hunting grounds in the eastern states and Florida, they would be escorted west, broken and hopeless, virtually all reduced to poverty.

The Government dumped them out in new, unbroken country. They went with chimerical and meager promises—basically a blanket, a calico dress for each woman, for each male a shirt, an axe, a plow and a rifle. Plus food rations until they could plant and harvest a corn crop. And, as soon as they became settled in their new land, the Government promised to pay cash annuities to be shared in common by the tribe. This money, fixed in the treaties, to be compensation for loss of their old homes and possessions.

Transportation for such a horde was haphazard at best, It was provided by widely varied means to accommodate the differing conditions. On river routes, the Indians went by crowded steamboats and keelboats. Across Tennessee, Cherokees were transported part of the way by railroad, then on horseback and in wagons hitched to four- or six-horse teams. At times many were forced to walk—and on bleeding bare feet.

The horror and shame of the Trail of Tears has been so vividly and repeatedly expounded by historians it needs no major elaboration here. In a typical traveling party of 500 to 1,000 emigrants, as many as 100 to 200 would fall ill. Four or five died each day, mainly children and old women and were buried randomly along the trail—in unmarked graves. Later Government doctors estimated 4,000 or more Cherokees died on the Trail of Tears. Other tribes suffered equally severe fatalities.

As for Dr. Brown, his red thread of destiny remained taut and unbroken. While he witnessed the horrors suffered by the Indians, he was not involved in their medical care. His exclusive assignment was to doctor General Scott's soldiers; the Government had hired other civilian physicians to travel with and care for the Indians.

On the trail, the enormous contrast between his current life of raw adventure and his old existence amid Charleston's aristocracy may have disturbed his dreams, and unquestionably stirred him to some nostalgia. He may have yearned, at least occasionally, for heavy silver on the table, a French wine in crystal goblet, the aroma of a good cigar, urbane conversation about large affairs, enchanting laughter, the musical voice of a pretty woman, the rustle of a silk petticoat . . .

Even if he missed such gentility, Dr. Brown had cast his lot with rugged life out West. He had steeled himself to be content as a military physician.

Thus in early March, 1839, he agreed to sign on again as a contract surgeon, at $100 a month, which was considered decent pay. This time he was taking assignment to another military post he had only heard about and not seen. It was Fort Illinois, a just-opened small Army post on the edge of the new Cherokee Nation out in the untamed Indian country.

ON THE CABIN'S dirt floor, in the crimson glow of the fireplace, a Seminole girl lay motionless on a wrinkled blanket. A cloth covered her face. Her father lifted it, and turned to Dr. Brown.

"*Tur-mérkv cuéhē*," the father said. [28]

As he later recounted the story, the physician had never seen anything like this. The girl's eyes were stuck wide-open, bulging, strange looking, clouded; she appeared in a coma. He bent for a closer look, while his brain swirled to translate the tribal tongue, which he barely knew.

Of a sudden the meaning of the words came to him. "Frozen eyeballs!" He turned to the father. "Good God!"[29]

Outside these log walls the ground was covered with snow and ice. Near-gale wind howled and hammered the hills and valleys around Fort Gibson. It was the worst Indian Territory blizzard in ten years. Dr. Brown had been summoned by the pleas of a runner, and responded by coming here on horseback over five miles of treacherous trail.

Dr. Brown quickly went to work. First he called for warm stones from the fireplace. These he wrapped in cloth and placed beside the girl's head. He dribbled warm water into her eyes, reheated the stones, bundled her body in all the blankets the Indian family could find in the cabin.

He several times had treated severe frostbite, and knew its dangers. Frozen fingers, toes, even feet usually had to be amputated. For eyes, obviously that was not an option.

Almost immediately he decided to resort to the treatment he relied on and was applauding in his book, venesection. He opened a vein in her wrist and drew blood. He didn't stop until his jar held what he estimated to be about one pound. The girl stirred and began moaning. He kept flushing her eyes with warm water, and muttering a prayer. Her chance of surviving, he felt, was slim. If she didn't die from shock or hypothermia, she might become blind.

For several hours he hovered over the girl, attempting to warm her gradually, keeping her eyes moist. He racked his memory for something else useful. Her pulse became gradually moderate, a good sign, but he was still fearful.

This poor girl had been out on the prairie several miles from home. The day was chilly and she was dressed for winter. But on the windy prairies of Indian country, the weather can change with fierce suddenness. The girl was caught by a blue norther! Within ten or fifteen minutes the sky turned black and the temperature dropped below zero. She became too chilled to walk. By rarest luck, a horseman chanced by and rescued her.

Several Seminole Indians huddled in the cabin watching the doctor work. With the father were two mature women, one likely the mother. Also the young man who come to summon him, and a slender girl with a round face and long black braided hair. She hovered at Dr. Brown's side. Over his shoulder, her wide brown Indian eyes intently followed every move of his hands.[30]

By daybreak, he was exhausted, and departed. He didn't bother to learn any names, not even the girl with frozen eyeballs. That could be done later; he intended to come back daily to see if his efforts would save her life and her sight.

By the second day, his patient was better. Dr. Brown mixed chemicals and herbs into a soothing solution with which he moistened bandages. Using these, he kept her blindfolded, the only thing he knew to do. Gradually he became hopeful; but not nearly as optimistic as the maiden with the long black braids and big brown eyes. She constantly looked over his shoulder and grinned often in apparent approval of his medical skill. She smiled at him and muttered in her tongue words he guessed were encouragement.

He took notice. She was lively, slender, neat and clean. By signs and using vague bits of English, she indicated her family had been brought to the frontier in the mass exodus from Florida. She spoke her name: *Kúnu Hvt'kē*. With considerable effort she finally made clear that translates to White Skunk.

Dr. Brown estimated she was about nineteen or twenty, and quite pretty. He sighed; he was at least twenty years her senior. Even so, studying her slender profile he felt an emotional stir in his heart. Something had clicked, he believed, between them—with her quick glances more telling than their scant verbal exchanges. He kept going back to the cabin to check on White Skunk's sister, even after the injured girl's sight seemed restored.

This was the winter of 1840-41, Dr. Brown's second year in Indian Territory. Much had happened. He had spent only a few months as a contract surgeon at Fort Illinois, a small and remote outpost, later renamed Fort Wayne. Next he had been assigned to Fort Gibson, near the junction of the Arkansas and Grand Rivers.

Fort Gibson, near what is now Muskogee, Oklahoma, was a large and important military outpost. Established in the 1820's, it served as the main "gateway" to the Indian country for travelers, soldiers, Indians, missionaries, adventurers—all arriving by riverboat, ox-drawn wagon, on horseback or on foot.

Gradually Dr. Brown had grown to appreciate and welcome life on the western frontier. He admired its valiant residents, their pioneer spirit and courage. He realized he was beginning to feel at home. At length, he made a crucial decision. He would establish a private practice, find a suitable residence, and finish out his professional career in the West.

When his assignment at Fort Gibson ended, he explored the nearby mountains and valleys. He wanted to find a place to build a log cabin. He was a white man, an intruder in the Cherokee Nation. That normally would be an obstacle. But in his duties at Fort Gibson he had met many of the frontier Indians. He gained trust and friendship especially among leaders of the Cherokees, Seminoles and Creeks.

He was attracted to a settlement called Park Hill, about fifteen miles from Fort Gibson. Its elevation was considerably higher than the Army post, and thus should be less subject to the bottomland fevers that perpetually besieged the fort's occupants.

He found a valley site near a sparkling mineral spring. That such a beautiful place had not already been taken surprised him. It would be ideal to build here a cabin facing west, which would provide a spectacular view of a grassy plain stretching two miles or more between wooded hills. In his mind's eye he visualized brilliant sunsets whose rays would flood *his* valley with a golden carpet.[31]

Through his adroitly developed and sincere friendships, Dr. Brown was able to obtain the site, erect a substantial log house, and go into private practice.

The Cherokee intellectuals were largely concentrated in Park Hill. He soon had many white and Indian patients, rich and poor. Some accused him of charging "stiff prices." [32] His genial response was that those fees permitted him to make calls to less affluent homes—such as those, he thought privately, where there were frozen eyeballs.

Now of a sudden he was smitten with White Skunk. What of her? Had she, too, fallen in love? He thought she had; but he needed to know for certain. Some of his Indian patients had given him certain tribal words so he could communicate with them. He opened this makeshift dictionary. Finally he found what he thought he needed: *Vnt-ce-tēhalv'tetv cvyac*—I want to marry you. [33]

Fearful of pronouncing the words wrong, he practiced his plea. When he faced White Skunk and spoke, her eyes dilated and flashed. She understood. She reached for his hand, and squeezed it gently. He took her in his arms, and squeezed, not gently.

At Fort Gibson, Dr. Brown went to the sutler's shop and bought the finest and most expensive blanket available; it was as soft as kitten fur and had blood-red checks along its border. He slipped a new silver-studded bridle on his most gentle pony, and led it behind his saddle mare as he went to the Indian cabin.

He approached White Skunk and affectionately wrapped the blanket around her shoulders. He understood this to be a tribal ritual of betrothal. He looked at the girl's mother and father. Did they understand, and accept? The mother smiled warmly; the old man nodded with majestic solemnity.

The maiden stood quietly beside him and Dr. Brown heard the strange words of the brief and simple Indian *etepáyetv*—marriage ceremony. [34] He then kissed her, put her on the pony, and they rode away for their honeymoon in Park Hill.

2

Facing the Firing Squad

FROM THE FRONT WINDOW of her Park Hill log cabin, White Skunk watched a sleek carriage pull up. The Negro coachman helped alight a stylish young woman with dangling dark curls. This was not a surprise. The wife of George Michael Murrell would be calling, White Skunk's husband had advised her. Dr. Brown's young bride trembled. She did not lack courage. In the Florida wars her own dagger had dripped blood. She was daring and had quick wit. But as an Indian, as a refugee from the brutal Everglades war, as a survivor of the cruel Trail of Tears, as the "child bride" of a white physician twice her age, and untutored in civilized society, White Skunk felt dismayed.

"Good morning, I'm your neighbor, Minerva Murrell." The woman at the door smiled, and held out a basket.[1] It contained fruit and cookies.

The Seminole bride relaxed, and ushered in her visitor. And thus began a lifelong friendship between the women—a camaraderie that markedly speeded and eased White Skunk's debut into the active and sophisticated life of the center of political, cultural, educational, and business affairs of the Cherokee Nation.

Entry into Park Hill society was a welcome achievement. But Dr. Brown's wife had good reason to retain some fear. The times were unsettled, dangerous. The Cherokee Nation was embroiled in a vicious struggle for power and headship. Much blood was being spilt.

Fortunately, Dr. Brown had managed to stay neutral, standing clear of the Cherokee internecine turmoil. The Murrells, White Skunk knew, were right in the middle of it.

Except for wealth and social station, White Skunk discovered things in common with Mrs. Murrell. Minerva, now twenty-two, also had been a "child bride," married back in Georgia at age sixteen. Also she had Indian blood—just one-sixteenth Cherokee. Currently she also lived in a log cabin. Both their husbands had Scottish lineage. There the similarity ended.

Minerva Murrell was the niece of John Ross, chief of the eastern Cherokees. His great-grandfather had come to Georgia from Scotland and married a Cherokee woman. Chief Ross was only one-eighth Cherokee, as was his brother, Lewis, Minerva's father. The Rosses had been wealthy merchants and plantation owners in Georgia and Tennessee before the Government propelled them west on the Trail of Tears. John Ross's wife died on the trip.

George Murrell was a white man from a wealthy Virginia family. As a Ross family son-in-law, he had come west to settle with the Cherokees. One of the wealthiest men in the Cherokee Nation, at this time thirty-three, he lived with the perks and in the style of the aristocracy of the Old South. He had a Park Hill plantation, with both grist and lumber mills, and a prosperous trading post. He brought along forty-two slaves, and had them erecting a two-story Greek revival style mansion. As a foxhunting aficionado, he would call it "Hunter's Home."

Nearby Chief Ross had built a much larger mansion with columns, "Rose Cottage." These two homes became the cultural and social apex of the Cherokee Nation. Clustered around these imposing structures were several dozen other substantial homes and buildings occupied by leading Cherokee influentials.

Situated in a valley of velvety prairie grass between thick woodlands on King Mountain and Park Hill Mountain, the settlement named Park Hill was five miles southeast of Tahlequah, the capital of the Cherokee Nation. Across the valley floor ran Park Hill Creek, emptying into the close-by Illinois River. This was an enchanted land; fish were plentiful in clear streams, game abundant, and the rich soil productive. Yet there were occasional untoward side effects—floods and storms, and blistering summers with occasional droughts.

Dr. Brown had a growing private practice and served periodically as contract surgeon at Fort Gibson. He rode horseback to make house calls. He spent much free time in meeting a personal challenge at home, smoothing off the rough edges of his aborigine bride.

"I am going to teach you the English language," he told White Skunk, who seemed happy with the news. She promised to reciprocate in Seminole. [2]

Both succeeded. She began to read and understand the white man's words; and to speak it fairly well. He did likewise in her tongue. From his Indian patients he already had learned a good smattering of their languages.

Who could whisper amorous compliments into the ear of a comely young woman named for a skunk, even though the skunk was white? Dr. Brown could not.

One evening he sprang a surprise. "We are going to give you a new name—an American one. I've talked to Minerva Murrell. Their family has a splendid name back among their grandmothers. I like it—Lucy." [3]

White Skunk appeared pleased. "Loo...cee," she breathed. "Sounds nice. . . Much nice."

That made it official. The Seminole name *Kúnu Hvt'kē*—White Skunk began to disappear into the dim recesses of Brown family history. She was thereafter identified as Lucy Greybeard Brown. The middle name was added because Lucy, for some vague reason, wanted it. In her tribal culture, she informed her husband, that word represented elements of honor and pride.

Theirs was an extraordinary, uncommon, and unorthodox love story, a rarity even on this wilderness frontier. Two disparate human beings chosen by Fate to star in a romance dominated by adventure, intrigue, excitement, and danger.

An Indian girl born into a savage Everglades family, a people who until two or three years ago had to run for their lives; a tribe all deft with knife and rifle, who killed and scalped the enemy, lived under the stars, and whose warriors sometimes impatiently snatched half-roasted meat off the campfire and quickly wolfed it, letting blood run off their chins.

A cultured aristocrat, old enough to be her father, a trained, skillful and highly respected physician, a white man, educated and well-read, whose library bookplate was a family Scottish coat of arms with the Latin motto meaning *"cautiously and carefully,"* who could quote with ease Sir Walter Scott and Shakespeare, who was handsome, well-dressed, mannerly, courageous as a lion, and could sit regally at a damask-covered table and choose a superior wine with élan and confidence.

When he wrote his family back in Charleston about his marriage, the disparity of his romance was hurled bitterly back in his face. One of his sisters railed in a letter: "You have married a savage! And a child at that!" [4] This estrangement from his siblings would follow him to the grave.

However, Dr. Brown and Lucy constituted an undeniably happy union. And they had children—two of whom were to become historically extraordinary, born with their own sensationally distinctive red threads of destiny, life skeins that would eventually propel them to the pinnacle of the Seminole Nation.

Each of these two, in turn, was destined to become Chief of the Seminoles.

THE FORCED WESTERN migration of sixty thousand Indians led to controversy, tragedy, violence and bloodshed that neither the Government nor its victims were prepared for, nor could easily abate.

From Park Hill, Dr. Brown and Lucy watched with dismay this sad spectacle. Government officials and the Army dealt with the Indians as a "problem," rather than as human beings.

In conversation with a select few officers at Fort Gibson, and to trusted Park Hill friends, the doctor expressed himself. The immigrants, he observed, were not being given even the slimmest chance to successfully begin a new life in this strange country.

"In intelligence and character they are far above the average aboriginal. Of course, that doesn't apply to all; even among the whites not everyone measures up. These tribes are much superior, certainly, to the wild plains Indians. And they would have no trouble adapting to this new land." [5]

His comments were private. He held no cards in this game. He stuck to practicing medicine, strictly neutral. He responded to all calls, Indian or white, regardless of tribe or the patient's purse or station in life.

Around the Brown cabin, for long months in the early 1840s, the territory remained dangerously enflamed. The Government went back on nearly every promise made the Seminoles. Money was not paid. Food and clothing were withheld or delayed. Likewise blankets, rifles, plows, axes, blacksmith tools. The Indians were unable to hunt game, plant corn, build cabins.

Seminoles came near starving when avaricious contractors shamefully cheated them on rations, when they could have fed the Indians for three and one-half cents a day.[6] Some intrepid tribesmen broke ground using as a plow the shoulder blade of a deer, and planted tiny corn crops. Arkansas River floods in 1844 washed them away.

To keep from starving, Indians scoured the bottoms for berries and roots, and dug a prairie "potato" similar to the tuber known as "coonty" that largely kept the Seminoles alive while hiding out in the Everglades.

No solution to any critical frontier problems could be obtained except in Washington. Tribal leaders donned their best attire and booked steamship and stagecoach passage to go appeal to their Great Father.[7] They would spend weeks beseeching the White House and Congress for help. Usually they came home denied, defeated and empty-handed.

The Seminoles felt, and were, homeless. Instead of being given their own land, they were ordered to crowd in amongst the unfriendly Creeks. The two tribes had once shared the same culture, language and leadership, but angrily broke apart around 1750, and mutual hatred lingered. The Seminoles in the main refused to accept permanent residence on the new Creek domain in Indian Territory, where they would be subjected with no authority. Most Seminole families instead pitched rag-tag camps up and down the Arkansas River around Fort Gibson in the Cherokee Nation.[8]

The Seminoles also were unhappy because the Creeks initially tried to push them up against the extreme western Creek boundary. That would put the Florida immigrants right on the edge of the buffalo domain of the marauding wild plains Indians. That would be dangerous; the Seminoles greatly feared Comanches and Apaches would raid their settlements, steal their horses, and kill all who resisted the depredations.

Among the Cherokees, a different turmoil raged. Which chief was in charge? John Ross, as head of the largest of the three contending tribal divisions, the eastern Cherokees, faced two rivals. Violent confrontations ensued; a dozen or so leaders were hacked or shot to death, usually mysteriously. In the end Ross would become principal chief, but still challenged.

Among all the Five Civilized Tribes slavery was a serious problem. In the 1840s through the 1850s, Seminoles who owned slaves struggled to retain the ones they brought from Florida. Bounty hunters were hired by Southern plantation owners whose slaves had escaped. These agents kept trying to snatch the Seminole's blacks. Some of these Negroes had been freed; others had intermarried with Seminoles. A similar troublesome situation existed in the Creek tribe.

Abolitionists were active among the red men, just as elsewhere across the country. Indians took sides against one another. This split grew worse, even violent, as the Civil War rapidly approached.

Another unyielding complication was that Indians grew suspicious, feeling that perhaps they could not trust certain tribal leaders. It became known that the Army was paying bribes. Washington's prevailing opinion was that under-the-table secret money was the only way to obtain surrender, movement, or agreement from the red brothers. Some of the most respected and able chiefs became visibly wealthy; several left estates of $100,000 or larger.

BY VALENTINE'S DAY, 1843, Lucy Brown, just twenty, was pregnant. She accepted the situation stoically. Having children was natural, what she expected. Dr. Brown, now forty-three, was overjoyed. He was eager to again have a child.

Their friend Minerva Murrell was envious. Now twenty-four, she considered herself hopelessly barren. She yearned vainly for a baby. So Minerva promptly began mooring her own maternal zeal on her Seminole neighbor. Over the months she would visit every day or two to observe Lucy's swelling belly, and to eventually feel the tiny kick. [9]

Inspired, Mrs. Murrell went even further. She got her husband to adopt her two motherless cousins, a boy Joshua, ten, and Jennie, nine.

On Monday, October 23, 1843, Lucy bore a boy weighing close to eight pounds. He was well formed, with coal-black eyes, a mop of dark hair. Dr. Brown examined him. "He's perfect. He will grow tall, and be strong." [10]

They named him for his father: John Frippo Brown, though as an adult he would change his middle name to Franklin to avoid being confused with his father.

Four years later, on Sunday, March 7, 1847, their first daughter was born. She was named for her mother: Lucy. Another daughter, Jennie, was born in July 1849.

THE MOST FEARED illness in the military was cholera. No region of the country was safe or exempt from an epidemic of the disease. It struck like lightning, a hit-and-run outbreak, suffocated most of the afflicted, and then mysteriously vanished—only to make an unwelcome reappearance perhaps years later.

Dr. Brown had battled cholera epidemics several times at Fort Gibson and elsewhere. In the last outbreak there, four Fifth Infantry soldiers suddenly began vomiting violently and fell out, prostrated. By nightfall, they were dead.

In the fort hospital, Dr. Brown found all these patients wretchedly dehydrated. The soldiers lay helpless, their tongues parched, eyes glassy, their dried-out skin looking like old parchment. He hovered over their sickbeds, taking care to not touch the diarrhea-stained, fishy-smelling blankets and sheets, staying alert to dodge frequent explosive bursts of greenish-black vomit.

Dr. Brown could do little for them. There was no cure for cholera.

The physician painstakingly explained to soldiers, and to Indians, that cholera could be avoided if they emptied their bowels a safe distance from their water supply. It saddened him that such a simple hygienic precaution was so persistently ignored.

Yet he realized that cholera did not infect only rustic and remote regions; New York, London, and other big cities with thousands of miles of plumbing and sewers were also stricken from time to time. The seriousness of the cholera epidemics that confronted Dr. Brown and other military physicians in the south and southwest was highlighted in an official document:

> Cholera . . . accompanied troops on their way to Texas from New Orleans in 1848 when that city was in turmoil as the result of simultaneous epidemics of yellow fever and cholera. When two steamships carrying 450 soldiers to Port Lavaca, Texas . . .[arrived] 350 men and camp followers had felt its effects and 150 died.
>
> [Soon] cholera appeared in Brownsville, Texas . . Brazos Santiago and Matamoros . . . Carmago and nearby Camp Ringgold. Dragoons leaving for San Antonio by way of Laredo took the vibrio with them . . . Estimates of the number of deaths in San Antonio from mid-April to the first week of June [1849] varied from 400 to 700; among them was that of a major general, William Worth.
>
> All told, 44 soldiers died of cholera in southern Texas and 173 in the western part of that state in the period of 1848 to 1854, after which the disease disappeared from the area. [11]

Dr. Brown recognized his limitations, but he struggled with a knowledge from his rapidly expanding wealth of experience and study, and a strong and willing heart. He did what he could do as a doctor. And often his house calls took him far from his home and family, and late in returning. He felt robbed on any evening he was unable to watch the dying sun spread a golden carpet across his grassy valley. [12]

IN EARLY JULY 1850 a Fort Gibson corporal rode seventeen miles out to Park Hill to summon Dr. Brown. Brigadier General William

G. Belknap needed the doctor to accompany a military expedition into the far reaches of Indian Territory and on into Texas. The offer was an attractive $100 a month contract; he was among frontier physicians who welcomed the certainty of Government income. That supplemented meager fees paid by the average Indian patient; the doctors' other revenue came from well-off tribal families and they were in the minority.

Dr. Brown readily signed his contract to become acting assistant surgeon to Company B of the Fifth Infantry, commanded by Captain R.B. Marcy. The physician knew he was obligating himself to leave his young wife and children, to face hardships and most likely danger, and to be gone from home certainly a year, and possibly longer.

What Dr. Brown did not know was that, despite undeniable success in fulfilling his duties, in the end he was to be cruelly demeaned, essentially fired, and cut adrift in a terrible winter, and cast off to make his way back home alone across roughly five hundred miles of frontier wilderness.

Officials in Washington were sending Captain Marcy to establish two or three new forts about four or five hundred miles west of Fort Smith. The forts were intended to stand guard against raids into Texas and Mexico by the Comanches, and likewise protect both immigrants heading to the California gold fields, and the Chickasaw and other peaceful Indians who were periodically attacked by the wild plains warriors.[13]

Dr. Brown was highly impressed by Marcy, young, intelligent, brave, and perhaps the Army's best woodsman. When the '49 gold rush had begun, Marcy and a Fifth Infantry detachment from Fort Smith safely led a party of 500 immigrants across the uncharted plains to California. Now he was again chosen chiefly because he knew the territory.

By August 26, 1850 the expedition had trudged 175 miles west of Fort Smith through wild country and camped in a timbered area on the south bank of the South Canadian River. Marcy designated this camp as the site for a fort. Dr. Brown, obligated to report regularly to the Army's surgeon general, Brigadier General Thomas Lawson, wrote, in part:

The spot at present occupied as a camp and which and where the captain proposes erecting the works is situated south of the Canadian River 1 1/2 miles, in a thick grove of timber suitable for building purposes, which extends north to the river. The grand prairie encircles us in every other direction.

There are several springs of water within a convenient distance, the supply ample although we have had but one shower since the lst July. The weather has been intensely hot and dry, but we have had very little sickness considering the exposure to which the men have been subjected, on two occasions having to march all night.

The teams consisting principally of oxen were compelled to travel very early in the morning and late at night in consequence of the nature of the country and the scarcity of water. [14]

Dr. Brown had learned to be circumspect with General Lawson, a crusty 60-year-old Virginian who had won praise for his medical skill and battlefield bravery from the War of 1812 through the 1847 successful American invasion of Mexico. Lawson was prickly with Congress, his superiors, his subordinates, and openly suspicious of all Army civilian contract assistant surgeons. [15] Under a tight budget, he closely monitored all expenses.

With one new outpost staked out, Captain Marcy was ordered to cross the Red River, go deeper into Texas and select another fort site. He explored a wide area on the edge of the Comanche hunting grounds. About 400 miles west of Fort Washita, he found a suitable location, a high, wooded area on the Red Fork of the Brazos River, about 15 miles north of present day Abilene, Texas.

General Belknap decided to leave Fort Gibson and go out to Texas and personally inspect his newest outpost. By the middle of May 1851, the general had arrived at Fort Washita. He promptly enlarged his expedition by bringing along five companies of Fifth Infantry from Fort Smith, one from Fort Gibson, as well as one from Fort Towson. His supply train included twenty-three wagons, each pulled by teams of eight mules or oxen, two artillery pieces and caissons with canister and grape shot.[16]

Dr. Brown reported to Surgeon General Lawson that he had been assigned to care for the Fifth's Company G and Company I.

He forwarded an invoice of precautionary medical supplies he had acquired anticipating that Belknap might explore even further west in Texas, explaining:

> We will commence our journey on May 28, crossing Red River at Preston, 20 miles from this place, thence following Captain Marcy's road 175 miles to his crossing of the Brazos and thence taking a course west of south to the Colorado River.
> Whether the General will have time or means to proceed further, I cannot tell. I should presume that a careful examination of the country at that point would occupy at least three months. [17]

On reaching the Red Fork in late June 1851, Belknap shifted the fort's site a few miles south and set soldiers to erecting the military works. Captain Marcy arrived then, and though ill, was dispatched with 25 men and eight Delaware scouts to explore to Pecan Bayou, a tributary of the Colorado River.

Belknap then decided to almost immediately return to Fort Smith with the bulk of his troops. General Matthew Arbuckle had resigned command of the Seventh Military District, and Belknap had been appointed his successor. [Arbuckle would fall victim to cholera and die June 11, 1851.]

Dr. Brown wrote the surgeon general that General Belknap departed Red Fork on June 24 after announcing his intention to bring his troops back to the new Texas fort in the fall. In the interim, in Dr. Brown's opinion, the Red Fork outpost stood in potential danger from the plains warriors.

> Our command now here is very small and it is perhaps fortunate that the Comanches have gone north to hunt the buffalo and that our force will be increased before they return. Their fall and winter range lies between the Brazos and Rio Grande from which they make incursions into Texas and Mexico for the purpose of stealing and it is very certain that as this is their only means of subsistence—trading their stolen horses, mules and boys for bread, blankets and such other necessities as they may require.
> As soon as they learn our object of establishing military posts in what they claim as their country, they will surely make a desperate effort to prevent it.

They are known as splendid horsemen and very bold and daring in their attacks. It is supposed they can muster over 10,000 warriors, though I cannot conceive how they can furnish subsistence for half that number for any length of time, when embodied.

It however shows the necessity of sending a strong force to accomplish the object of the government, the preventing the Indians from hostile incursions into Texas and Mexico.

There is no correct map of the country lying between the Brazos and Rio Grande. The courses of the rivers and the distances are entirely incorrect. I think it a very fortunate circumstance that Capn Marcy was sent to examine the country south of this as he has good judgment, is an excellent woodsman, and indefatigable in his explorations, and will be able to make valuable additions to his map.

We expect the company from Gibson, the one from Towson, and the two from Washita will join us about the end of this month when Capn Marcy will have returned and the companies that are ordered to Pecan Bayou may proceed in time to erect huts before the winter as I myself and some portion of this regiment have been deprived of vegetable food. The only antisorbutics are 3 pounds citric acid and 1 bottle limejuice. The company has some kraut, a few jars pickles and 10 bushels dried fruit which I have recommended be offered to the men once a week for the present as they get three days rations (in the week) of fresh venison or beef. [18]

By October 1851, General Belknap had returned to the Red Fork, now garrisoned by five Fifth Infantry companies. There had been no Indian raids; calm prevailed. The General, however, was showing erratic behavior. Fifty-seven years old, he had fought with valor in both the 1812 and Mexican wars. Belknap apparently recognized he was perhaps mentally ill. He turned over Red Fork command to a Captain Stevenson, and set out to return to Fort Smith, traveling in a wagon ambulance drawn by four mules, accompanied by thirty mounted troopers.

His unseen companion was the Dark Angel.

On November 10, the Belknap caravan had passed by Preston, Texas, crossed the Red River by ferry and was traveling east in a heavy rainstorm. Within three or four miles of Fort Washita, the tongue of the ambulance wagon snapped. The medical steward riding with the general hopped out to help fix it.

"It couldn't have been more than ten minutes," he testified later. "When I got back in the ambulance, General Belknap was dead."

The soldiers hauled his corpse on to a shocked Fort Washita. Two days later General Belknap was buried in the post cemetery with full military ceremony.

Repercussions from General Belknap's death disastrously and unexpectedly jolted Dr. Brown's career as a civilian physician in the Army. In a manner that to him was unnecessarily demeaning, Dr. Brown was fired.

The action was taken by the commander at Red Fork, Captain Stevenson. He summoned Dr. Brown and told him that since Dr. E. J. Bailey had arrived with the new Fifth Infantry troops, the captain did not feel authorized to retain Dr. Brown.

Such abrupt annulment of his contract astonished and infuriated Dr. Brown. He protested, and asked Captain Stevenson to refer the matter to General Lawson in Washington. There is no indication Captain Stevenson did so. Being left in limbo, Dr. Brown finally saddled up and began the long ride to his Park Hill home in the Cherokee Nation.

"I left the Brazos on the 10th December and returned home over the bleak prairies during the most intense cold weather," Dr. Brown asserted later in an angry letter to General Lawson.

> I was indebted to a mere accident for the transportation of any baggage.
>
> Some little consideration should be shown under such circumstances for the feelings and interests of a professional man and a gentleman, particularly as I remained at Camp Belknap by General Belknap's order, who thought the emergency for which I was employed still existed when both Dr. Bailey and myself were together.
>
> I was anxious to return home in the fall when the weather was pleasant but was prevented from consulting my own convenience and pleasure from the circumstances of there being no other officer to attend the sick.
>
> But in the depth of winter, for fear of responsibility, I am discharged as there was an Army surgeon at the post. [19]

36

Because of his difficult journey home, and waiting for promised word from Captain Stevenson, Dr. Brown did not send his stinging letter until April 2, 1852 when he turned in his papers and supplies at Fort Gibson.

In the formal obeisance of the day, he signed off with the customary "Very respectfully, I remain, your obedient servant."

But any criticism from a civilian employee apparently did not set well with General Lawson. The surgeon general's resentment appears to have resulted in Dr. Brown being black-balled by Washington, even though his service as an acting assistant surgeon in the Army spanned fifteen years.

At any rate, five long years went by before Dr. Brown got another contract!

ON FRIDAY, OCTOBER 10, 1852, the stork again hovered over the Brown cabin in Park Hill. This would be Lucy's fourth child. First-born John F. was nine, Lucy, her mother's namesake, five, and Jennie three.

Lucy went into labor and delivered a great surprise—twin girls. The parents immediately settled on names—Zora and Alice. It became a day of tragedy. In early afternoon, Zora began gasping for breath and died. Dr. Brown and George Murrell got shovels and took the corpse to Park Hill cemetery, while loyal Minerva remained with Lucy as she began nursing infant Alice. [20]

Minerva grieved over the loss of Zora as deeply as the Browns. She had no inkling then that the Dark Angel would very soon write her own name on his Doomsday list. The first of June 1854 Minerva developed a fever and cough. Dr. Brown was summoned to "Hunters Home." His diagnosis was malaria, a severe case.

In the journal he kept to detail patient treatments, he wrote:

> Saw Mrs. Murrell on Thursday, 1st—Has taken sick with severe chills followed by fever. Violent headache. Vomiting. Pain in back. Took calomel gr. xx. Found her free of fever. Pulse slow but excitable. Tongue coated in center. Gave quinine gr. viii, paregoric, spirits nitre. Rested well until about midnight when she became restless. [21]

37

Next day, Friday, Minerva was feverish, with head pain, and vomited bile all day. "No relief from usual remedies," Dr. Brown noted in his journal. He spent the day at her bedside. At night her headache stopped, fever abated. She had slept little so he gave her morphine and she rested well.

He became hopeful Saturday, writing she was "comparatively easy." But when he returned at 11 A.M. Sunday "she was worse" with slight fever, headache, gastric irritability. At 4 o'clock he gave her a sedative. He noted a derangement of her liver and jotted down that Minerva was depressed, doubtless because of confinement to bed, since she "hitherto enjoyed uninterrupted health."

By Monday she was "quite easy—convalescent." Dr. Brown kept her on quinine. He was hoping against hope. She was young, had always been strong, was intelligent—she would fight to live. But he was fearful. He realized malaria remained one of the trickiest scourges physicians then confronted. He would monitor her closely, and do the best he could.

For a few months Minerva seemed to be recovering. Then suddenly a relapse. Dr. Brown was regretful, but not surprised. Then she rapidly went downhill. With laudanum, opium and morphine, her pain was eased. But she was dying. Lucy came to the sickroom, feeling bewildered. She made an attempt to console George Murrell, and left crying. [22]

Nothing could be done. On a snowy Sunday morning, January 7, 1855, Minerva died. She was barely thirty-six.

More heartache was ahead for the Chief John Ross's clan. Daniel Ross's small son Johnny suddenly developed ulcers in his mouth. He was taken to Dr. Dwight D. Hitchcock in Park Hill, who became alarmed.

He called in Dr. Brown. "I've never seen a case like this," said Dr. Hitchcock. "Johnnie's mouth has mortified. It's probably *cankerome orisi*. In animals we call that *black death*." [23]

Whatever had enflamed the boy's mouth was fatal. Neither doctor could save him. Johnnie choked to death on a flood of his own saliva.

Life went on placidly in the Brown cabin. At thirty-two, Lucy was pregnant for the fifth time. On Saturday, March 3, 1855, she delivered another son. The squalling infant was named Andrew Jackson Brown, in honor of the seventh President.

Dr. Brown now had two sons, the eldest just turning teen-ager, and three daughters. That constituted a reasonably large family; but it would grow bigger. Lucy was destined to bear two more Browns, both boys.

The future held not only additional children for the Browns of Park Hill, but a disastrous onrush of untold, unexpected, and cataclysmic changes in the lives of all of them, not yet evident but coming at breakneck speed.

In May 1856 Dr. Brown was employed for two months once again as an Army surgeon at Fort Gibson. But even that work led to a confrontation and screw-up.

It revolved around getting timely payment from the government. Mail was slow, requiring three or four weeks for a letter from Indian Territory to reach Washington, and an equal time for the reply. To overcome the delay and get immediate needed cash, Dr. Brown often assigned his salary claim to friends such as George Murrell. Comfortably fixed, these friends didn't mind handing him the nominal one hundred dollars. Without hardship, they could wait the usual two months for the pay to arrive from Washington.

At the end of his last contract, he arranged for the sutler at Fort Gibson to advance him $200 in exchange for the doctor's valid claim. When the sutler submitted this to Washington, the chit was rejected.

Stunned, Dr. Brown wrote a protest, but belatedly discovered he was ignorant of a new necessary form of notification required by the Government cashier. The sutler finally got paid, but Dr. Brown still upbraided Surgeon General Lawson:

> The refusal to pay my accounts for services rendered might have subjected me to severe inconvenience, by injuring my credit and character with those to whom I was unknown, but happily I am among old acquaintances.

> Your obedient servant,
> John F. Brown
> A.A. Surgeon, U.S.A.

Dr. Brown, with the needs of a growing family and only the uncertain income from a frontier medical practice, apparently was now encountering financial straits. No available Cherokee Nation records or memoirs shed light on particulars of his plight.

However, on January 6, 1857 he felt it actually necessary to beg for Army work, obviously a traumatic embarrassment.

From Park Hill, he wrote Surgeon General Lawson in Washington:

> Dear Sir:
>
> I have at various times, to the best of my abilities, faithfully discharged the duties of a medical officer both in hospital practice and in the field to which no doubt you can testify.
>
> Being now out of employment, I would respectfully solicit your assistance in giving me any situation in your gift that would be to my benefit and the interest of the service.
>
> I am willing to go anywhere and to do any duty which may be required of me.
>
> I read occasionally of the movement of troops accompanied by acting assistant surgeons. Can you not for auld lang syne remember me and my past services should any opportunity occur?
>
> Any communication addressed to me at Fort Gibson will be thankfully acknowledged by,
>
> Your obedient servant,
> John F. Brown [24]

No reply from the Surgeon General can be found in official records that still exist. But Dr. Brown was hollering down an empty well, anyhow. In that very month, the Surgeon General was recommending that Fort Gibson be closed because of its unhealthy, swampy climate.

Barely six months after Dr. Brown's begging letter, the troops were withdrawn on June 23, 1857. The abandoned fort was turned over to Chief John Ross on November 5, and the area converted into a town called *Kee-too-whaw*, with lots sold to Cherokee citizens.

During the remainder of the time the Brown family spent in Park Hill, in the grassy valley that got splashed with those magnificent golden sunsets, there were no other Army contracts.

However, within a few years the shoe would be on the other foot. The Civil War was about to erupt, and drag the people of the Indian Territory squarely into the bloody conflict. Then John Frippo Brown would not have to beg for work as a United States Army assistant surgeon; the Army would, in fact, have urgent need of him.

WHILE THE PARK HILL BROWNS' solvency was sinking, Dame Fortune at last smiled on Lucy's tribe, the immigrants from Florida. For fifteen years the Seminoles as a complete and distinct tribe had been callously kept in general disarray.

Now came a change—a tripartite treaty was signed in Washington August 7, 1856. Severed were all ties between the Creeks and the Seminoles, who had been under Creek law with no vote in their councils. The Seminoles could now set up their own government. [25]

Most importantly, the Seminoles were given their own land, a snake-like, skinny swath that stretched one hundred seventy miles across the middle of present day Oklahoma, in width wobbling from about fifteen to fifty miles.

In doing this, the Government had ulterior motives. One was to create a lure to bring west the one thousand Seminoles still remaining in Florida. Sending tribal emissaries from Indian Territory to argue for removal, and offer of generous bribes had failed. Also creating this new Seminole Nation would bring together and move westward the Seminole "squatters" who had been living scattered among the Cherokees and Creeks. [26]

About 2200 Seminoles—half of them female—had been brought out from Florida. Because of uncertainty, few had built cabins, or tried to create settlements while unwillingly mixed into the Creek Nation.

Boundaries of the new Seminole Nation were defined in the treaty: due north from the mouth of Pond Creek (*Ock-hi-appo*) to the North Fork of the Canadian; then up said North Fork to the southern line of the Cherokee country; thence, with that line, west to the one hundredth meridian; then south to the Canadian River, and thence down that river back to the mouth of the *Ock-hi-appo*. [27]

When surveyed, this new Seminole Nation was found to comprise 2,170,000 acres. Today that area, between the North Canadian and South Canadian Rivers, would extend from about eight miles east of Shawnee to Oklahoma's western border, not including the panhandle. Within those boundaries lie present-day Shawnee, Tecumseh, part of Oklahoma City, El Reno and western towns like Camargo and Shattuck.

The treaty, signed by the Government, the Creeks, and the Seminoles, also defined the Creek Nation.

Further, it also contained the guarantee from the United States to the Seminoles that no part of their new nation would ever be sold without the consent of both tribes.

This latter provision, however, was doomed to be ruthlessly broken by Washington in another of the shameful string of injustices done Indians by federal officials. And within less than a decade.

The treaty gave money to the Seminole tribe: $90,000 for losses suffered in the forced removal from Florida; payments for ten years of $3,000 annually for schools, $2,000 for agriculture, $2,200 for blacksmiths; plus, to be paid *per capita* as annuity, 5 percent interest on $250,000 invested by the Government for the Seminole Indians. If the Florida Seminoles joined their "western brethren," the Government would add another quarter-million dollars to that annuity fund, and promised to give the new arrivals , as a tribe, twenty thousand dollars, plus rations for one year, and the usual clothing, axes, rifles, cards and looms.

Despite trips to the Everglades by Seminole emissaries from the west, repeated arguments, rich promises, and handsome bribes, the Government's hard sell was never to succeed, and a sizeable and influential contingent of Seminole Indians remain today in Florida.

Importantly, the treaty provided for the Government to construct two substantial buildings to serve as the new Seminole Nation's headquarters—an agency and a council house.

For their government seat, the Seminoles chose a site just seven miles inside their new eastern boundary, and fifteen miles north of the South Canadian River, on a timbered prairie near a splendid spring and creek. They dubbed it "Council Town," and there built houses for the leaders.

The two-story stone Agency, built first, was on the prairie just one mile west of the boundary and four miles north and two miles east of the present town of Wanette, Oklahoma, on the Canadian River. Occupied by Indian Agent Samuel Rutherford, and also housing the commissary, the Agency was in use by 1858— two floors, each thirty-two by forty-four feet, with a log kitchen sixteen feet square. A blacksmith shop also was built.

One year later the imposing Council House was completed, twenty by thirty-six feet, two rooms, with a rock fireplace in each. It was furnished with tables and chairs. Council Town also had a trading post and blacksmith shop. A wagon road running atop the ridges connected the Agency to Council Town.

ON HORSEBACK in the summer of 1857, Dr. Brown rode into the Seminole Nation. From a half mile away, he could make out the outlines of a new two-story stone building. Carpenters were noisily hammering shingles onto the roof. It was the Seminoles' almost-completed Agency—his destination. The structure looked sturdy and roomy, and by frontier standards, handsome.

Twenty minutes later Dr. Brown drew up at the new hitching rail, slid off his bay mare, and tied her up. The carpenters kept banging away, but someone at a window caught his arrival. An impressive looking Indian, at least six-four, two hundred pounds and broad-shouldered, wearing a double-breasted vest and coat and a wide-brimmed hat, emerged from the door.

They introduced themselves. The Indian was John Jumper, principal chief of the Seminole Nation. Their handshake was warm and friendly. They had heard of each other; each had a favorable impression. Chief Jumper led the way to log benches in the shade of the building. As the chief observed, they would "make talk." [28]

This was an enchanted day. The sky was a huge inverted bowl of blue, songbirds were active, wildflowers danced in the gentle breeze, the crystal creeks sang over sun-dappled rocks. For more than a week Dr. Brown had been riding around exploring the new boundaries defining the Creek and Seminole Nations.

43

He had come to try to gain from Chief Jumper a clear insight into the character, and prospects, and leadership of the Seminole territory. He wanted to hear the facts from a candid and authentic source. The doctor had boned up pretty well on the chief's background, and had been impressed.

The chief's heritage stemmed from an uncle in Florida, known only by the single name "Jumper," who had been a sub chief; the principal chief was a full blood named Micanopy. The original Jumper, however, had fought in the Florida wars alongside such notables as Osceola, Wild Cat, Alligator, and King Phillip—and had personally in combat taken lives of several soldiers. He was described by the Army as "influential and exceedingly intelligent."

The Florida chief Jumper did not surrender until 1838. As a prisoner, he was included in a party of sixty-four, including slaves and his two nephews, Jim and John Jumper. Soldiers escorted them out of the Everglades onto schooners chartered by the government for the Gulf of Mexico voyage that launched their sad journey to Indian Territory.

On reaching New Orleans, Jumper, the sub-chief, abruptly died of consumption. His nephews and the others continued on to the new land. During their hiatus around Fort Gibson while in conflict with Creeks, Chief Micanopy became known as an idler, a hard drinker and careless administrator. When he died in 1848, the Seminoles elected Jim Jumper.

That turned out to be unwise. Jim Jumper was not forthright and honest. He attempted to pull off a crooked deal that would surrender Seminole slaves to the brother of the tribe's Government agent. That plot was detected, publicly exposed, and thwarted. Further, he was shown to be a coward, afraid to get a tooth pulled without drinking a quart of whiskey. Within his first year, he died, possibly from tuberculosis as had his uncle.

The Seminoles then chose carefully, and elected John Jumper, who was thirty-four, healthy and intelligent, industrious and honest. Historians term him "the most influential chief among the Seminoles." He had vision. He fully realized the Seminoles could never get on their feet and prosper unless the tribe broke totally free of the Creeks.

So it was his determined and constructive maneuvering that prompted George W. Manypenny, U. S. Commissioner of Indian Affairs, to develop the 1856 tripartite treaty.

Dr. Brown knew also that Chief John Jumper was deeply religious. In 1857, Chief Jumper had been induced by a missionary to join the Presbyterian Church. He studiously read the Bible, and his aborigine mind began to trouble itself with critical questions. One difficult point for him was being unable to reconcile the Presbyterian ritual of baptism with his understanding of Matthew, third chapter. He determined to find out if the Baptist church's system was more true to the Scriptures.

Chief Jumper was a father with a fairly large family. On the day he conferred with Dr. Brown, two of his young daughters, Winnie and Lizzie, were with him. The physician had no inkling on that day that Lizzie's red thread of destiny would lead her into his family.

The physician was looking over the Seminole Nation with a clear purpose. He had a decision to make, a very serious and important decision.

If his professional life in Park Hill was going to continue its sad decline, should he think seriously about pulling up stakes, and moving elsewhere?

On the long ride home, he finally thought through his dilemma.

Back in Park Hill, he assembled the family while another of the glorious sunsets he so prized washed gold over their log cabin.

First-born John Franklin was now fourteen, tall, broad-shouldered, keen-eyed, and sharp like his papa. Little Lucy was twelve, Jennie ten, Alice five, and Andrew Jackson three. The newest baby, Robert, was two. Their mother was now thirty-four.

The doctor got them quiet and then made his announcement. "We are leaving Park Hill, and moving to the Seminole Nation." [29]

FOUR YEARS LATER the doctor's son John, shy of his eighteenth birthday by fifty-four days, stood amid an excited throng of Seminole men outside the Seminole Council House. It was August 1, 1861. The Civil War had broken out barely six months before, and was harshly spilling over into the lives of the Five Civilized Tribes.

Troubling every mind was the paramount question—should the Indians remain loyal to the Great Father in Washington and his

American soldiers, or should their interests lie with the Confederate rebels? The conundrum left the Seminoles agitated and excited, unhappy and angry. Strong arguments were being shouted—going both ways. The Indians believed their decision could put everything at risk—their lives, families, possessions.

Young Brown and the others watched a swirl of dust arise from the ridge trail. A large caravan was approaching. The boy was thinking about his parents and his brothers and sisters. They had moved four years earlier to Council Town, where his father had set up his medical practice. They lived in a comfortable log house, and were contented. What would this war do to them?

Approaching on the ridge road was a military wagon ambulance drawn by four white mules. Directly behind came a squadron of gray-clad cavalry on matched horses. A stunning spectacle this, clearly meant to be colorful and impressive.

When the ambulance wagon whirled in off the ridge road and came to a dramatic jolting halt, the boy watched it discharge a tall, heavy, bearded man in dark clothes. He had long wavy black hair and wore four finger rings. His step was sudden, quick. His eyes flashed; he was obviously ready to do important business.

To John Franklin Brown this was perhaps the most formidable and kinglike individual he had ever seen—Albert Pike, fifty-two, from Fort Smith, the Indian Commissioner for the Confederacy. Pike was scouring Indian Territory vigorously attempting to forge military alliances with the Five Civilized Tribes. The Seminoles had expressed a preference to remain neutral, as had the Cherokees.

From the Council House, Chief John Jumper emerged to greet his visitors. John Franklin knew Jumper well; so well he could actually recognize his shadow. He had been spending many evenings and some Sundays at the Jumper home. He was courting pretty Lizzie.

Watching this Council House scene, John Franklin was torn by conflicting emotions. He felt anger because the Great White Father was clearly mistreating his children. The Government made promises, and didn't keep them. The annuity payments for 1860 never arrived and still were being withheld. That created a double hardship on the Seminoles. For this was the third straight summer of drought. Crops failed; corn, the tribe's food staple, was scarce. Everyone suffered.

Even so, the boy had been taught that Indian honor was sacred. When a Seminole gave his pledge, it could never be broken. Not even a bad treaty could be ignored. He knew many of the young Seminole men felt the same. But they, too, were muttering discontent, and were decidedly ambivalent about allegiance in the war.

Like him, nearly all were superior horsemen. Should they forget the treaty and volunteer for the Union cavalry? He looked closely at the Confederate troopers chatting and watering their horses in the Council House yard. They were Indians, too—and they had decided to fight on the South's side. That was something to think about.

His brain felt heavy; his thoughts jumped from place to place. He pondered it all—life, love, honor, and war. He knew his father's intentions were unequivocal. Dr. Brown intended to remain neutral, despite having been born in the Deep South, where his in-laws owned slaves. To John Franklin, his father explained: "As a healer, I must be unbiased, and help all, with no distinction."[30]

The Seminoles milled around waiting for the meeting in the Council House to end. After about ninety minutes, the doors opened. Chief Jumper and Albert Pike emerged. John Franklin's father had explained that Pike was an ambitious man of remarkable talents and skills. Born in Massachusetts, he turned himself into a brilliant teacher, poet, author, lawyer, editor. While young, he had gone to the Staked Plains as a trapper—but by 1849 had converted himself into a lawyer and had the distinction of being admitted to the bar of the Supreme Court of the United States alongside young Abraham Lincoln. As an American soldier, he had fought in the Mexican War. He was somebody!

Outside now under the August sky, Pike's features seemed to soften. His face exhibited a smile. Chief Jumper held up a paper, and waved it like a banner. It was a treaty he and his council had signed. Turning to face Pike, Jumper handed him the document. Pike then produced a Bible and had the Chief place his hand on it. Then he swore Chief Jumper into the Confederate Army with the rank of major, second in command of a combined Seminole and Creek mounted battalion.

With a swift move, Pike produced a new saber that sparkled impressively and handed it to his newest officer.

John Franklin Brown felt no surprise; this had been predicted. The boy watched the Confederate troopers mount their horses and form up behind Pike's departing ambulance wagon. Stirring up the dust again, the Confederate contingent disappeared back down the ridge road. Even though the Council had voted to support the South, the boy knew their action didn't speak for the entire tribe.

The Seminoles were not of one mind on North versus South. Two of their town chiefs, Billy Bowlegs and John Chupco, were agitating loudly for staying loyal to the federal government. Heated dissent was rising in the Creek Nation, too. There could come serious trouble.

Young Brown rode home. His mind was still in a swirl of uncertainty. He yearned for an answer, but he decided to seek no counsel—not from his father, nor anyone. He was a man; he could make his decision. Other young Seminoles looked to him as their leader. He would act, and do the right thing. He vowed to honor the Seminole pledge to the Great White Father. [31]

After dark, without even a goodbye, he mounted up and set out to round up other young Seminole horsemen he would take with him into the United States Army.

"Hold up, Brown!" He had gone hardly two miles from home. Three mounted Indians emerged from gloom onto the wagon trail, and hemmed him in. Somebody must have been spying on him; he had been perhaps too open about his pro-North feelings. "Council wants you. Come!"[32]

Escorted back to the Council House, young John found himself facing a battery of interrogators. In the yellow gleam of the table lamps, they eyed him with suspicion. What, they asked, were his intentions? His honor was at stake; he would tell no lies. His answer was quick, strong, and truthful. Yes, he intended to gather volunteers and take them to ride with the cavalry of the United States Army. For him, there could be no breaking a solemn treaty.

Chief Jumper sat at the end of the long table, apart from the "jury" of five full blood Council members who questioned the boy. Finally the jurors arose, gathered in a corner of the room and put their heads together to consider a verdict. After only a few minutes of discussion, they returned looking grim.

John Franklin Brown was ordered to stand.

The foreman spoke. "You be foun' guilty desertion Seminole Nation. An' spyin'. Penalty is firin' squad." He turned to Chief Jumper, and added: "If Chief agree." [33]

The chief sat staring at, and gently stroking the blade of his shiny new saber lying on the table. For a minute or two, he said nothing. Finally, he lifted his head and drilled the boy with hard eyes. Still he said nothing, but cleared his throat, seeming to ponder his response.

John Franklin felt a sudden tremor. Death by firing squad was a strict Seminole tribal punishment. Perhaps he could visualize a heart-shaped target being cut from paper, and pinned on the left side of his shirt. How does it feel when a bullet smashes your breastbone? He might have imagined the pain facing his parents, his sisters, his new baby brothers. He doubtless thought of Lizzie, and lost love.

Chief John Jumper turned to the jurors and spoke. "There is another way." He paused, looked down and let his fingers again gently touch the silver blade. He lifted his head, and raised his voice. "This young man could here and now raise his right hand, and swear faithful allegiance to the Confederate States of America . . . and ride with me!" [34]

3

'The Wolf Has Come'

I N FREEZING WEATHER on December 9, 1861, Lieutenant
John Franklin Brown of the Confederate Army got his first taste
of bullets and blood on the battlefield.

And, astonishingly, it was red brother killing red brother!

He was galloping with Major John Jumper's just-commis-
sioned Seminole battalion flanking other Southern soldiers push-
ing a fierce attack on an "enemy" caravan in wild country near
present day Tulsa.[1] The *whoosh* of a bullet past his ear startled
Lieutenant Brown, but invigorated him. He kept riding fast and
hard; he didn't flinch.[2]

This was a test of courage he gladly welcomed. Especially
since he was a Seminole warrior just turned eighteen years old. In
the Florida Everglades, young Seminole men earned essential distinction by exhibiting skill as warriors or hunters. In the West there
had been scant opportunity for young Brown to show the tribe his
bravery or keen mental powers. So in this war as a lieutenant he
hoped to find glory that would demand the respect of elders.

All around him, guns were flashing. Out of the corner of his
eye, Lieutenant Brown caught sight of a fellow trooper being
shot out of the saddle. This was a running battle, furious and hard
fought.

50

In this din and clatter, his jejune mind had no inkling that this fighting would be recorded as perhaps the cruelest episode in the history of the Civil War in Indian Territory.

The "enemy" that Lieutenant Brown and his fellow Indian soldiers were chasing and shooting actually were Creeks and Seminoles, their own tribe members who were fleeing north mainly to avoid being involved in the war. The pursuers intended to stop their kinsmens' escape—by capturing or killing them.

Warriors fell on both sides. But the real horror was the terrible toll of casualties inflicted by this few days of fighting on non-combatant and refugees —hundreds of women, children, and the aged.[3]

Outbreak of the war brought chaos to the Five Civilized Tribes. They felt the federal government abandoned them by withdrawing U.S. troops from their three Indian Territory forts, on the theory the frontier soldiers might be needed for action up north. That left the Five Tribes again unprotected from raids by the wild plains Indians. Washington also withheld all 1860 annuity payments, hurting Indians' pocketbooks and confidence.

In the midst of this anger and confusion, Confederates came among them seeking alliances. The war pulled tribes apart. Slavery was not the only issue; old feuds and simmering rivalries were re-ignited. Anguish was rampant when a tribesman had to choose between North and South.

Out of this dangerous welter arose a singular leader—Opothleyahola of the Upper Creeks. He stood with Chief John Ross of the Cherokees in wanting to remain neutral. That wasn't possible. Under Confederate blandishment, roughly half of each tribe sided with the South. Opothleyahola lost the Lower Creeks of Chief Roley McIntosh, who was his personal enemy because of a 1825 family killing back in their Georgia-Alabama era. The Lower Creeks joined the Confederacy, as had the large band of Seminoles who were followers of Chief John Jumper.

Unable to reconcile his own conflicts, Opothleyahola had written on August 15, 1861 asking help from President Abraham Lincoln and dispatched by courier his letter, which said:

Now I write to the President our Great Father who removed us to our present homes, and made a treaty and you said that in our new homes we should be defended from all interference from any people. And that no white people in the whole world would ever molest us unless they come from the sky but the land should be ours as long as grass grew or waters run. And should we be injured by anybody you would come with your soldiers and punish them.

But now the wolf has come. Men who are strangers tread our soil. Our children are frightened and their mothers cannot sleep for fear. This is our situation now. There our Great Father was strong and now we raise our hands to him for help to keep off the intruder and make our houses happy as they used to be. Our Great Father was always near and stood between us and danger.

We his children want it to be so again and we want you to send us word what to do. We do not hear from you and we send a letter and pray you to answer it. Your children want to hear your word and feel that you do not forget them.

I was in Washington where you treated with us and now white people are trying to take our people away to fight against us and you. I am alive. I well remember the treaty. My ears are open and my memory is good.

This is a letter of
your children by
Opoth le hoyola* [4]

Lincoln eventually answered that it was "a white man's war" and did not involve the Indians. Opothleyahola was not reassured; he could plainly see the war was killing Indians, ruining lives, property. About sixty years old, the Upper Creek chief was, says historian John Bartlett Merserve, "cool, cautious and sagacious and displayed talents of a superior order . . . never bribed or corrupted." [5] Eschewing white man's attire, he at times wore a blanket, gracefully, leather leggings and a bright shawl as a turban. He was considered the wealthiest of all Creeks, but the war eventually wiped out his estate, consisting mainly of a vast array of horses, cattle, and sheep. [6]

The Upper Creek's best option, the chief finally concluded, was to round up their livestock, load all household goods in wagons, and flee en masse north into Kansas where Union forces would protect them. He sent out runners inviting other like-minded Indians to join his caravan.

Colonel Douglas H. Cooper, head of Confederate operations in Indian Territory, got word of the scheme. With an armed force of 1,400, he hurried to Opothleyahola's camp at the North Fork and the Deep Fork of the Canadian River (near present day Eufaula). On arrival November 15, 1861, Cooper found the site deserted.

Opothleyahola's "loyal" Indians had already started north, a four- or five-mile long train of covered wagons drawn by oxen and mules, plus buggies and horsemen, with hundreds walking, followed by droves of livestock. [7] These "loyals" numbered about 9,000.

In the caravan were a large number of Seminoles, men, women, and children, under leadership of town chiefs John Chupco, Billy Bowlegs, and Halleck Tustenuggee, who were responsible for splitting the tribe.[8] They had revolted against Chief Jumper's decision to lead Seminole tribesmen into the Confederate army.

Colonel Cooper turned north and led his troops after the "loyals." Four days later the Confederate soldiers caught sight of Opothleyahola's train at the Arkansas River near present Tulsa, and attacked, but they encountered shocking return fire. The "loyals" were well armed. Their rear guard drove off Cooper's forward detachment.[9]

Cooper paused and then withdrew, intending to marshal a larger force. When next he resumed pursuit, his command was stronger, including a mounted regiment of Choctaws and Chickasaws, Texas cavalry units, and the smaller Creek-Seminole column, commanded by Major John Jumper. Lieutenant Brown rode in the Seminole battalion.

On December 8, Cooper again caught up with the "loyals." Opothleyahola had set up formidable defenses behind boulders and trees in a bend of Bird Creek (south of present Skiatook). By clever strategy, the Creek chief seduced Cooper, who was camped six miles away, into sending one of his captains to talk peace. That parley came to naught, but the incident disturbed Cooper's Cherokee soldiers, and that night 300 of them deserted, unwilling to kill friendly fellow red men.[10]

On the morning of December 9, 1861, Cooper attacked with three columns, the Major Jumper-Lieutenant Brown cavalry being on the left flank. The battle see-sawed furiously. Opothleyahola's warriors, estimated at 2,500, were protected by a 30-foot high creek bank and deep ravines, and could not be dislodged. At sunset, Cooper, low on ammunition and with 15 dead and 37 wounded, drew back and bivouacked on the prairie. Next morning when the Confederates returned to do battle, Opothleyahola had vanished, again disappearing in the dark of night. [11]

Fearing further defections by his Cherokee soldiers, Cooper quit the chase and started a long march back to Fort Gibson to reorganize. [12] There he requested help from Colonel James McIntosh, the Confederate division commander. Instead of giving Cooper more men, McIntosh decided to take on Opothelyahola himself. He sent Cooper's regiment up the north side of the Arkansas River to be ready to attack from the rear. McIntosh led 1,600 troops north and on December 26 found Opothleyahola's forces well dug-in along Shoal Creek, but low on food and ammunition.[13] Without waiting for Cooper to get in position, McIntosh launched an immediate assault.

The ground was snow-covered, and a northwest wind drove sleet into the soldiers' faces. The Union Indians fought fiercely, but this time they could not hold off the stronger enemy. By four in the afternoon, Opothleyahola's lines were broken in several places. His men began running. It turned into a devastating rout, a total Confederate Indian victory.

The "loyal" women and children fled in every direction, but the Confederates captured 160 of them, and seized virtually all cattle, ponies, wagons and supplies. Colonel McIntosh lost nine dead and forty wounded. The "loyal" dead he estimated to be 250.

Only later did Lieutenant Brown learn the full extent of the horror that took place within thirty miles of sanctuary the "loyals" were trying to reach—the Kansas state line.

As historian Edwin C. McReynolds described the battle's aftermath:

> The flight of Opothleyahola and his people . . . was a time of indescribable horror for the fugitives. Frozen bodies lying in the snow marked the route north, and often the garments of the dead

were removed to supplement the meager clothing of survivors. Of the Indians who reached Kansas a large percent had frozen hands or feet, which had to be amputated . . .

Some of the Seminoles and a few Cherokees who had not succeeded in joining Opothleyahola before the march northward began, arrived in the refugee camp later. By April 1862, there were 7,600 Indians in the camp. Medical attention could not be given to all who needed it; shelter, clothing and food were inadequate; and several hundred of the Indians died, including Opothleyahola, after they had reached a place of safety from the Confederate bullets.[14]

Although this battle occurred roughly thirty miles south of the Verdigris River near present Coffeyville, Kansas, the surviving "loyals" trudged afoot across the snowy prairie two or three miserable days to reach the Union haven. Babies were born to naked mothers in the snow; some died. Ponies that died of starvation were eaten by the Indians. It was as bad or worse than the Trail of Tears.

Refugees who reached Kansas found very little of the help expected from their Great Father. No housing was available. The few available physicians were overloaded with emergencies, kept busy amputating frozen toes and fingers. Both feet of an eight-year-old Creek boy were cut off. Scores of escaping refugees died even after reaching Kansas. It was up to the Army to feed the refugees, but miserly rations were distributed. Once a week the Indians were given condemned Army bacon "not fit for a dog," plus one pound of flour, scanty salt, but no coffee, sugar, vinegar or pepper.

All of the able-bodied male survivors, about 800, were taken into the Union Army. The other refugees, Government agents estimated, could be fed for ten cents a day but that would come to $292,000 a year. [15] Thus short rations continued, and hundreds more of the "stranded" Indians were destined to fall ill and die in Kansas.

AT FORT GIBSON in early 1862, Dr. Brown stood and watched the U. S. Army ambulance wagon come rumbling in through the main gate with a load of wounded. It was trailed by two wagons stacked with the dead, both Yankee and Confederate.

Seized by anxiety, he rushed to the wagons and quickly scanned the faces. Such personal trepidation he had never before experienced. Was his son among the incoming "enemy" dead or wounded?

At the outbreak of war he had been summoned by the U.S. Army from his home out in the Seminole Nation to return to duty at Fort Gibson. Once more he was employed in his old role, as a civilian contracted acting assistant surgeon.

Just now he turned away from the wagons with a sigh of relief. He has ascertained that CSA Lieutenant Brown was not among these just-arrived dead and wounded. He ran to the post hospital and began trying to save lives. He did not consider himself a Yankee; he was neutral, a humanitarian, a military surgeon trained and willing and able to deal with the horrific damage of war. Inflicted by either North or South, it made no difference to his neutral surgical hands.

It dazzled his mind that—technically, at least—he and his first-born son were on opposite sides in the Civil War. He prayed that good luck would be on young John's side. Deadly skirmishes were erupting around the re-opened and rebuilt Fort Gibson. But he had learned that his son and Major Jumper and their Indian troops were now primarily away from danger, being on home guard duty down along the Red River near the Texas border.

Dr. Brown expected to be at Fort Gibson for the duration. Hence he had brought his wife Lucy and their children temporarily back to Park Hill. All around Fort Gibson life was dangerous. The Cherokees were violently split into rivalry over secession, and partisans of both the North and the South were spilling blood across their Indian nation. Nightriders and bushwhackers pillaged and burned homes and murdered innocents.

On the traditional battlefields, Confederates furiously tried to cut Fort Gibson's supply line from Fort Leavenworth in Kansas. This led in the summer of 1863 to a series of bloody battles near Fort Gibson. [16] On May 25, 1863 a Union train of 200 wagons from Leavenworth was attacked but got through to Fort Gibson after killing 35 Confederate Indians. A month later another supply train of 218 mule wagons and forty ox wagons from Kansas was attacked by Confederate General Stand Watie, a wily and powerful Cherokee whose hands already were bloody in the internecine fighting with Chief John Ross.

"Stand Watie," Union Cherokee agent Justin Harlin reported in 1863, "entered the Territory in three different raids, took everything he could ride, or drive, or carry off, and destroyed their crops. . . Watie with 700 ragamuffins was permitted to rob at will over the whole Territory. If anything was left by Watie, it has not yet been found."[17]

Although he led 1,600 warriors, General Watie's attack was stymied because a flood on Cabin Creek prevented a supporting Confederate column of 1,500 on the opposite bank from coming across the stream to help him. The train's defenders prevailed and the supply wagons escaped, leaving one hundred fifty attackers dead.

General Watie attempted one year later, September 19, 1864, to again waylay Federal forces at the same Cabin Creek site. In this battle, he had with him Major John Jumper and Lieutenant John Franklin Brown, and their Confederate cavalry battalion.

For almost two hours, the clatter of musketry echoed up and down the stream. In the end it was another Confederate defeat. Major Jumper and Lieutenant Brown were among the lucky soldiers who escaped unscathed.

About then the war began to subside in Indian Territory. Dr. Brown occasionally was ordered to grab his medicine bag, saddle up and go out into the countryside to treat civilians—essential laborers, hay-cutters or salt workers. He disliked this duty, and vigorously protested, but to no avail. [18] This travel added an additional $13.83 to his $100 a month paycheck.

In the waning days of the Civil War, Dr. Brown was sent to Vicksburg, Mississippi on May 15, 1865 to be one of that city's two military health officers. [19] His Vicksburg duty lasted but a month, ending about the time the last Confederates in Indian Territory surrendered.

Once more Dr. Brown was abruptly let go by the Army. And that again got his dander up.

He was on duty at the Fort Gibson hospital when notified that his contract was annulled. He complained: "I do not therefore consider the reason assigned a good one, tho' the order like all military orders is supreme." [20]

And in a postscript he got in another dig. He had heard "nothing of my pay accounts from 15th August 1864 to 14th May 1865 inclusive." He ended his letter with a quote from Solomon's *Proverbs:* "Hope defer'd maketh the heart sad. J.F.B."

WHILE THE WAR wound down on distant battlefields, Lieutenant Colonel John Jumper had time to study his well-thumbed Bible. He often pondered over Matthew, third chapter. In this period, the Confederacy was collapsing, but blue and gray soldiers were still killing each other on battlefields from Mobile Bay to Richmond, Virginia. Jumper's small battalion, however, was rarely called out, and usually for home front excursions. He had just received his promotion to lieutenant colonel, authorized by the Confederate Congress. He was aware his new rank was largely honorary, carrying no increased authority or pay. That wasn't what was on his mind.

"Let me read this to you," he said to Lieutenant Brown. "It says, *Then Jesus came from Galilee to the Jordan to be baptized by John...As soon as Jesus was baptized, he went up out of the water.* So you see, that is the difference—'out of the water.' That disturbs my mind." [21]

When he later became an Indian preacher himself, John Franklin Brown would sometimes refer to this conversation, their earnest discussions of differing conversion rituals of the Baptists and the Presbyterians. The latter only "sprinkled." Jumper was explaining why he had switched from the Presbyterian to the Baptist faith.

Infrequently summoned for action, they had a good deal of time to talk. Jumper's admiration seemed to grow for his young protégé. He expected Lizzie to marry John. The lieutenant was brave, smart, and handsome. Schooled by his father in classic literature, Lieutenant Brown was likewise fast and sure in the Seminole tongue—and ways. Jumper could see that the lad's mother had extensively shared tribal lore with her half-blood son. It was clear he could walk with equal ease in the footsteps of both Indian and white man.

Often the Seminole battalion mounted up and rode out to chase away invaders. Plains Indians sneaked in at night stealing cattle and ponies. So did Kansas Jayhawkers and Texas bushwhackers. In daylight, brutal murdering renegades brazenly plundered Seminole Nation homes and fields.

These lightning depredations became so difficult to prevent or punish, a large number of Seminole families abandoned their homes around Council Town. The tribe sent the Confederate government a $3,225 bill for thirty-two horses stolen by the Comanches. Then the disheartened Seminoles packed their belongings and trekked south toward the Red River.

Creek refugees already were clustered around Fort Washita. The Seminoles headed further west into the Chickasaw Nation. They discovered a place called Oil Spring amid timbered hills and thick-grass prairie. Observing tall trees, they knew the land was fertile. The Seminoles built cabins and planted corn, vegetables, and cotton. Their settlement was only fifty miles from Fort Washita, which was occupied by Confederate troops. The nearness of these soldiers gave them hope of protection.

It was no mystery to either Colonel Jumper or Lieutenant Brown why their cavalry was for such long periods kept out of action. In private, they deplored this secret prejudice. It was clear that white Confederate officers disliked working with Indian soldiers. Most Southern commanders seemed to characterize the tribesmen generally as undisciplined and undependable.

Desertions actually were abnormally high in the Indian ranks. One reason was existence of this racial discrimination that robbed them of a fair share of rations and supplies. "We only get the crumbs," lamented General Albert Pike, "that fall from the white man's table." Failure to receive clothing and pay for his Indian soldiers so disgusted Pike that he resigned. [22]

Colonel Jumper took a less jaundiced view, writing: "The Confederate States have not deserted us; we have been provided for; our women and children are fed . . . The Government is engaged in a great war; she cannot do any more for us now than she is doing." [23]

Lazing about at Camp Jumper, Lieutenant John Franklin Brown found himself almost forgetting a war was still going on; his mind was inclined to stray. An unbidden pleasant reverie might start while he was gazing on a field of sun-lit wildflowers that waltzed in the prairie breeze. Or while basking in the silvery glow of a coyote moon. [24] One day his grandchildren would be told of those dreams, of hearing a soft, gentle voice, of tenderly touching warm, velvety skin, and of drowning in the mysterious depths of dark, shining eyes . . . the love bug had bitten him.

WHEN THE END OF THE WAR terminated his contract at Fort Gibson, Dr. Brown in the late summer of 1865 loaded up his family to return to the Seminole Nation and pick up their lives in the home place they had left at Council Town.

On arrival they got a severe jolt of surprise, shock, and anger. [25]

The homestead they had always kept neat and well-attended first came into view about dusk. As their wagon and riding horses topped the crest of ridge road, everybody looked and gasped. Their house was a shambles!

Whoever had wrecked it —most likely renegade army deserters, Comanches or Kiowas raiding from the plains, bushwhackers from Texas, perhaps even enemies from the "loyal" Seminoles —inflicted terrible damage.

The front door hung askew by a single hinge. Glass in every window was shattered. Part of the roof was smashed. The well house and the privy had been toppled. Fence rails were broken. Dried weeds clotted the fields.

When their noisy little caravan pulled close to the front gate, a dark cloud erupted from the burnt pasture, hammering their ears with a thunderous burst of chirping. The purple-greenish cluster for a long moment blotted out the golden horizon. Then the malignant curtain swirled briefly overhead and fluttered off toward the north. "Grasshoppers!" someone shrieked. "Millions of grasshoppers! What next!" [26]

As if the war hadn't been bad enough, the drought was hanging on, the worst dry spell, everyone said, in thirty years. It was too late to plant crops, anyhow. Times would be hard. Dr. Brown had just seen, however, as their wagon passed through the Creek

Nation, that conditions there were even worse. The Creeks' greatest asset, 300,000 cattle worth $4,000,000, had been left on their pastures largely untended. Organized rustlers boldly came in and started driving them off to Kansas. Agents were hired to try to stop these raids; but civil and military authorities gave no help, seeming to condon the theft simply as expectable wartime plunder. Finally every pasture was emptied of livestock. [27]

Starting over was not going to be easy, Dr. Brown knew. Especially without any appreciable help from his first-born. John Franklin was caught up in charting his own post-Civil War life, trying to sort out his most promising opportunities. He was spending a good deal of time with the John Jumper family. Love had triumphed; he and Lizzie were now married.

Dr. Brown, at sixty-five, no longer felt the excess vigor that propelled him in earlier times. But his long years of practice enabled him to now move more quickly in diagnosis and treatment, so the calendar had diminished his effectiveness very little.

Now just forty-two, Lucy Greybeard Brown had borne eight children, seven living. John Franklin would be twenty-two this coming October. Daughter Lucy had just turned twenty and Jennie was eighteen. The doctor usually smiled when he gave extensive thought to Alice; she was thirteen, and a surprising whirlwind, inquisitive, active, and studious. Andrew Jackson was eleven, Robert ten. A just-born son, Stanton, was six months old, still nursing. Dr. Brown was pleased with them, and enormously proud of all. And of his wife Lucy, especially because she had so conscientiously imparted to the offspring in the most frank but appropriate way, the values of their Indian heritage.

His Scotch taciturnity kept him on an even keel. He didn't panic. Repairs to their home place required much labor; but he could do it. Rain would come again; at least in time for Spring planting. The grasshoppers hadn't destroyed crops; there had been nothing growing in their burnt fields. The insects would vanish, mysteriously, overnight—and, if the legends were true, not come back for seven years.

Dr. Brown observed that John Jumper had caused John Franklin to become deeply involved in religion, as was now the chief himself. What inspired Jumper's deep interest in religion was an unusual story. It was triggered by the arrest of the Seminoles' interpreter, Major James Factor, an Indian and native of Florida and known, because of his strong bloodlines from the Conquistadors, as "The Spaniard."

Factor had been converted by a Presbyterian missionary, Ross Ramsey, who had come to the Creek Nation from Georgia. The Creeks, however, let it be known "we don't want the ways of the white man, such as schools, preaching, fiddle-dancing and playing cards." [28] The Reverend Ramsey quickly packed his wagon and moved to the Seminole Nation.

In this period Christianity and other aspects of American culture were achieving scant acceptance among the Seminoles. Not many of the tribe spoke or read English; most chiefs had to sign treaties with their X mark (attested to by interpreters). Only about two percent attended preaching services conducted by missionaries.

When it became known Factor had been converted, he was put on trial before the Seminole Council, convicted of being "bewitched," and punished by being publicly whipped. Intrigued by these circumstances, Chief Jumper sought Reverend Ramsey to question him about religion, and was himself converted to Christianity.

No one, of course, would dare take the chief to the whipping tree. Two Baptist missionaries also had come into Indian Territory, John Bemo and Joseph S. Murrow. Bemo, a nephew of Osceola, led a charmed life. Kidnapped as a lad in the Florida wars, he was shanghaied as a cabin boy, became an ocean-going sailor, fell in with influential citizens in Philadelphia, who saw that he was well educated. He became a Christian and came out to the Seminole Nation as a missionary. Murrow, then about thirty, quit college in Georgia to come to Indian Territory and convert natives.

In 1860 Murrow established in the Seminole Nation a Baptist church at Ash Creek, near Council Town. Chief Jumper joined his small congregation. Murrow, a skinny fellow five feet, not much over 110 pounds, led the chief out into the creek for the baptismal ceremony. Jumper at six-four weighed at least 225 pounds.

The little missionary easily managed to submerge the big Indian. Then Murrow panicked. He could not raise Jumper back to the surface.

"Help! Help!"

Bemo instantly leaped into the stream. He was quick and muscular. He had Jumper up in a flash.

REPAIRING DAMAGE done his Council Town home kept Dr. Brown busy, but he resumed his practice among the Indians who were returning to their homes. He continued also to closely direct the education of his children.

Also he found time to maintain his literary interests. Mail was slow and infrequent, usually arriving by stagecoach or military courier. By reading journals and newspapers, he remained aware of new books being published.

To his library he hoped to add a few of the new: *Letters From The Underground* by Russian novelist Fedor Dostoievski, Jules Verne's *Journey to the Center of the Earth,* the first of Anthony Trollope's six Palliser novels, *Can You Forgive Her?* [29] He read with interest about Robert Browning's newest book of poetry *Dramatis Personae,* with one critic slavering over the poem "Rabbi Ben Ezra" which included the lines:

> *Grow old with me!*
> *The best is yet to be,*
> *The last of life, for which*
> *the first was made.*

His own quill pen was busy enlarging his "Therapeutics." The manuscript now ran 900 or so pages. As he re-read his work, new thoughts, rationales, or experiences prompted additions and revisions. Medicine was not seamlessly scientific or rigid. He felt doctors should experiment. How many home remedies "Therapeutics" contained surprised him. For example: To treat catarrh, his prescription called for cooking in three pints of water two turnips, two potatoes, four stalks celery, one medium onion, one slice of bread, boiling all down to one pint. This was to be strained and served to the patient on toast. This, he found, was highly curative. [30]

For certain fevers, he prescribed shaving the patient's head, applying cold compresses, and a blister, which should be left in place twenty-four hours. A "very good unguent" for treating hemorrhoids can be made of hog lard mixed with spermaceti, laudanum, and Goulards extract of lead, applied every two or three hours. "I have done much good with a bread and milk poultice smeared with laudanum and lead water. In very old cases where every remedy has failed, Dr. Physick is in the habit of recommending a long journey on horseback, and with success." [31]

Dr. Brown devoted a long chapter to menorrhagia. "By this is meant the flow of blood from the unimpregnated uterus." Even here he was committed to the practice of blood letting, writing, "Copious V.S. is necessary especially where it is attended by an acute pain in the head, loins and limbs, giddiness, dyspnoea, fever, with a corded pulse. The bowels should be kept open, repose and a strict adherence to the antiphlogistic plan should be resorted to."

This included saccharum saturni [lead sugar], 3 to 4 grains combined with one-eight grain of opium taken internally ever hour or two.

> This will often display extraordinary powers. It is very often also applied to the pudendum or injected into the vagina and here it is very serviceable.
>
> The powers of ipecacunanha in checking uterine hoemorrhage are frequently astonishing. In many cases, I have remarked that the moment nausea could be induced, the hoemorrhage ceased.
>
> We are to make use of topical applications. Of these the most efficacious is cold, which may be applied by cloths wet in cold water or with vinegar and water, to the abdomen or pudendum. Ice introduced into the vagina is often productive of great advantage.
>
> But by far the best method of applying cold is to pour water from a height on the pudendum and abdomen. The shock thus induced seems to act very powerfully in stopping the hoemorrhage.
>
> All these remedies failing, however, much good may be derived from plugging up the vagina. [32]

AFTER THE FAMILY returned to Council Town, Alice elected to spend more time in her father's company. She fetched his medicine bag before he mounted up to go visit a patient. She peeked around the corner to watch him shave. In the evenings when he took up his quill pen, she would sit near him and read.

Almost fourteen, Alice was beginning to blossom, but more as a tomboy than a beauty. She had not only a mesmeric brain but muscles. She could run like a deer, and held her own in sibling controversies. [33]

Alice had her mother's deep-set wide-spaced dark eyes, and long black hair, and identical narrow mouth and thin lips. But her face was more angular; the girl's nose a trifle longer, and her chin not so rounded. The daughter's close-set ears were already pierced, from which she proudly dangled silver earrings. Though long-legged and slender, it seemed obvious Alice would reach only moderate height, probably no more than five-six.

Her facial features were unmistakably Indian, but her smooth and light complexion was from her father's genes. She was attractive enough to be self-confident, with moods ranging from giggly or adventuresome to solemn and studious.

When Alice examined her father's leather-bound books she knew beyond doubt that his family had brought from Europe to America an aristocratic heritage.

Often she took down his three-volume edition of Sir Walter Scott's *Guy Mannering* just to again marvel at the Brown family crest displayed on the flyleaf. A family crest! The thought made her glow with pride. [34]

Enchanted, she dove into Scott's other works on her father's shelves. In *Marmion* she found herself pondering at length over the esoteric implications of romantic hero Young Lochinvar's utterance, "Oh, what a tangled web we weave... " yet was stirred by the poetry.

She felt vaguely guilty that she somehow knew more of her mother's days in the wild Everglades of Florida, than she did of her father's years back in Charleston.

From the crest on the flyleaf, she read the Latin motto: *Caute et Sedulo.*

"Tell me again what it means."

Alice was asking for perhaps the twentieth time. [35] Her father, understanding, answered patiently, "Cautiously and carefully."

Often she wanted to discuss his profession. He was intrigued by her interest in medicine, as well as pleased. She pumped him, and listened avidly. Those conversations stayed vividly alive in her memory, as she demonstrated years later by repeating them to her grandchildren. She often recalled the amusing tales her father, with a mischievous twinkle, told one pleasant evening.

"This happened several years ago in Park Hill. You were just a baby then. Doubt if you ever heard this. I'll never forget it.

"An Indian came running to me for help. He thought he was done for, I guess.

"He had got hold of a bottle of red liquid. Thought it was whiskey. He drank it all down. Then he discovered it was red ink!

"That's when he rushed to me—and wanted to know quick what to do.

"I looked him in the eye, and said: 'The thing for you to do is eat some blotting paper.'

"The Indian looked even more scared. You know Indians do not have much of a sense of humor. But in a minute or two, he got it. His face twisted up in a great smile. He mumbled thanks, and quickly left."[36]

Her immediate thirst for medical lore quenched, Alice remembered going off to bed while her father again dipped his quill in his silver inkwell to write more on "Therapeutics." [37]

4

Hark! The Dark Angel

TWENTY-THREE MEN, Indians and Government officials, filed into a Washington, D.C. conference room, shuffled the chairs noisily around and sat down. They spread out documents on a massive rosewood table that gleamed in morning light from tall windows.

This day, Wednesday, March 21, 1866, was crucial for the Indians. They were Seminoles who had come to sign a new treaty, even though by its terms their Great Father intended to punish them for their Civil War rebellion—and severely so.[1] The Indians were disappointed and unhappy, but powerless; they had no weapon capable of holding off Washington's revenge.

By far the youngest person in this historic session at the Department of the Interior was John Franklin Brown. Though barely midway in his twenty-third year, he ranked equal in importance to any Indian in the room.

This youngster, whose boots left dusty footprints on the rich Aubusson carpet and whose neatly pressed coat sleeves slid on the table's high polish, was not out of place. He had been sent to Washington as the sole delegate to act for the several thousand Seminoles who cast their lot with the Confederacy—and lost. [2]

Much like his father, John Franklin Brown stood six feet tall, broad-shouldered with almost a barrel chest. His Indian strain was obvious, but his complexion was not dark, rather that of a plainsman, often called sun-tanned or swarthy.

Out of bright black, deep-set eyes he took in the scene stoically, rarely excited. His head was large, thickly covered by a black wavy mane, with close-set ears. His mustache and goatee looked like fine black wire—scraggly, untrimmed. Close friends dubbed him "John, The Silent." But in private his natural Scottish wit and humor came easily to the surface. [3]

In the throng at the table, he perhaps sat most erect; [4] his movements were fluid, graceful, and unhurried. His coat, trousers and cravat obviously were new, but fit handsomely. His status was no secret in Washington. Such a young delegate would not be negotiating for the "southern" Seminoles except for two facts of privilege—he was married to John Jumper's daughter, and he had been the chief's wartime lieutenant and protégé.

John Jumper had stayed home. He was still chief of the southern Seminoles, but no longer principal chief. The Government gave that office and authority to John Chupco —sometimes called "Long John"—who had remained loyal to the Union.

Brown and "Long John" no longer were fighting each other. The Civil War was over. Together here in Washington, they agreed it was urgent to sign a treaty and have a better and immediate chance to get on with reconstructing their tribal lives.

Chief Jumper's son-in-law did not like the deal being jammed down their throats by Dennis N. Cooley, United States Commissioner of Indian Affairs. The Government had the Seminoles with their backs to the wall, with little wiggle room. [5]

But Brown tried to put up a fight. As the story was told to descendants, Chief Jumper's young son-in-law lifted the treaty off the rosewood table and waved it before Commissioner Cooley. He put his forefinger on Article Number Three of the treaty's eleven.

The document, Brown inquired pointedly, would mandate that the United States Government "buys back all our land at fifteen cents an acre—and sells us new land at fifty cents an acre?" [6]

Cooley, the story goes, gave a stiff, solemn nod.

"And," Brown continued, "we give up two million one hundred sixty-nine thousand acres, and get back much, much less— only two hundred thousand acres?"

The Commissioner of Indian Affairs responded with a haughty stare, as reported by the Washington newspapers. "By joining the Confederacy," Cooley said, coldly, "your people forfeited all rights under your old treaties with the United States." His expression grew even sterner. "You must now consider being at our mercy... at the mercy of the Government."

There was no doubt of that. The Seminoles realized almost from the start of negotiations they would finally have to give in and sign.

The formalities took less than an hour. Only John Franklin Brown and the officials from the Department of Interior actually signed their names. All the other Indians made their "X" mark; they did not know English. Even the interpreter for the "loyals," Robert Johnson, signed with his "X."

As bad as the new treaty was, it could have been much worse for the Seminoles. Losing no time after the end of the Civil War, as early as September 1865, the Indian Commissioner had summoned tribal leaders to confer with him at Fort Smith. He wanted to discuss the wartime defections. Cooley made a startling and unwelcome demand—that the five tribes consolidate on one reservation, under one chief. That was intended to give the Government better command and control of Indian Territory, as well as to take back and free up land on which to relocate Indians from Kansas and elsewhere. And to free up Indian Territory on which it would be eventually simple and easy to bring in white settlers.

The "one-tribe" idea was recognized by all as too onerous; it got lost in the shuffle, without much ado.

The Seminole Nation lost more than 1,500,000 acres, and was brazenly bamboozled on the low price it received for land sold and the higher cost of the new territory the Great Father made them buy. Otherwise they were not greatly hurt by the Treaty of 1866.

The document granted amnesty for all offenses committed during the war. It also spelled out mutual pledges of peace and friendship. Slavery was abolished, of course; the Government wanted freedmen made equals of Indian tribesmen.

For surrendering all the territory granted by the 1856 treaty, the Seminoles were to be compensated a total of $325,362. But the Seminoles would not get their hands on this money directly. First, as payment for their new reservation (which turned out to be approximately present Seminole County), a deduction was made of $100,000.

The Government, through the Department of Interior, would dole out the remaining $225,362 as follows: $30,000 to establish the Seminoles on their new reservation; $20,000 to purchase stock, seed, and tools; $15,000 to establish a new mill (which in the end turned out to be an old mill that never worked); $50,000 to be invested by the Government as a school fund, and $20,000 invested as a tribal fund, with only the 5 per cent annual interest earned by each to be spent; $40,000 for subsistence; $50,000 to repay "loyal" Seminoles for wartime losses, which were to be determined by the Secretary of the Interior; and $10,000 to construct new agency buildings. [7]

Article Five called on the Seminole Nation to grant a right-of-way three miles wide for any Congressionally approved railroad. The price of the land required was to be determined by the President of the United States.

For a half-blood who had never before ventured beyond Indian Territory, Brown found the ten weeks he spent in Washington enlightening. Also somewhat frightening.

The experience provided a clear opportunity for him to recognize how broad was the scope of his informal education. He could now fully appreciate the enormous value of his father's literary sophistication. And of being schooled amid such a considerable library of worthwhile books. [8]

When the Interior Department's learned satraps casually threw into the treaty discussion such terms as *pari passu, pars pro toto, persona non grata,* or *pro et contra, ex curia* and similar legal terms, most Indian delegates looked blank.

Not Brown. Fortunate for him, his father, largely because of being a medical man, was an avid student of Latin, and had spent hours instructing his son in that language.

In his walks on Pennsylvania Avenue, John Franklin Brown watched in wonder and admiration the elegant broughams gliding by bearing top-hatted dignitaries and their stylish ladies. [9] They were wheeling to the theatre, to embassy parties, to the White House, to the Capitol.

President Andrew Johnson, who had succeeded the assassinated Lincoln, invited the treaty delegates for a brief "hello" visit to the White House. They spent many hours on Capitol Hill, discussing their hardships out West. The help or sympathy they received from Senators or Representatives was negligible.

Brown was almost overwhelmed, as were most Indians, by the apparent power of the federal government. Likewise his first sight of the unaccustomed modern aspects of American civilization awed him.

With Chief Chupco, he wandered out of curiosity into a Fourteenth Street hat shop. The John B. Stetson "ten-gallon" hat was just out. It cost five dollars. Chupco was tempted to buy one.

"If you get it," Brown told him, "the first thing you'll do is stick a few eagle feathers in the band." [10]

"Long John" broke into a twisted grin. "Make 'um war bonnet!" he said, cheerfully.

John Franklin Brown wrote home about the Washington excursion and such experiences. Although enthralled, he had been lonely for Lizzie's tender embrace. He was overjoyed to finish signing all the papers. Now he could head back to the Seminole Nation.

ONE KEY PUNISHMENT the 1866 Treaty imposed on the Seminoles as a tribe turned out, oddly, to give a lucky break to the Dr. Brown family.

In squeezing down the size of the Seminoles' new reservation, the Government cut adrift the handsome Council House and the Agency, each built new less than ten years earlier, by moving the new boundary about twenty miles to the east, leaving the buildings vacant in a no-man's-land.

Dr. Brown quickly struck a deal to rent the Agency. It was a large, substantial, two-story stone building, with two stone fireplaces, and more than a dozen five-foot tall windows. A covered verandah surrounded the lower floors, three steps above ground.

By far it was the roomiest and nicest home they had ever had, he told Lucy and the children, a fact already obvious to them.

Their new abode had convenient stables, fenced lots for livestock, and a dug well, with a nearby spring, corncribs and smokehouse. It provided an ideal location from which Dr. Brown could continue his wide-ranging medical practice.

The family moved into the Agency in early 1867, not yet two years after the end of the Civil War, and forty years before Oklahoma was to become a state.

This land was rolling forested hills and verdant plain, soon to be strewn with spring blossoms. The territory was still untamed. It was dangerous from both occasional Comanche raiders and outlaw six-guns, to say nothing of blizzards and tornadoes, of rain, hail, and flood, of wild beasts and rattlesnakes.

That the Seminoles had split into opposite sides in the Civil War brought the tribe fresh difficulties and suffering. Their homes, crops and livestock had been pillaged and ravaged. And now their Great Father in Washington was piling on new punishment. Though only half of the tribe had been "disloyal" and sided with the Confederacy, Washington was punishing all of them by greatly reducing the size of their reservation.

Early on the Browns had become friendly with the noted Cherokee trader and scout, Jesse Chisholm. He was their neighbor, having a trading post and ranch just four miles southeast of their new home in the Agency building. [11]

Alice greatly admired Chisholm's gruff-gentle solicitude, his quick-draw, his masterful horsemanship, his courage and wit. His daughter Jennie became Alice's best friend, and almost daily companion. [12] They were the same age, both eagerly galloping their ponies, jet black braids flying, hyper and outgoing, full of fun, just getting into the adult world. In whispers, they exchanged gossip, even their puberty secrets.

Jennie spoke enthusiastically of the trail her father developed to bring thousands of Texas cattle across the Indian country to the nearest railheads in Kansas. This trail would become famous and bear his name. It ran north and south and crossed the prairie a few miles west of the famous scout's current spread at Chisholm Springs. [13]

Jennie and Alice were agog over fascinating tales told by warriors and soldiers about the great mystery horse that ruled the wild herds running free across the prairie. Everyone wanted to capture the White Stallion of the Plains. Nobody had; perhaps nobody could. The girls pestered Jesse Chisholm to tell them how to track the White Stallion to his lair. And then some clever way to capture him.

Chisholm would readily and jovially comply. He answered not in Seminole, Creek, or English, which the girls understood, but in one of the other tongues in which he was fluent—Spanish, Comanche, Cherokee, Caddo, Choctaw. [14]

Jennie would pound him with her fists in frustration, and pretend to grab the lethal Bowie knife from his gun-belt.

Occasionally Jesse Chisholm would titillate the girls with snatches of his own observations of Indian tradition, culture, and customs.

Helping the girls sort through a stack of animal skins at his trading post triggered one memory. "Know what the braves sometimes do when they kill a deer—or a heifer?"

Jennie and Alice looked at each other, and shook their heads.

"Bucks—if they was real hungry—rip the critter open and while blood was just pouring, they'd reach inside, pull out the liver and heart, and eat 'em blood raw.

"Many a time I've seed a buck give his half-growed son the heart while it was still quivering and tell him, 'Eat much quick—make 'um strong!' They would take that hot liver and tear great chunks offen it, and eat 'er down, blood running everwhere." [15]

Alice in later life recalled how she exchanged tremulous glances with Jennie, but was certain neither asked the intrepid scout to elaborate on his story.

In a playful mood, Jennie would taunt Alice about which was the more Indian. *"Cvcke, Muskogee catvesfvckusat tos. Vnt catv esfvckattomes,"* Jennie jeered, grinning. *"Cent Catv envrkvpv ont ches!"*

That was correct; as Jennie Chisholm had just said her mother was a full blood Creek, making the daughter all Indian; Alice was just a half-blood. [16]

But Alice reverted to English for her ready comeback: "You no Scotch! Pooh on you!"

73

Being the half-blood daughter of a descendant of an aristocratic Scottish clan was, in fact, a heritage full of amazing and confusing contrast for Alice. When spellbound by the splendor of a sunset, she probably pondered and marveled at the mystic turn of Fate that had set in motion her parents' most unlikely romance.

Alice surveyed her own Indian face in the mirror and pondered the imponderables. How many obstacles the Army surgeon and the Seminole maiden named White Skunk had to conquer. Her father recounted their improbable love story many nights in the fireplace gleam as Alice grew up. Her mother listened usually in silence, always with a gentle smile. It was truly a good marriage. In Alice's view, a *wonderful* marriage.

From Alice's earliest memory, her father had been "an old man." She was just as proud of him as Jennie Chisholm was her dad, but she still felt a little guilty comparing the physical prowess of the two men.

In no way could she imagine John Frippo Brown, M. D., strapping on a pair of Colts revolvers, grabbing up a Winchester, jumping on a horse and racing out into the night to duel to the death with desperadoes or scalp-taking Plains Indians.

Instead, Alice's father was the soul of gentility, soft of voice, careful and calm in action. Usually he was able to mask every feeling of anger or disgust. Heavyset, bearded, lovable—but, yes *old,* having just recently turned sixty-seven.

Jesse Chisholm might best him in knowing horseflesh, and certainly in tracking any quarry through the badlands of the Territory; but the neighboring Cherokee stalwart was not even in the game when it came to quoting the classics, knowing the true geography of the earth and the heavens, definitely not with the ability to divine the aberrations of body and mind, or to concoct regimens and potions to restore health.

Over her dad's shoulder, Alice often watched as in a magnificent, precise calligraphic hand Dr. Brown thoughtfully set down on foolscap his regimens and medicines for treating a large array of ailments and medical misfortunes. This priceless document had grown, Alice knew, to close to a thousand pages. Dr. Brown told her his work, if printed, would fill at least two or three volumes. Alice felt a warm glow of admiration as her eyes traveled over the even lines of pen strokes, as beautiful to her as an artist's painting. Only in one of every ten or twelve pages was even one word scratched or blotted out. That was where the physician had changed his mind or had made an error.

Baffled by medical jargon, Alice would lift a puzzled face from the page. Invariably, Dr. Brown would give gentle reassurance, and caution her not to fret, promising more instruction when she was older. "Especially of the marvelous healing herbs and roots that grow all around us." [17]

When her father had mentioned the names Renfrewshire and Paisley on The Clyde, she concluded in juvenescent innocence that they were unimportant towns or places in far-off Scotland, a country she never expected to see, but to only read about in the Sir Walter Scott books.

Her juvenile brain captured not too much of what he said about his life in Charleston, South Carolina. That coastal city had a bustling harbor, she dimly remembered, thronged with three-masted schooners that could transverse the Atlantic Ocean in fourteen days, sometimes less. She vaguely recalled some bits of history her dad had recounted. Especially the death of the Seminole Chief Osceola in the prison at Charleston's Fort Moultrie, and the fact that it was not known until later that the attending Army physician cut off Osceola's head and kept it as a medical specimen.

Of her father's first marriage she was told little, except that he had a daughter named Clara. She would be Alice's half-sister! And not a half-breed, but all white. Imagine that! The name Clara struck a chord with Alice; she promised herself that if she ever had daughters, one would be named Clara.

Alice had no feelings of condemnation. She placed no blame on anyone for whatever might have happened back in Charleston. Forces beyond the control of any individual could beset—and upset— the most solid family. She had only recently witnessed, because of the outbreak of the Civil War, just such a devastating dilemma.

It was the wild debate that had split the Seminoles right down the middle. Half of the men in the tribe, disgusted with years of

Washington's broken promises and near-starvation neglect, saw fresh hope in the Southern rebellion. They switched sides and volunteered to fight for the Confederacy.

One of these boys in gray, of course, was her own brother. First-hand, Alice had seen the anxiety and tension—and tears—imposed on her family by this filial rupture. Fortunately her brother endured three years of warfare and came out unscathed. Likewise, her father, wearing the Union blue, escaped harm.

During lulls on the battlefield, Alice had occasionally been permitted to visit, with her mother and siblings, inside Fort Gibson. So she knew first-hand that her father patched up soldiers, doing hated amputations and probing for shot and shell, whether the wounded man was Yank or Rebel.

COPIES OF *The Arkansas Gazette* that straggled west by stagecoach in early Spring 1867 brought dire news of a cholera epidemic in Chicago. Dr. Brown read the newspaper with dread. In less than a year, the Windy City scourge had taken 678 lives.

Dr. Brown shuddered. He had seen enough cholera to last a lifetime; and he still felt helpless against the disease. No doctor he'd ever heard of had any ammunition that was effective in this deadly battle.

In isolated tents and cabins, in Army camps—and especially at Fort Gibson's hospital—in recent years he had hovered over scores of cholera sickbeds. Every battle against this malady, regretfully, he had lost. No magic conjured up by his brain or hands, as far as he could see, did much to help.

Surprisingly, he had known a few victims to survive. His private opinion was that each of these recoveries was entirely due to the individual patient's unbreakable red thread of destiny, or Fate's careless toss of the dice, or God's whimsy—perhaps all of these combined.

His earnest hope was that he never again would see a case of cholera. His wish was in vain. For in April 1867 cholera hit the Seminole Nation. The epidemic erupted right at his doorstep in the strip of no-man's-land containing the Agency, which served now as his home, and abandoned old Council Town.

76

Dr. Brown was the only physician for miles around. His first summons was to examine two middle-aged Seminole brothers; they were already prostrated and in their final throes. Despite knowing the futility, and deeply feeling his patients' anguish and misery, he did all he could. His doses of opium and laudanum would ease pain if those stricken could keep the drugs down. But almost invariably the medicine was vomited up in explosive bursts of greenish-black bile. And the sick folks died wretchedly.

Calls for his help then came often and steadily. But, of course, his black satchel contained nothing that would eradicate cholera. Yet he mounted up and made his house calls, day and night.

By the time some twenty had died, and her father began to look haggard and weary, Alice leaped on her pinto and rode along to help. She was no more effective as a nurse than he was as a physician in these rooms of death. But they worked closely as a team. They kept struggling . . . long desperate hours.

In their comfortable home in the old Agency building, Alice's mother Lucy watched these events unfold with nervousness and a sense of foreboding. [18] Something in her Everglades heritage triggered bad vibes. Her aboriginal instinct detected dark and dangerous clouds approaching their prairie abode.

It had become a routine scenario—the doctor and Alice on the go. Every day, sunrise to after dark. And this had gone on for five weeks. Lucy knew the days exactly. Under her bed lay a bundle of small sticks from a blackjack tree. They numbered thirty-five; it was the Indian way of keeping the calendar.

Later she told the family of her mounting dread—having to add stick after stick to her bundle, the sorrow of doing that. Alice was young enough to bear up under the burden of the house calls, but her husband, Lucy could clearly see, was totally worn out. [19]

On this night, in the middle of May, father and daughter did not return at sundown. Lucy went out on the verandah and sat in the moonlight, waiting and worrying.

Finally their horses clopped in off the trail. It was near midnight. Dr. Brown slid out of his saddle, staggering in weariness. He dropped his medicine bag. Alice jumped off her pinto pony, picked it up. She grabbed her father and helped him up the steps, and through the door.

Their arrival triggered a stir. Dim figures began moving in the yellowish gleam of tallow candles. The eldest daughters, Lucy, twenty-two, now nicknamed "Sukey," and twenty-year-old Jennie hurried outside to stable the horses. The youngest boys, fifteen, twelve, and two, already were asleep upstairs.

The doctor's wife came forward with a bowl of chicken and rice. He smiled wanly, waved her aside, and fell into bed without removing his coat or boots.

"Cvrke hotosuse tos," Alice said to her mother, *"Vtoketvn esseelectanhakes."*

Lucy answered with anguished eyes. *"Cvcus-hokte, mehenwvn opunayetskes,"* she agreed.[20] Their words were true. Dr. Brown was totally exhausted. More to the point, as Alice had just lamented, he was literally working himself to death. Lucy also thought so. In her native tongue, she had responded that her daughter spoke the truth.

While the rest of the household slept, Lucy sat beside her husband's bed. The dark hours dragged on. The night wind usually came up in gusts strong enough to rattle the corncrib door and to fling about the bucket hanging from the well rope hard enough to make the pulley squeal. Lucy struggled to keep her tired eyes open. A stronger sense of foreboding stabbed her heart. What of the new day—the thirty-sixth stick? She realized that at daybreak this conscientious healer, regardless of exhaustion, would struggle up and again ride out to make more house calls. [21]

But now he lay quietly in his bed, with closed eyes. His breathing, as she could clearly observe, was quiet and gentle.

An hour or so later, an owl perched in the tall sycamore gave an ominous hoot. Dawn was about to break. In the barnyard, the big speckled rooster would strut and finally crow to confirm the rapid approach of sunrise.

Lucy looked down, expecting to see her husband snap awake as he always did. He stirred not, as she later told the family, nor gave the slightest heed to these everyday sounds and signals. Of a sudden, she felt alarm, and quickly looked closer. He didn't seem to be breathing. His lips looked bluish. And his eyes remained closed.

She leaped up and cried out for Alice.

JOHN FRIPPO BROWN, M.D., about midway in his sixty-eighth year, was buried in a small cemetery containing about six graves located 300 yards from the old Agency building. His grave was dug next to a stone marker on which is chiseled: "In Memory—W.L. TEMPLETON—bir June 30, 1819; de Ap 2, 1861."

For Dr. Brown a shaped sandstone two feet tall and about nine inches thick was raised, but not marked.

The physician's grave is between Asher and Wannette, in what he called Greenhead Prairie, an area later included in Pottawatomie County, Oklahoma. Well over 130 years later it could be found, marked by its crumbling stone, amid tangled brush on a farm whose owners discouraged trespassers, even Brown descendants. [22]

His demise plunged the widow and children into a crisis. What of their future? The breadwinner was gone. What would happen next?

Decision-making fell almost exclusively on young John Franklin's shoulders. It seemed likely that residency in the Agency building would have to be given up. He would contact the Department of Interior in Washington and try to obtain a lease extension allowing time for them to chart the family's future.

Everyone agreed that Alice was correct.

John Frippo Brown, physician and humanitarian, had literally worked himself to death.

THREE MONTHS LATER a distraught Alice was whipping the team as it tore over the rough trail toward the little town of Wewoka, the new capital of the Seminole Nation.

In the back seat of the buggy, Sukey held her mother tightly against her breast, trying to protect Lucy from hard jolts as the wheels crashed against ruts and rocks, over bumps and gullies.

During the night their mother had collapsed. Now she was only semi-conscious. They were racing to see the Government doctor in Wewoka.

They did not arrive in time.

The red thread of destiny of the Seminole maiden who survived primitive life and soldiers' bullets in the Florida wilds, who had by the freakish kind of fortune married an aristocratic white doctor, who had managed to charm Park Hill society, had borne eight babies, had endured the Civil War and innumerable Territory hardships . . .

Her life skein was now broken. And she was not yet forty-seven years old.

Lucy Greybeard Brown was buried in a small Indian cemetery, located about one mile north of Wewoka.

At sundown Alice returned alone to the cemetery. She kneeled on the raw dirt of her mother's grave.

"*Nerrv hervn, cvcke vcakat, nocepvs,*" she said. [23]

Alice laid a single red rose on the grave, and arose, repeating, "Good night, dear mother, sleep."

5

Falling in Love in Sasakwa

JESSE CHISHOLM GOT HUNGRY and ate some bear grease. That gastronomic incident played an oblique role in John Franklin Brown's first business venture. The bear grease was cooked, unfortunately, in a brass kettle. That's a sure-fire way to turn bear grease into poison. [1]

Chisholm didn't live to see the next sunrise. (Comanche chief Ten Bears and other friends dug a hole beside a bend of the North Canadian River, wrapped Jesse in a blanket and buffalo robe, and buried him in true frontiersman style.)

John Franklin Brown already had been thinking about establishing a trading post on Greenhead Prairie, near the Agency building. Trader Chisholm's death left an opening for a new store. John started one.

This was a young man who had just spent four years as a Confederate lieutenant. Where did he get enough capital to open a trading post? Family memoirs hint of a legacy from Charleston. At an earlier time that would have seemed unlikely, inasmuch as Dr. Brown's aristocratic South Carolina siblings had ostracized him for marrying a "savage...and a child at that." But the years softened a few of their hearts. His parents apparently left him a few thousand dollars, which his eldest son had now inherited, and used.

81

John's trading post on Greenhead Prairie got off to a good start. He was smart, a quick learner, and friendly. He demonstrated that it was easy for him to get the knack of trading with the Indians and whites, and turning a profit.

Yet he had a problem. His trading post was remote, his Greenhead Prairie territory too small to develop the large-scale operation he had in mind.

"I think we ought to move," he told his six siblings. "Should we go to Wewoka or to Sasakwa?" [2]

The new Seminole Nation had about a dozen settlements considered towns, called *tvlófv* in their language. Young Brown considered only Wewoka or Sasakwa capable of supporting a general store. These two towns were connected by the Seminoles' principal wagon road running from the northern border at the North Canadian River about forty miles to the South Canadian River, which marked the southern boundary of the nation.

On horseback, John Franklin Brown carefully surveyed his prospects in both locations. Wewoka was his first choice—for several reasons. It had just been designated the new capital of the Seminole Nation. Carpenters and masons were erecting in Wewoka a new Council House to replace the one that the Government had caused to be abandoned on Greenhead Prairie.

Further, Wewoka was a midway point on the well-traveled military road between Fort Gibson in the east and Fort Sill 200 miles to the southwest, on the buffalo lands of the Plains Indians.

Because of its convenient location, the United States Army had established a remount station in Wewoka. This consisted of six buildings of hewn stone surrounded by a stone wall. Several officers who were later to become celebrated in the Indian wars in the West were at different times in command of the remount detachment. One was Colonel George Custer, whose exploits were to fill countless pages in the history of frontier Indian warfare. General Phil Sheridan also was briefly in charge of the remount station. His Wewoka duties included designating the site for the new Seminole Agency building. [3]

The small village of Wewoka had a checkered history. It began not as a Seminole Nation citadel, but as a Negro settlement started by a freedman called Gopher John. In the Florida wars, he had been an interpreter between his Seminole tribe and the Army. He had come west over the Trail of Tears.

Gopher John showed more bravado than the main body of the Seminole immigrants. Most of them balked at settling on land offered by the Creeks. The Seminoles regarded the area both too small and too close to the dangerous Plains tribes. Thus for several years the reluctant Seminoles remained in "squatter camps" around Fort Gibson. Gopher John, however, had gone as early as 1849 seeking land on which to settle the band of 255 ex-slaves of which he was "chief."

Near the remount station, he found a likely site on the banks of a small creek where the sparkling water surged and snapped over a rocky ledge. He dubbed the place We-wo-ka, which is Seminole for "barking water." [4]

John Gopher led his black people there. They built cabins and began farming, raising livestock, and hunting. The Seminoles had always permitted their slaves to have their homes apart from the tribe so there was nothing unusual in Gopher John establishing the town of Wewoka for them.

But now on his inspection trip, John Franklin Brown found that Wewoka already had a trading post; and he could see the village wasn't large enough for two.

The general store in Wewoka had been opened by a middle-aged frontiersman named Elijah J. Brown, who was in no way related to the Dr. Brown family. Elijah Brown was born in New York but had gone west in the California gold rush. Later he had commanded wagon trains of immigrants leaving Missouri for Santa Fe. At the end of the Civil War he was commissioned by the federal government to serve as guide and escort to bring the "loyal" Seminoles back from Leroy, Kansas to Indian Territory.

His efforts earned him considerable respect among these Seminoles. So much so that he became the first white man ever "adopted" into the tribe. Elijah Brown found those circumstances favorable for opening a trading post in Wewoka and promptly did so. [5] He soon built a house and married the daughter of the Reverend John Lillie, a Presbyterian missionary among the Indians. Through his good con-

83

nections in Washington, Elijah Brown arranged to open a post office in his store and on May 13, 1867 was appointed Wewoka's first postmaster. The mail was brought by horseback from Muskogee.

John Franklin Brown, in view of the circumstances, decided to move his Greenhead Prairie establishment to his alternate choice, Sa-sak-wa, which means "wild goose" in Seminole. [6]

The hamlet of Sasakwa was in the heart of a vast prairie with rolling hills, which John saw ideal for ranching and hunting. The area was also verdant farmland, with thick groves of valuable and productive pecan and walnut trees. Indians eventually would be induced to cut hundreds of walnut trees for shipment to Germany where they would be manufactured into furniture and gunstocks.

John found that his trading post needed to stock a wide variety of goods, and he did so. His favorite saying: "We sell everything from a needle to a threshing machine." [7] To determine the extent of inventory carried in a typical Indian Territory trading post in the late 1800's, historian Grant Foreman examined thousands of old yellowed invoices to write this description:

> One could find snuffboxes, shirt bosoms—plain, calico, and fancy linen—saleratus, saddlebags, silk hats—and remember these were Indian merchants—shell side combs, Sioux twills, sidesaddles with full quilted seat, silk cravats, strouding, stirrup leathers, silk gloves—and their customers were Indians, too—sulphur, shoe hammers, silk handkerchiefs, shaving boxes, satin vests, skeins of silk, Sappington's pills, spurs, shawls, super-fine blue cloth coats, surcingles, plain fancy stocks, summer stocks, candle snuffers, percussion caps, dirk knives, figured bobbinet, powder flasks, cassimere pantaloons, nail rods for fabricating homemade nails, bunches of bonnet wire, Osnaburgs, domestics, bodkins, martingales, hoops, beaded reticules, velvet vases, white Russian hats, quills, ink powder and sand for blotting, sealing wax and wafers, candle molds, bombazine pants and vests, neck combs, fish lines, Godfrey's cordial, linen pants, bar lead, Chickasaw plaids, bear oil, Turkey red, cambric, tuck combs, buffalo robes, bed cords, lace, ribbons, furniture fringe, peppermint, alpaca, horse collars, porter, calfskin boots, hair oil, prunella shoes, cologne, bear traps, paregoric, frock coats, and an endless list of merchandise in use today. [8]

Indian trading posts, of course, purchased practically anything worthwhile the natives brought in—garden vegetables, eggs, poultry, pecans, animal skins. In the mid-1800s this was a typical scale of peltry prices: Indian deerskins, 18 cents each; country deerskins, 16 cents; No. 1 otter skins, $2; Nos 2 and 3 otter skins, 75 cents; opossum skins, 6 cents; cat, wolf, and fox skins, 20 cents; bearskins No.1, $2.50; cub skins, 75 cents; country raccoon skins, 15 cents; Indian raccoon skins, 25 cents; beaver skins, 75 cents. [9]

ON A SPRING morning in 1870 John Franklin Brown walked into a grove of elm, catalpa, and huckleberry trees on the hill he considered the most picturesque in Sasakwa. He studied them admiringly, perhaps lovingly; the trees were stately and beautiful, some fifty or sixty feet tall. He had a serious concern, which occasionally he discussed with wife Lizzie. How many would he have to cut down?

His frequent strolls among the trees, which were across the road from his trading post, were intended to help conceptualize the dream home he was eager to build on this site. [10] He was not thinking small. He told Lizzie he wanted a mansion—maybe twenty rooms. Two stories, maybe three. Verandahs all around, with elaborate steamboat filigree.

Having to cut down trees to make room for the house shouldn't be too worrisome. For he had in mind planting more to create a sizeable orchard of cherry, apple, and peach trees, as well as additional walnut and pecan.

His trading post was busy and profitable, but he was not yet in financial shape to build his mansion. He dreamed of it constantly, even seeing a private room for himself, high up, with a copper bathtub and basin. He had in mind a white-painted six paling fence in front, to keep out livestock. Also a concrete walkway to the front entry. He wanted fireplaces, large windows, dormers, plus a laundry house and servant quarters, as well as barns and stables.

He had already staked out a large plantation on tribal common lands, an option available to any tribesman with ability and means to convert it to his use. He had fenced fertile fields for crops, and pastures with luxuriant prairie grass for a large herd of cattle and many horses. [11]

It was convenient that he had located near his wife's family. Chief John Jumper's Spring Baptist church was within two miles of the store. Both he and Lizzie were members there and regularly heard her father preach.

Nothing, he thought, would stop him from building his dream house. And nothing did.

As had been his father, John Franklin was eager to have a large family. Lizzie had borne their first child in 1869, a boy they named John James. Now she was again pregnant.

Though only twenty-seven, John was rapidly gaining stature both as a merchant and as an influential strategist in Seminole councils. His start came, of course, from being John Jumper's fair-haired boy. The Southern chief admired him not only as his son-in-law but also for his brainpower.

Ordinarily, because his father was white, John Franklin Brown might have been not as much respected as were Seminole leaders who were full blood. However, his mother was a full blood; additionally he had already passed an important tribal test of manhood. By serving as a lieutenant in the Seminole cavalry battalion, he had clearly proved his bravery in battle.

Likewise, he was looked up to for the skill he demonstrated in Washington as the Seminole point man in negotiating the 1866 treaty. There he was considered the tribe's star delegate, knowledgeable and effective in facing up to hard-line Interior Department officials.

His Indian Territory companions and his Government adversaries keenly recognized his intellect, and his vision. Nobody in the tribe came close to having his white man's education, his poise, or his mastery of English, his skill as a speaker, his ability to seize an audience. [12]

In reading and speaking the Seminole language, most tribal leaders, of course, could easily out-shine him. This had been their tongue since childhood. When John was growing up, his father had prohibited any conversation in Seminole in their home. The doctor wanted to make certain his children were well versed in English. Their canny mother had openly instructed John and his siblings fully in all essential Seminole traditions and customs. And secretly Lucy had also given John a good grasp of her native tongue.

Alice, on the sly, was also her mother's proficient language student. John felt somewhat deficient in his limited ability in discussions with Indians who spoke only Seminole. So he had for years worked diligently to broaden his native language skill—both spoken and written. To increase his vocabulary, he often spent time writing useful Seminole words. One of his lists, found by a great grandchild and now a treasured keepsake, reads: "horse" *(co-rak'ko)* and "hay" *(pv'hē)*, "important" *(herēmáhē)* and "infant" *(estŕcē)*, "July" *(Hiyucē)* and "June" *(Kv'co-hvsē)*, "it is not" *(tóko)* and "it is so" *(mómusen)*. [13]

CHIEF CHUPCO ripped open the Department of Interior envelope, yanked out the letter, glared at it, and shoved the paper across the table to John Franklin Brown.

On this day in early 1870, the chief was inside the Seminole Council House at Wewoka with John Franklin and John Jumper, both members of the Seminole Council.

These frequent Government letters, making inquiries or demands confused and irritated the chief. "Long John" did not read or speak English. Nor did he see any need to acquire those skills as long as he had a dependable man like Brown to explain and advise him on communications from Washington. John read the letter carefully, and then told them: "No surprise here. The Great Father says, 'Don't do it!' " [14]

In question was a proposal by the chiefs to create one constitution that would apply equally to all members of the Five Civilized Tribes. The idea had been under discussion by the Indians for several weeks. At Chupco's request, John was writing a draft of the constitution. The five tribes would soon meet in Okmulgee to take action on the document. Chupco was sending John to represent the Seminoles.

Discussing the federal objection to such unification, John pointed out that the five tribes were trying to be forthright, only desiring to keep their lands for themselves, and to exclude the whites and the railroads. He predicted the Government's response to the proposed constitution would be tedious, tiresome, and oppressive. He was proved correct. From the time the petition was dispatched from Okmulgee, it was destined to travel through official channels at snail pace. It would take two years for the Five Civilized Tribes' constitution proposal to reach the desk of President U.S. Grant. There it ultimately would die in a pigeonhole. [15]

It surprised John Franklin how well he got along with Chupco. The principal chief could have had valid reason to hold deep enmity. In the Civil War they were actual deadly enemies. When Chupco was fleeing to Kansas with the "loyal" Seminoles, Lieutenant John Franklin Brown, C.S.A., was at a hard gallop to chase him down. And in the Confederate lieutenant's rifle was a bullet meant for "Long John" or any other "loyal."

Then, too, rivalry might have popped up leading to a struggle for power between Chupco and Brown's patron and father-in-law. John Jumper had been unfairly deposed, his friends thought, as principal chief because of the war. But no such feud had developed; Jumper, now pastor of Spring Baptist Church, could have been antagonistic in tribal politics just to frustrate Chupco, but he was not.

Reverend Jumper was by now mainly concerned with preaching, and in gaining new converts and leading them down into the river and baptizing them.

Chief Chupco had quietly taken John Brown's measure by observing his skillful manipulation of Interior Department officials in the 1866 Treaty negotiations, and came to respect and admire him.

For his part, John Brown recognized the chief's strength and wise judgment. Chupco was handsome, intelligent, mild-mannered—and a superb athlete. John had seen the chief, even in his sixties, seize a typical 150-pound or 200-pound Indian male and easily lift him over his head. Chupco's run from Wewoka to Fort Gibson in twelve hours was a much-heralded frontier legend.

JOHN FRANKLIN BROWN was succeeding splendidly both as merchant and as tribal leader. He was still hiking around in the shade of his hilltop trees, dreaming of his mansion-to-be. He was not yet ready to build, but he was glad to see he would have use for those extra bedrooms. Lizzie had given birth in 1871 to their second child, another boy they named John W. She was again pregnant, and due in 1872.

In his busy waking hours and in the evenings as he toiled over his ledgers, John Brown would turn introspective. Of course, he was scheming to assure his personal business success. But often he pondered the progress and future of his tribe. [16] The Seminoles had been in this new land almost forty years. Yet in significant ways were still hamstrung and hobbled by native customs and beliefs that were ingrained during their years in Florida. Their mode of life was now drastically changed. In the sunshine of the Everglades they could go virtually naked. In Indian Territory they were beset by uncertain weather—from blizzards to droughts. They had to bundle up against the cold. Food in Florida had been more abundant; now, though wild game was plentiful, the Indians must plant crops, build secure shelters and work more than in the old days.

The Seminoles, he believed, would eventually achieve the necessary acculturation. But they were severely handicapped by inability to comprehend the whites' language. Learning English was absolutely essential. Their children must also be taught some arithmetic. Tribesmen were not simple, but they were too trusting and relied also on others to be honest. In Brown's trading post, as well as in transactions elsewhere, the Seminole customer tossed his money on the counter and expected the store's clerk to make change, taking only the correct amount. The Indians never haggled, merely accepted the merchandise at the posted price.

Obviously the Seminole Nation needed to establish schools so their sons and daughters could get at least a basic education—the three R's. To establish tribal schools was a major project on which John Brown worked hard.

At times he mused the Seminoles might as well be living on the moon as in Indian Territory for all they knew of the outside world. The majority could not comprehend at all civilization's enormous and rapid advances.

A few of his colleagues on the Seminole council could read newspapers. Most other tribesmen were largely ignorant of what took place elsewhere in the United States in the early 1870's, unless some elder learned news and passed it on. The ordinary Indian tending his crops, his cows, pigs, and chickens had not the slightest inkling of the great historic Chicago fire that killed 250 people and destroyed three and one-half square miles of buildings.

That the typewriter had been invented. . . that the Union Pacific Railroad had cut from three months to a mere eight days the time required to travel from the east coast to the Pacific Ocean . . . .Queen Isabella II abdicated her thirty-year-rule in Spain, and France had gone to war against Prussia . . . the Suez Canal opened. . . Jesse James pulled his first train robbery out in Iowa . . . Brigham Young was arrested for bigamy for having twenty-seven wives . . . That the population of the United States grew to 39,000,000, largest in the world except Germany's 41,000,000.

Of all this, and more, John Franklin Brown took notice. As a merchant, he was personally interested in reading about the startup of important stores like Marshall Field and Montgomery Ward in Chicago, Macy's in New York, Rich's in Atlanta. He also noted the appearance of new products like Mueller's pasta, Arm & Hammer baking soda, Underwood canned ham. John D. Rockefeller had created the Standard Oil Company, and he wondered what effect that would have on his business in Sasakwa.

His literary taste was piqued by publication of Jules Verne's *Twenty Thousand Leagues Under The Sea,* the exploits of Captain Nemo and his submarine. He ordered several new books for his library.

Considering ways to augment his business enterprises. John Brown saw two immediate possibilities. One was cotton. The Negro freedmen and slaves had induced a number of Seminoles to plant the crop. The blacks had, of course, gained their extensive knowledge working on plantations in the South before running away. Now cotton was being grown in the Seminole Nation. If the production continued to expand, it would be worth his while to build a cotton gin in Sasakwa. Larger crops, he believed, would soon be grown. [17]

More importantly, he decided to get seriously into the cattle business. Every condition and aspect was favorable. Steers could be grazed and fattened on Indian Territory grass at practically no cost. They could be sent north and sold for a good profit. A ten-dollar Seminole steer brought thirty dollars in Kansas, as much as forty in Chicago.

It was to his advantage that the Five Tribes had a unique communal land system. Each of their domains was owned collectively by all tribal members. No individual could for any reason obtain title to any land, not even one acre. Yet any tribesman was free to use whatever acreage he needed—especially for building a home, and for grazing livestock.

John Brown looked over the limitless prairie surrounding Sasakwa, and vowed to bring in thousands of steers, brand them, and fatten them for market. Another favorable aspect for Indian Territory ranchers was that because of available water and abundant grass, steers on the range could successfully "rough over" the winter and be sold in the Spring markets.

"Here's my chance to make much money," he told John Jumper. "Enough, I hope, to build my big house. And a cotton gin, too."[18]

One big problem concerned the Indian ranchers—cattle rustlers. Thieves, who mostly were white men, organized into gangs and boldly raided pastures, driving away hundreds of cattle. Eventually the Indians retaliated, and with force. Choctaw Chief William Bryant sent out an Indian posse that captured forty rustlers, fifteen of whom were shot forthwith. [19]

Indian ranchers would continue to graze several hundred thousand steers on their pastures, but not without trouble. For nearly three decades, the Five Tribes would be called on to continually fight off rustlers.

ALICE BROWN, twenty-one, was clerking in her brother's Sasakwa trading post when George Rollin Davis banged open the door and swaggered in.

The stranger announced he was on a search for wholesale furs and pecans.

"I'll buy all you have," he said, with a dazzling smile. [20]

Alice drew back, and directed him to her brother Andrew Jackson, eighteen, who also was behind the counter, learning to become a merchant. But she kept a speculative eye on the brash visitor.

George Rollin Davis was worth a frontier girl's dreamy appraisal. He was young and handsome, twenty-four, with nice manners and a bravado air. He was tall, with bright eyes, a neat mustache and stylish clothes.

Though born in Indiana, he was from LeRoy, Kansas, where his saucy Irish mother ran a boarding house and his Welsh father was a merchant and railroader. Young Davis was now working as a traveling agent in Indian Territory, employed by J. E. Jones, an Okmulgee trader.

George Davis went over and started a conversation with Andrew Jackson. After a lengthy discussion, they arranged a shipment of pecans. With side-glances, he gave Alice the same introspective study she was giving him. Before departing, George Davis took time to chat with her, and pay her a compliment on something or other, and let it be known that his friends called him "Roll." When Roll mounted up and rode away, he carried in his mind's eye a distinct vision of a bright half-blood maiden; and his heart strings apparently felt a quirky flutter.

Alice was an exceptional young woman. Though an outdoors type, athletic and robust, she was studious, inquisitive, and keenly intellectual. Her parents had tutored her at home in Park Hill. She had also attended Cherokee seminaries. During the Civil War she was in classes at Fort Gibson taught by Carrie Bushyhead, sister of Dennis Bushyhead, a Cherokee chief. After the death of her parents, she spent a year as a student at the boarding school north of Wewoka operated by Reverend Ross Ramsey, a Presbyterian missionary.

She later worked part-time as teacher in a fledgling school for young girls in Sasakwa, as well as clerking at the trading post. All of the siblings lived together in Sasakwa with their older brother, his wife Lizzie and their two sons.

Alice could ride a horse as well as the average cowboy, had biceps that enable her to accurately swing a two-blade axe. She could swim like a fish, and often did in the South Canadian. She was not known to often back down in any wrangle, but was soft-spoken, a vivacious conversationalist, courteous, with full knowledge of and acquiescence to the dictates of etiquette, knew how to sew brilliantly and understood trends in ladies' fashion.[21]

Moreover, she had pored over her father's extensive library and could discuss and moderately quote from Shakespeare, Dickens, and other celebrated writers. Much of the Bible was also in her quick recall; she had begun reading a chapter every morning, a practice she would maintain for her lifetime.

At fifteen, Alice had been baptized by the Reverend James Factor—"the Spaniard"—and joined Chief Jumper's Spring Baptist Church. Reverend Factor, incidentally, was now courting Alice's twenty-four-year-old sister Jennie. Alice was a strict moralist, influenced by her father's strong beliefs.

She felt haunted by bittersweet memories of her father's labor of love on his "Therapeutics" manuscript. Neatly stacked and tied with pale blue ribbon, she kept it in the top drawer of her bedroom dresser. Lately she had felt inspired to examine it again, and wonder what use to try to make of it. That it had never been published saddened her. Just at the time he was felled by overwork in the cholera epidemic, Dr. Brown was poised to finally complete his book. "It would be of interest," he had told Alice, "if I could write a bit about the herbal remedies of the medicine men. Some of their potions seem to be quite effective." [22]

Alice had watched tribal doctors preparing herbs, some times boiling them, blowing in the water through their cane "bubbling" tube, and also grinding plants, roots or leaves into curative powders. Likewise she heard the ceremonial chanting that was an integral part of their technique.

But she knew little of their actual "medicine." She decided to learn more, and try to write an insert or additional chapter to her father's work. With the help of friendly elders, she managed to spend time with two or three Seminole medicine men, and discover a good bit of their lore.

Some chants and formulas were considered too secret or sacred to disclose, but she acquired an extensive knowledge of a wide variety of organic and animal matter considered useful and helpful. Many were plants, shrubs, and trees that she had often passed without a second look.

The root of the lowly milkweed, for instance, could be boiled into a tea to cure kidney ailments. The wide scope of the armamentarium of the medicine man stunned her. To acquire beneficial ingredients, he could choose from needle grass, cattails, thistle, sage, snakeroot, sassafras, farkleberry, ragweed, as well as the bark from bois d' arc, cedar, cottonwood, slippery elm, pussy willow, and peach trees. And more. The fields and forests offered him a portfolio of nearly 200 other curative products. [23]

As a traditional war medicine to staunch bleeding, the heads of prairie parsley (*mabilanoji* in Seminole) are chewed and then the pulp is stuffed into the arrow or bullet wound. Turkey weed (*pthlngeska*) reverses fainting spells. Farkleberry (*owisa*) cures a deranged person, when the roots are boiled and the infusions are applied to the head.

Black nightshade (*hthllthls hvtki*) is doubly powerful. A small amount placed under the lip cures a nosebleed. And if the roots are boiled and if a man uses the infusion as a hair tonic it becomes a lure known as "woman-catcher."

When making a sassafras (*wthlso*) tea, the medicine man chants four times: *Cthllfi-ki nok'kati* "big heart hurts" *Cthlfikoji nok'kati* "small heart hurts" and then once *fthlnuk fthlnuk* "beats beats." The tea is then drunk to treat gallstones, coughing, as well as pain in the bladder or the bowels. Before making a journey, a Seminole faces the direction he is heading and places four bois d'arc (*tulani*) "stickers" in the front of his hat band. This guarantees that dangerous snakes will get out of his path.

Love magic is created by rolling special tobacco in a blackjack oak (*sthlcv*) leaf, lighting it, taking four drags, and blowing smoke toward a desired woman. Slippery elm (*lupaka*) sap is used as a vaginal lubricant, and men rub their penis with the slimy sap of spiderwort (*thllmpvkpvki holati tihvs eakita*) to increase its size. A man who has sore testicles or urinary pain boils cream wild indigo (*yaha mileka*) and drinks the infusion. [24]

Alice received a startling insight on how portions of the bodies of animals, birds and insects are used by medicine men. A skunk's scent sac is carefully removed, and one drop of the fluid mixed with a quart of water. Drinking this several times a day is supposed to cure tuberculosis. A sharp piece of turtle shell is used to make four curative scratches on the spine of a patient with back pain. Children who wet the bed are fed burnt chicken feathers. The "daddy-long-legs" spider—with the legs pulled off—is baked in a biscuit and eaten to prevent boils.

Alice perused the pages she had compiled of this and similar material. She felt uncomfortable trying to evaluate these ancient tribal remedies, especially in relation to her father's more scientifically advanced procedures. She did note, however, that the Seminole medicine men frequently employed her father's standard panacea—venesection. The Indian practitioners used a herbal wash to clean the skin, scratched it with a shard of broken brown glass, and cupped it with a cow horn which they filled with blood by sucking a hole in the small end.

For the time being, she put this material aside. Perhaps later she would figure out whether it would enhance—or diminish—her father's work.

ALICE HAD NOT SEEN the last of the brash young traveling agent George Rollin Davis. With extraordinary frequency, "Roll" could be observed dismounting after a 100-mile ride from Okmulgee and tying up at the Sasakwa store hitching rail.

There didn't seem to be all that many deals being made to buy pecans or animal pelts. But young Mr. Davis came to the John Brown Trading Post anyhow. He would look around to see if Alice was behind the counter. If not, he waited until she showed up. And then began trying to impress her with his charm and good looks.

Alice could not remain aloof forever. She melted a bit. Roll was genuinely entertaining, she concluded, and fun to talk with. She began looking forward to his visits, and her heart would jump when she recognized the distinctive clop of his mare's hooves.

On one bright Sunday, Roll came for a surprise visit. He accompanied her to church; she was amused by the look on his face when he discovered that Indian men and women sit in segregated pews. But she and her suitor sat side-by-side on the afternoon buggy ride that took them down to the shady shore of the river.

When Roll started his long ride back to Okmulgee, all he could think of was her sweet breath and the moist warmth of her lips. And a radiant Alice rushed to tell her brothers and sisters that she was engaged. [25]

George and Alice were married January 20, 1874 at Okmulgee by one of the most distinguished men in the Creek Nation, the Rev. Sam Chocote, who said the rites at his home. Not only was he pastor of the Indian Methodist church, but also the long-time principal chief of the Creek tribe.

The young couple took up residence in Okmulgee at the home of a Captain Belcher. George continued to work at the trading post of J. E. Jones, and later was employed by Captain F. B. Severs and the Moore family, all prominent in the Creek Nation.

On October 21, 1874 in Okmulgee, Alice went into labor. With difficulty, she bore their first child, a girl. The infant was tiny and appeared exceedingly frail. They named her Katie Jane. From the start, the new parents were apprehensive. Their baby could gain no weight, and remained sickly. Finally, at three months, Katie Jane gasped her last breath.

Despite the heartbreak, George and Alice put this tragedy behind them, still hoping to have a large family. On January 26, 1876 their second child, a boy, came, and was named George Lytle Davis. The parents were overjoyed that he had lusty lungs, a thick mop of dark hair, and sterling health. They did not know just then how completely their wish for a sizeable brood was to be fulfilled. Through the years this boy would be followed by nine siblings.

The clock was ticking. Unknown to her, Alice's own red thread of destiny was slowly propelling her to unexpected, unorthodox, and unbelievable heights—to chief of the Seminole Nation.

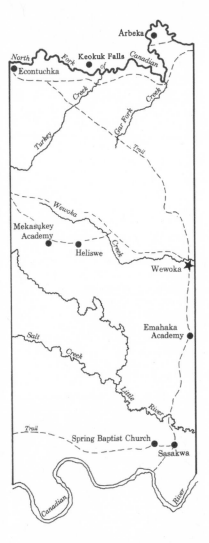

[*Above*] The Seminole Nation as established between the North and South Canadian Rivers by the treaty imposed by the federal government in 1866.

[*Top right*] The noise of these little falls in a creek just north of Wewoka gave the town its name, which translates from Seminole to "barking water."

[*Lower right*] Elijah Brown (no relation to Dr. John F. Brown) was Wewoka's first postmaster and established the first trading post later sold to Dr. Brown's sons.

Photos courtesy THE SEMINOLE NATION MUSEUM
and Gene and Martha Aldridge

97

Alice Brown Davis at age thrity-nine in the Arbeka period when she was already mother of eight of her eleven children.

John F. Brown at the time he was elected Principal Chief of the Seminole Nation at age forty-seven in 1885. He adopted the title "Governor" and served as chief until his death in 1919.

Family portrait of *Kúnu Hvt'kē* (White Skunk), the Indian teenager who married Dr. John Frippo Brown. He changed her name to Lucy.

George Rollin Davis [*Above*] in the 1890s at Arbeka.

[*Right*] In later years, with the favorite cane he passed down to a grandson.

[*Below*] Andrew Jackson Brown, the governor's favorite brother.

On the porch of his Sasakwa mansion, Governor Brown (*center*) enjoys the late 1880s sun with his family (*from left*) Henrietta Brown, Solomon Brown, Jennie Brown, Lizzie Brown, Josie Brown, J.F.B., Andrew J. Brown, Oliver Factor and John Brown, Jr.

Farmers and blacksmiths in front of Sasakwa's livery stable with some of Governor Brown's prize draft horses.

The abandoned Seminole Nation Agency building in present day Pottawatomie county which was rented as an office and residence by Dr. John Frippo Brown after the end of the Civil War. He died there in 1867 during a cholera outbreak.

Seminole Council House, Capitol of the Seminole Nation at Wewoka. It was built in 1899 and razed in 1932.

Two Principal Chiefs of the Seminole Nation; John Chupco [*Above*] died in office at age 82 in 1881. He was affectionately known in the tribe as "Long John."

John Jumper [*Right*] filled out Chupco's term, and was elected Principal Chief in 1882. He retired at the end of his term to become a missionary, opening the way for his son-in-law, John F. Brown, to be elected chief. J.F.B. was chief until his death in 1919.

Pictured just prior to completion in 1902, the Wewoka Trading Company was an impressive edifice. The main building and its satellite structures encompassed almost an entire city block.

[*Right*] Interior of the Wewoka Trading Company. Customers could purchase everything from bed frames to automobiles. A. J. Brown is pictured to the far right of his staff.

[*Right*] Ruins of the Wewoka Trading Company, destroyed by fire October 1925 with many tribal records.

Note of script issued by the Wewoka Trading Company, which could be redeemed for either cash or merchandise.

The note is signed by Cortland L. Long [*Right*], a partner in the million-dollar rated business.

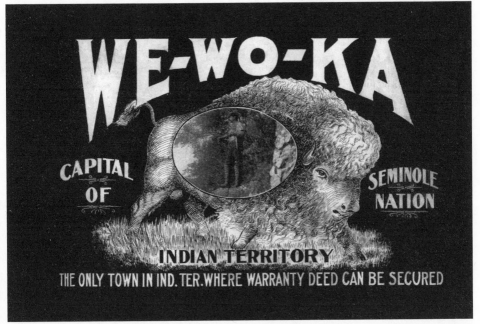

In an effort to promote the opening of the lands in the Seminole Nation prior to statehood, Governor Brown contracted with the Jennings Company to produce a brochure that extolled the great opportunities for wealth by settling around Wewoka. The above image is the front of the brochure and features an image of A. J. Brown in hunting attire in the center medallion.

Seminole tribal elections were quite transparent. Candidates announced for office but did no substantial campaigning. On election day (as above in 1902) tribesman lined up on opposite sides of the street to indicate how they wanted to vote. Tellers came out, usually at 11a.m., and counted noses.

Close up of voters waiting to be counted.

The voting took place on Wewoka's main street. This photograph was taken atop the Seminole Council House. The Wewoka Hotel can be seen (*center*) and the Wewoka Trading Company in the background.

Corn was the major staple in the tribal diet. Here grain is being pounded to a fine grit in a hollowed-out section of log known as a *cudjo*.

Typical dress and mode of transportation for the tribe in the late 1800s.

This photograph is of Palmusky, the last convicted murderer who faced the firing squad under Seminole laws. The "execution tree" was near the "whipping tree" along Wewoka's main street. It was chopped down to create a site for a building. A bullet-pocked section of the tree was exhibited by the Seminole Nation at the 1904 St. Louis World's Fair and is now a part of the permanent collection of the Oklahoma Historical Society.

Photos courtesy Gene and Martha Aldridge
and THE SEMINOLE NATION MUSEUM

6

'She's a Witch! Kill Her!'

S HOULD A "WITCH," an ugly old Seminole crone, be put to
death by the Seminole Indian firing squad?

Such an execution was challenged dramatically in June
1880—and John Franklin Brown, one of the most powerful men
in the Nation, was caught in the middle. His personal answer was
gauche, and worsened the muddle.

Led by a mounted Light-Horse sheriff, the broken-down, gray-
haired Indian woman was afoot and stumbling along the main street
of Wewoka. Her life was at stake. She was being taken to the Seminole Council House to be tried as a witch.

Watching in disbelief from her window facing the street was Antoinette C. Snow Constant, thirty-eight, the teacher at the Seminole
mission girls' school.[1]

She was outraged. Her history books said persecution for witchcraft ceased in America two centuries ago after the 1692 Salem gallows outrages.

This Seminole hag was accused of blowing her breath on a
piece of bread and giving it to a long-sick tribeswoman who tried
to eat it. She immediately choked to death. Superstitious kinsmen
accused the woman, at least eighty, wrinkled, with long straggly
hair, of being a witch.

Indian punishment was relentless and severe, Antoinette Constant knew. In four years since coming from Kansas to teach the Seminole children, she had seen tribesmen given as many as 100 lashes by a Light-Horseman for lying, stealing, selling whiskey, etc. And she saw several executed by gunfire for the crime of murder.

Even knowing all that, Antoinette Constant became more incensed by the hour over the outrage of the "witch" trial. But this white teacher stood alone. No one else seemed concerned. The "witch" was found guilty. Chief Chupco set the execution date— Tuesday, June 8, 1880 at 2 o'clock in the afternoon.[2]

Antoinette was overwhelmed, but decided to try to halt the execution. She knew three men to whom she could appeal; one was the Reverend Ross Ramsey, the Presbyterian missionary who founded the little school where she had fifty pupils, mostly girls who chattered constantly about their sympathy for the supposed "witch."

The others were Chief John Chupco, and the most learned and important "white" half-blood in the tribal leadership, John Franklin Brown.

When she went to the preacher, he rebuffed her. By interfering in tribal affairs, he warned, she could lose her job. At the Council House, she asked to speak to Chief Chupco. He refused to see her. She promptly formalized her protest in a letter to the chief. In part it said:

> I appeal to you this morning in the name of the women of this community and in the cause of our Christian faith and Indian civilization, to spare the life of that unfortunate woman now under sentence of death to be executed for this so-called crime of witchcraft.
>
> There is no such thing as a witch. . . . You now represent a civilized tribe. You have friends at home and abroad who are pleading for Indian rights. But when you, in the light of this Christian age, surrounded by elevating influences, schools and churches in your midst, will condemn and shoot to death a defenseless old woman for the superstitious idea of witchcraft, what more can your friends say in your defense?
>
> Be wise. Be above this cruel act, so that civilization may not be impeded and false impressions made on the young who are

111

the hope of your race. . . . stay the hand of the executioner. If evil comes of this act, remember your friend warned you in time to avert it.

In the cause of Indian civilization, I am your friend,
Mrs. Antoinette C. Snow Constant [3]

Fearful of failure, and with time running fast, the teacher made her second appeal without waiting for the chief's reply. She wrote and dispatched this letter to Sasakwa:

Hon. John F. Brown
Dear Sir:
In behalf of the wives and sisters of the Seminoles, I appeal to you as the representative man of this tribe, to use your influence with the council, to have them reconsider this action in reference to the sentence of death passed on that unfortunate woman for the crime of witchcraft, so called.
In all kindness I urge this appeal to you for the sake of humanity. I fear it will result in evil and evil only in your tribe. There is already an increasing interest in the Indian work and many friends are coming forward in the aid of Indian civilization who will be shocked at this act of a civilized tribe.
Please accept this appeal to you, with no motive only for good and a desire for the welfare and elevation of the Indian race.

Your friend,
Mrs. Antoinette C. Snow Constant [4]

It was strenuously fretful to wait for answers to her letters. But Antoinette's anxiety turned to blinding anger on Sunday as she sat with her children and husband in their pew in the mission church and heard the Reverend Mr. Ramsey announce from the pulpit in a matter-of-fact tone: "For all who wish to watch the execution of the witch, I can tell you that it will take place on the Council House grounds on Tuesday, at two in afternoon." [5]

Chief Chupco ignored her letter, but a rider brought a response from Sasakwa. Antoinette Constant was stunned by John Franklin Brown's reply. His weird letter said:

112

Your sympathetic appeal for the life of that poor victim of superstition who in this day of grace stalks abroad in our land penetrating the light and sanctum of our council chamber, planting his banner upon the confines of our capital, unfurling his banner to the midnight breeze—oh, foul air!—and clamoring with murderous voice for the life and blood of even our grandmothers who in their helplessness and old age in days gone by it was our custom, our pride and our joy to love and respect, reverence and protect, was handed me en route for home, deserves well to be remembered.

It finds a responsive beat in the ebb and flow in every impulse in my nature and existence. But I fear fate is settled beyond the reach of any aid I might be able to render and her life doomed to pay the forfeit of a credulousness I cannot trust my pen to name, nor can I bear to think of the retribution to Seminoles just consequences of the act assuredly will deal out.

John F. Brown [6]

When Antoinette prayed for guidance a light dawned. The United States Government might help her. Fortunately she knew Major A. W. Tate, the United States Indian agent headquartered at Muskogee. In haste, she wrote to him:

The Seminole Council has arrested, tried and condemned an old Indian woman for witchcraft. The chief has already signed the death warrant and she is to be shot to death in a few days. I have appealed to the chief, the councilmen and missionary, Reverend Mr. Ramsey, but no one will listen to my appeal for her life. Will you not use your official authority and in the cause of humanity and Christian civilization come to her rescue and save her life? Let this be confidential.

Your friend,
Antoinette C. Snow Constant. [7]

She found a horseman willing to carry her letter to Muskogee. She would have swooned if she had known Major Tate was away from his headquarters. She waited in vain all Monday for a response.

113

On Tuesday, execution day, a steady stream of buggies, wagons and riders on horseback began arriving by mid-morning. It was a warm day, and men in shirtsleeves, clustered in the vicinity of the Council House. Women and children, mostly silent with apprehensive faces, found places to sit on the Council House grass. People sat in second floor windows to watch from across the street.

At noon, the "witch" arrived, calm and resigned to dying. In the family wagon was a rough pine coffin lined with muslin. The old woman sat on the coffin, and waited. The captain of the Light-Horse police summoned two Light-Horse privates with loaded rifles. The weapons had been handed over to a medicine man the day before to be "purified," to remove the stigma attached to their use to kill a fellow Indian.

To her kinsmen, the Light-Horse captain explained that the condemned would sit at the foot of the "execution tree"—a thick oak just off the main street. White paper cut in the shape of a heart would be pinned on her bosom. She would be blindfolded, but not bound. The riflemen would kneel a few yards away and fire in unison.

With the execution barely an hour away, came cliffhanger drama. A United States Army corporal knocked at Antoinette Constant's door and handed over two wax-sealed letters. To her, Major Tate wrote:

"Your note I received this morning as I returned home from Washington. I send an order by special messenger to the chief. Please direct him where to go to find him, and any other advise you can give him. Thank you for your note. It will be confidential."

The trooper rushed the second letter across the street to the Council House. Chief Chupco handed it to John Franklin Brown to read. Major Tate had sent an order "to stay the execution," warning that if the "witch" was shot he would "hold the Seminole Council responsible for this illegal act."

"The order came like a thunderbolt," Antoinette Constant wrote in her memoirs, published in 1923. [8] Though surprised and infuriated, the chief called off the execution. The "witch" was sent home. The teacher was promptly discharged and left Wewoka.

Never again was a "witch" put on trial in the Seminole Nation.

114

DR. VIRGIL BERRY, from his Wewoka office doorway, watched a lanky Indian walk up to the Seminole Council House "whipping tree" and take off his coat and shirt, exposing his bare back to the morning sun.

The Indian had been convicted a week or two earlier of some crime, such as pilfering, stealing a neighbor's pig, fighting, perhaps attempted rape. He had been sent home, with no bond or bail, told to return for his punishment at a certain day and time. Here he was.

This exact scenario Dr. Berry had seen played out perhaps a hundred times during his years as the Government physician for the Seminoles. The culprit always showed up for his whipping, riding horseback, in the family wagon, or in rare instances on foot after walking miles across the prairie.

It was a matter of honor. The Seminole Nation had very few written crime laws, not more than one hundred. But when violated, the guilty readily paid. Not to do so would disgrace the family. (A search of available tribal records discloses but one instance where a Seminole, a young man named Tommy Larney, ran away to escape punishment.)

Dr. Berry threw a clean sheet over his examining table, and got out bandages, salves and lotions. Within a half-hour or so he would have another dangerously lacerated hide to treat. [9]

The Indian miscreant stood under the "whipping tree," a towering pecan. Beneath a stout, low limb, he was ordered to raise his hands above his head. Light-Horse privates tied them with a rope, the end of which was tossed over the limb, and pulled tight to suspend him. His feet, not quite touching ground, were tied together and a long rail inserted between his legs. On each end of the rail sat a Light-Horse. Thus the culprit was stretched, immobile and steady.

Forward stepped the Light-Horse captain, usually brawny, and strong-armed. In his hand was a green hickory switch, three feet long. He swung it in a high wide arc and brought it down with great force on the Indian's back.

Dr. Berry was always impressed that the criminal uttered no outcry. The Indian would remain stoic, though not exactly mute. His breath would be rhythmically knocked out in guttural groans. The whipping continued. The Indian's skin began falling away in strips.

115

When a hickory switch broke, the Light-Horse picked up a fresh one from his nearby pile. If the lasher became exhausted, another of the ten Light-Horse sheriffs took his place.

First offenders usually received twenty-five or fifty lashes. For third convictions, the penalty was 100.

Spectators drawn by curiosity, the thrill of exotic excitement, or sympathy, gave the whippings a Roman circus atmosphere. Even small children crowded the scene. From her second floor window across the street, Pearl Marie Sampson, a seventeen-year-old who had just arrived from Missouri with her parents and four siblings, watched in awe.

"I saw the whippings," she wrote in her memoirs. "They were extremely severe. Their backs would be a bloody froth from the lashes." [10]

Dr. Berry expands on that in his memoirs of frontier medicine.

"It usually took five switches to finish the whipping," he wrote. [11] "By the time five switches were used, the back would be beaten to a pulp and blood would stream down around the man's feet.

"It was a horrible and brutal sight to watch, but of course I never tried to interfere in their tribal punishment. The victim would be cut down and carried to my office. I would dress the wounds as gently as possible.

"Although the wounds were ugly, I can't remember any resulting in infection, although their scars were carried to the grave.

"Some who got one hundred fifty lashes were unconscious by the time I saw them. In my cases, no victim died from the whipping. Though I was told one woman died from being whipped for adultery. Her death was considered a blessing by her family."

THE DEATH PENALTY was not uncommon under Seminole law. The botched effort of Chief John Chupco and John Franklin Brown to execute the "witch" was a rare anomaly. Chiefs did hold the power of pardon, but rarely granted clemency.

Every captured murderer invariably was backed up against the "execution tree," a cutout paper heart pinned on his chest, and shot. How many Seminoles were executed is not precisely known; but there were a few hundred. Their names are not available; most tribal records were destroyed in a 1905 fire.

One "execution" literally stunned the crowd of spectators and the Light-Horse riflemen. As intended, their bullets whistled straight into the culprit's paper heart, pinned on his left breast. The Indian stood up and walked away. The shots had not pierced his heart; the organ was on the opposite side, Dr. Berry later discovered.

The last Seminole executed before tribal government was abolished, according to a memo left by an elder, was a man named Palmusky, and the last whipped was a Solomon Mitchell, who received fifty lashes.

Although few in number, the Seminole Nation's laws were tough. [12]

For any persons to "band together" to "obstruct or oppose" tribal authorities or "disturb the peace" within the Nation, the penalty for first conviction was fifty lashes; for second, 100; third, 150. "And for the fourth (4th) offence," reads the law, "he shall suffer death."

Light-Horsemen could shoot to death anyone resisting arrest, as could tribesmen chasing horse or cattle thieves. Convicted thieves got fifty lashes and if unable to pay for what they stole fifty more. Liars got up to 100 lashes. Any law-breaker testifying against a co-conspirator escaped whipping, but was made to pay damages to his victims. Rape was punished with fifty lashes, 150 on third offense. Indians guilty of encouraging commission of a crime, or failing to report knowledge of one, could get 150 lashes.

"Anyone marrying a woman," said the law, "must do so with the full knowledge of her parents or relatives." Couples were permitted to break their engagement, but any meddler in a romance was subject to twenty-five lashes. Divorce was permitted, but only after a sixty-day wait, and payment of $50 to the deserted spouse.

Over the Christmas-New Years Day holidays, "dancing after the music of the violin" was banned, subject to $5 fine. No swaps or trades could be made "sight-unseen" and buyers could back out in five days by paying $5. In ten days, the deal was final.

Councilmen had to toe the mark. Missing a meeting cost a fifty-cent fine; drinking whiskey at a session one dollar. Savage punishment was meted out to adulterers—eighty lashes to both man and woman. If the offense was repeated, a woman could find the end of her nose cut off. Sometimes her ears. Old settlers in Wewoka gossiped about one Indian woman who went around town with a shawl wrapped around her ear-less head.

AS TO SUPERSTITION, the most prevalent and oft-repeated phenomenon among Seminoles in Indian Territory was the existence of fairies, called the "Little People." [13]

Queer stories abound of the strange behavior of ghost-like great horned snakes, sacred fire that "ate" the unwary, night creatures and dreams that sucked the dreamer into the afterworld, perhaps a thousand wild and unbelievable tales of magical episodes.

But the tradition of the Little People was said by elders in the tribe to be perhaps the oldest, dating back to times long before the coming of the white man.

The universal belief was that the Little People bring Indians disease or bad luck, or, coming under the proper auspices, they bring good fortune.

An old Seminole named Tom Lowe lived north of Wewoka for years and reared a large family. Suddenly in 1921 he burned his house and moved to a new home southwest of town, because, he said, the Little People were bothering him and bringing him poor health.[14]

Old Tom said they came in the dusk of evening and sat in the trees in his yard and looked at him with wide, unblinking gaze for hours at a time. He told Wewoka lawyer-historian C. Guy Cutlip: "I could tell they were still there after dark, by their noise—a low murmur, as though they were whispering among themselves."

Another authentic account was given by London Coker, an old Creek who lived many years among the Seminoles, and ran a prosperous trading post in the 1890s at a place that became known as Heliswa.

Coker told friends that the Little People were casting a spell on him; that they marched past his door in countless numbers every afternoon, and that they were led by a man who was an enemy of his.

"I warned the Light-Horse I was going to carry a gun for protection, because I knew that man meant to try to destroy me," Coker said.[15]

As the old Indian told Cutlip: "It was the strangest thing. At times they sat up in the trees. They were no bigger than children, but they looked old. They wore peaked caps, and had strange pointed features.

"Other times they come into the road, and either stand or march around in single file. They are always silent, always sober and earnest. They have prominent, slow-moving eyes. First they look at each other, then they gaze for a long time at me, just as though in wonder."

Coker, himself one of the strangest and most picturesque figures on the Indian frontier, died in 1919 at age 105. [16]

When Seminoles became ill, they frequently summoned an elder known as "The Prophet." This was a person, usually old, who studied the trees and the wind and the weather, and sometimes killed animals and dissected them, looking for signs that would tell which Medicine Man would be best for the afflicted Indian.

Quick action was essential. The Medicine Man must come to the bedside within twenty-four hours and start making his medicine. This "doctor" went through certain incantations, sang and danced until he had properly diagnosed the case. Next he medicated the water. A real good Medicine Man was one who could sing the longest without taking in his breath, and then blow in the water. He filled a ritual basin with water and then began a slow dance around this medicine bowl, chanting in low tones. Finally after he got properly worked up, he sang in a loud voice.

The words generally ran: " They have cast a spell on him, they have cast a spell on him," repeating until his breath was almost gone. Then he would scream, "Away!"[17] And begin blowing in his medicine pipe, which was usually an elder stem with the pith blown out. One end went in his mouth and the other into the basin. Thus he medicated the water by blowing his spirit into it. Then the patient drank the water.

Not always did the Little People bring bad luck. At least not to Isaac Bottley, an old Seminole employed by Wewoka businessmen as an interperter. Riding into town, Isaac encountered a pony picketed on the side of the road. Astride was a "queer little fellow" bending over talking to another of the Little People standing on the ground. [18] When they saw Isaac, they scampered into the bushes. The pony-rider was wearing a pointed cap, a little brown jacket and tight-fitting knee britches.

Elders had told Isaac it was bad luck to reveal you had seen a fairy until four days passed. So he kept his mouth shut.

He then told the story to an old Indian named Deer. "You lucky," said Deer. "You no tell four days . . . Go hunting!"

Isaac immediately did so. Half a mile from his house he killed a big gobbler. Next day he found two gobblers in a fight with their necks twisted together. With one bullet, he killed both. Three days later he stumbled on a flock of fifty-six gobblers and got two. [19]

7

Chupco to Jumper to Brown

O N A CHILLY MORNING in early February 1881, John Chupco sauntered out to the pasture next to his Sasakwa home, carrying a spade. For perhaps an hour he strolled around looking over the lay of the land. At length he stopped in the shade of a tall pecan tree, and after a moment's hesitation, jammed the spade into the ground. He left it there, and went back inside his house.

Unlike the Plains Indians, the Seminoles never sing a "death song." They attempt, however, to make preparations for their journey to the afterworld. The principal chief of the Seminoles had just planted the spade to designate the location for his grave.

Next Chupco began examining his prized possessions, and selecting those to be buried with him. He did not intend to be as extreme as had some tribal leaders, especially in Florida. In some instances, in earlier times the chief's favorite pony was killed and buried with him. That occurred when famed Everglades warrior Billy Bowlegs died en route from Florida to Indian Territory in 1859. As the Reverend J.S. Murrow, a missionary, described that event:

> " . . . A few of his followers were with him and buried him in the true old Seminole style: viz. with everything he had with him. They first killed his pony, and were hardly prevented from

killing a Negro man whom he had with him in attendance. His rifle, money, and everything else were buried." [1]

Chupco was in his eighty-second year. His knife and his rifle had drawn blood in two wars—in Florida resisting the United States Army, as well as for the North against the Confederates. He likewise had lived in peace, and helped lead his people toward a brighter day. He knew death is inevitable, and he did not fear it.

Only days earlier, with surprising suddenness, his strength had vanished. He became light-headed and walked with a stumble. His vision flickered. Hard pain seized his chest; each new breath brought pain. "Long John" heard the ominous and repeated—and significant—hoot of the night owl. He now felt resigned to his final journey, and gave his afterlife instructions to his family. He went to bed to wait.

On Thursday, February 17, 1881, Principal Chief Chupco closed his eyes at 5 o'clock in the afternoon and never opened them again.

The women washed and dressed the body. His sons sawed and nailed lumber for his coffin. Inside with the corpse were placed his reading glasses, his knife and rifle, tobacco, and a small jar of his favorite food, hickory nut *sokfe*. His friends came and began a wake that ended with a feast. Men filing past his bier dropped cornbread crumbs into the coffin; he would need food for the four days the Seminoles believed it took to reach the Great Spirit.

Chupco was buried facing east. A small fire—to light his way—was kept burning at the head of his grave for four days. For the same period of time, bowls of food were placed there.

Official word of Chupco's end was dispatched on February 21 to the other Five Tribes by Fus Hutche Harjo, signing his letters as "second chief of the Seminoles." To the Cherokees he wrote:

> It is my painful duty to inform you of the death of our Principal Chief John Chupco who died after a short illness Feb. 17 5 P.M. In him we have lost our most influential man ... He had endeared himself to us by his uprightness and many other virtues. We feel that we are unable to replace him.

Second chief Harjo's last statement was somewhat a misnomer. Actually an excellent replacement was available—John Jumper. Whether the Government would let him return as chief was in question. Washington had "fired" Jumper and replaced him with Chupco after the Civil War. Was Jumper still to be punished—sixteen years after Appomattox—because he had led half the Seminoles in defecting to the South?

Letters went back and forth between Wewoka and the Secretary of the Interior. In a short time the word came; the ex-rebel chief was acceptable to Washington.

For years John Jumper had been an active member of the National Council. Thus he was well aware of the myriad problems that continued to beleaguer the tribe. His heart, though, was in religion. He was pastor of Sasakwa's Spring Baptist Church, and busy doing Indian missionary work, extending even into the Choctaw and Chickasaw Nations.

Jumper was now sixty-three and healthy. He consulted his conscience, and prayed to the Great Spirit. In the end, he agreed to take over as acting chief, counting on continued help from John Franklin Brown. After filling in the last of Chupco's term, Jumper ran officially in 1882 and was easily elected. [2] But three years later he retired as chief and returned to helping Indians toward Christianity.

Chupco's demise and the end of John Jumper's reign brought the Seminole Nation again to a leadership crossroads. Prominent elders felt they knew the appropriate candidate. If they had been able to speak English, they would describe him as "quite literate, and a businessman and statesman of the highest calibre."

They referred, of course, to John Franklin Brown, who at this time—1885—was forty-two years old, and had been for two decades a strong tribal activist. Where could the Seminole Nation look to find a stronger, more learned and loyal advocate to wisely shield the tribe from the continual harsh mistreatment showered down by their Great Father? It didn't take a lot of looking around.

AT THE TIME John Franklin Brown became chief, the Seminole Nation remained in 1885 largely a wild and untamed frontier. The clear valley streams sparkled. Grass grew lush and tall. Hills were wooded, and dazzling flowers blossomed abundantly across the prairies. Yet the average Indian found his life still largely primitive, hardscrabble, and somewhat chancy.

In the main, the Seminoles lived simply, tending their livestock and crops, usually small plots. They at times fished and hunted game. Their ambitions or dreams rarely extended beyond the next sunrise. Only their few literate leaders had traveled much, mainly to see the Great Father.

Among newspapers, journals, and books in his office, Brown would ponder the plight of his tribe. The typical Seminole would not have been able to visualize that in the East existed paved roads, running water, streetcars, hospitals, millionaires building mansions, high society balls, theatres, French cuisine, a sixty-mile-an-hour train between Washington and New York, electric lights—even electric flat irons.

Governor Brown (on being elected he had abandoned the title of chief and adopted "Governor") realized the Seminoles could advance only through education. He was keenly aware the Indians were held back by their inability to comprehend the white man's language, laws, and customs. Schooling was too late for the grownups, but not for the boys and girls. His main objective was give the children at least the basic Three R's.

Confusion and distrust was not one-sided. From his own travels, Governor Brown knew the picture the average Easterner had of all Indians was of stoic faces and war paint. The trauma of the massacre of General Custer and his cavalry at Little Big Horn still rankled the American conscience. General Phil Sheridan's quip, "The only good Indian is a dead Indian," was often grimly quoted. Geronimo, the renegade Apache chief, eluded U.S. Cavalry on the Mexican border, triggering angry news headlines.

Other extremes resonated nationally. Buffalo Bill Cody, famous for killing and scalping Cheyenne Chief Yellow Hand in a duel, caught attention by launching the world tour at Omaha of his Wild West show, starring Annie Oakley and Sioux Chief Sitting Bull. That, too, Brown believed, tended to exacerbate unwarranted hatred of the red man.

In the Seminole Nation, travel continued to be mainly by wagon or horseback. There were ridge-top trails, but few good wagon roads.

The going was slow. Rivers had to be forded at shallows or crossed by ferry.

Railroads had come to the Territory, but many chiefs, including Governor Brown, considered them ill advised, if not dangerous. They were believed precursors of an invasion of unwanted homesteaders. The M-K-T [Katy] pushed south from Kansas through the Cherokee and Choctaw Nations toward Fort Worth, chiefly to haul cattle up north.[3] That signaled the death knell for the Chisholm Trail drives. The tracks brought telegraph which put the spurs to news and communication.

From personal experience, Governor Brown knew how travel difficulties hampered frontier medicine. By 1885 physicians were generally available, but often a day's ride away. Dentists were not so handy. A monk at Sacred Heart School on the western edge of Seminole Nation suffered a serious toothache. To reach help required a two-day wagon trip to Atoka where he boarded a Katy passenger train for Texas. It was ten days before he came home with a sore jaw minus seven teeth. [4]

Young dental students made quick "bushwhacking" forays into Indian country. One came to Wewoka, rented a room for a day or two, and distributed handbills to attract customers. Patients were seated in a rocking chair, which was steadied by chocking it with four sticks of firewood. A pail was hung on the chair's arm as a spittoon, and the drill operated by a foot treadle. Instruments were sterilized in a bucket of Lysol solution.[5] Dentists often worked cheap. Extractions were fifty cents to one dollar, according to published recollections of those days. Dr. F. C. Holmes recalled being called thirty miles into the hills to help a farmer whose angry and combative son-in-law had broken his jaw. It took two days to fashion and fit a rubber and canvas mask to hold the jaw for healing. The dentist asked $25; the patient pleaded poverty. A year later the dentist got ten dollars. [6]

AT THE TIME Governor Brown became chief, the federal government rolled out a powerful new legislative offensive to drastically change the way of life for the Five Tribes.

Hence the Seminoles urgently needed a leader with a sharp and serious mind and a strong and steady hand. They got such a chief. And he kept the job, despite one glitch, for thirty years.

His length of tenure was unprecedented—not equaled by any Seminole Chief, before or since.

Governor Brown would be called on to guide the tribe through the upheavals triggered by a literal "war" with the powers in Washington.

Over the course of relatively few years, the Congress would undertake to abolish tribal governments and substitute federal law. Legislation also was written to break up the commonality of reservations and the open range by allotting Indians individual plots of land. The "twin" Indian and Oklahoma Territories would come, followed by the land rushes of "Boomers and Sooners" that would lead to the 1907 creation of the state of Oklahoma.

In this period, Governor Brown was enveavoring to expand his own business interests. Essential to this was devoting time to reading, keeping up. He spent many evenings at his desk, in lamplight. One corner was piled with ledgers, books, and newspapers. Lizzie at times joined him. He was concerned about her; lately she looked so wan. Not yet forty, she was the mother of eight, the youngest five. Tuberculosis ran in her family; he would shudder at the memory of three Jumper siblings dying young.

To brighten her mood, he showed newspapers reporting exotic doings of the rich. New York magnate William K. Vanderbilt threw a fancy dress ball that cost $250,000, including $155,000 for costumes and $65,000 for champagne, music, and food. Cyrus McCormick died in Chicago, leaving his widow and seven children $200 million.

The Indians ate up newspaper coverage of national politics. Grover Cleveland had been elected President in 1884, a surprise and the first Democrat to reach the White House since James Buchanan in 1856. Tribal leaders in the Territory speculated what this would mean to their people. Would the new administration soften the Government's harsh Indian policies? Governor Brown opined there'd be no letup.

Looking ahead, Governor Brown had guided his siblings into his business enterprises. His brother Andrew Jackson, nine years the

126

Governor's junior, and generally called "Jackson," became his right hand man, in tribal affairs as well as at the trading post. Jackson was treasurer of the Seminole Nation almost as long as John Franklin was chief. The Indians viewed Jackson as a mathematical "wizard" because he could calculate three columns of figures in his head as fast and accurately as a bank clerk. [7]

Nepotism didn't seem to be a dirty word in tribal government. Alice would assume an important role in Seminole education; she likewise was to be active as a businesswoman, though not in the Brown Trading Company. She became also an interpreter in the courts, and later ventured into Mexico on land quests for the Seminoles.

Two other brothers were involved peripherally. Stanton, sixteen years the Governor's junior, clerked in the trading post and later would become superintendent of tribal schools. Robert worked in the trading post until he was killed December 10, 1885 at age twenty-eight. The two remaining sisters, Lucy and Jennie, were not to become distinctive in public life; both married and added to the bountiful crop of children and grandchildren. The Browns were enormously fecund.

Governor Brown in the course of three marriages would sire seventeen children, seven of whom were boys. Curiously, he repeated given names—two Ruths, two Solomons, two Jameses, and two Marthas. His last child, a James, was born in 1913, but died in infancy. (Information on his marriages and children is difficult to verify because of inconsistencies in the available sources, viz: Government Indian enrollments, the official census, and Brown family documents and memoirs.)

Alice, married only once, would bear eleven children, the first of whom died as a baby. Jackson, married twice, fathered three children. Stanton had five, and Robert at his death left two small daughters. [His widow, Eliza Coker, later remarried.] Jennie Factor had twins who died at birth and later a son. Lucy Crain, described as the most beautiful of the Dr. Brown daughters and known as "Sukey," had three children. Her life ended tragically; after a mental breakdown, she would die in a South Dakota Indian insane asylum at age sixty-eight.

TRADING POSTS were essential on the frontier, meeting needs of Indians, and the growing influx of whites. Sister Alice now followed Governor Brown into business with a general store.

In reality, she was not impinging on his business. She and Roll Davis had cast acquisitive eyes on the lush country about twenty miles north of Wewoka. Along the meandering banks of the North Canadian River, they searched for a large acreage. They had in mind both a trading post, largely to serve nearby Creek Indians, and a cattle ranch.

By buggy they reached the river on a Spring morning in 1882. Hobbling their team, they set out exploring on foot. The North Canadian was full, clear and wide. They came, as Alice would later relate to her children, to a limestone falls, where the stream gurgled noisily, sparkling in the sun.

"Look! A cave!" Alice cried. [8]

"Must be the 'robber's cave' some of the Creeks told us about," said her husband.

They had to stoop to enter, but the cavern's interior was almost as roomy as a barn. At the top was a yard-wide opening. Daylight streamed in, illuminating the cave. "What would the kids think of this?" Alice said.

Outside, to the west, they saw a vast pastureland. Wooded hills fringed the falls and robber's cave.

"This is it," said George Rollin Davis. Alice remembered nodding with vigor and delight.

Alice was thirty and Roll three years older. They were in their prime and ready for adventure and prosperity. They did not lack business ability. George was a "graduate" of trading post "school." His reputation for integrity was first rate across the frontier, and, importantly, he had established good credit. He knew cattle and horses. Alice had a keen business mind, and the energy of an athlete.

They had three living children, ages six to three—George Lytle, born January 26, 1876; Clara Estelle, who was named as promised for Dr. Brown's lost Clara, and would grow up as "Kitt," born December 6, 1877; and Jesse Edwin, born November 22, 1879.

Only a few days before starting out on this exploration, Alice had happily discovered she was again pregnant.

In the shade of the buggy, they got out a tablet and pencils and made notes on how to create their prairie trading post. They could see that the buildings would be far enough from the riverbank to escape Spring floods. They would require a warehouse, quite large, connecting to the back of the general store. Alice had her heart set on a two-story house, painted white, with a paled fence enclosing a front yard. They'd need barns, stables, a washhouse, and privies.

"Pretty big bunkhouse," said Roll, as she later remembered it. "We'll probably need twenty cowboys. I may graze five or ten thousand steers." [9]

The Davises would also utilize the Brown family influence in Washington. Having a post office in the trading post would bring customer traffic. This area of the Seminole Nation currently had no mail service, and needed it. Alice felt sure Governor Brown could make that happen.

What about names?

George had already picked one for the ranch—Bar X Bar. "The blacksmith can make our branding iron with just four straight pieces of iron, one bar on top of the X and the other on the bottom."

And the trading post and the post office?

Alice knew and admired a friendly Indian elder known as Yar-Beka.

"How about honoring him?" said Alice. "We'll call our place Arbeka. Of course the Indians don't pronounce the 'r'. They'll call it Uh-beck-uh." [10]

With fancy dreams and laughing spirits, Alice and Roll set to work at once.

DESPITE HIS OWN robust health, Governor Brown felt hounded by the Dark Angel. His daughter Ina, born in 1876, died of tuberculosis as a baby. Now three of his other children—John W., fifteen; Solomon, fourteen; and Ruth, twelve—were ill with tuberculosis. Dr. Virgil Berry, the government's tribal physician, looked grave when he examined them.

129

"How bad are they?" the father asked.

Dr. Berry recalls in his biography that he looked down, and took his time wiping his thermometer with alcohol. Finally, he shook his head sadly. "Only the Lord knows. . ."

Governor Brown's first-born, James, had fallen off a horse, and died of a broken neck. Now his immediate family consisted of the three tuberculars and three daughters—Henrietta, thirteen; Jennie, nine; and Martha, seven—and their mother.

Lizzie had a cough that intensified. She lost weight, and her strength ebbed. At times she talked irrationally. She suddenly started vomiting blood. Dr. Berry, worried and weary, couldn't seem to do much for her. Sadly, she suffered the curse of the Jumpers—tuberculosis.

In her sick bed, Lizzie Brown, wife for not quite twenty years of the Seminole Chief, lapsed into a coma. Governor Brown was holding her hand when her spirit departed on the long journey to join her ancestors. [11]

Not much later his mourning was interrupted by a business emergency. An important opportunity came up that he had to carefully examine.

This concerned the Wewoka Trading Company that had been launched in 1866 by Elijah Brown. The store was busy and prosperous, but seemingly wearing on Elijah. To him came another white man, Courtland L. Long, from the Midwest. Like many another newcomer to the frontier, Long was an ambitious adventurer. He wanted to buy into the trading post. Elijah checked Long and found that he was honest, upright, and extremely capable in business. He had capital, so Elijah Brown sold half-interest and took him in as partner. [12]

Then Governor Brown got the word that Elijah wanted to sell his remaining half interest in the Wewoka Trading Post, and retire from business.

"Mr. Long," said Governor Brown, walking in, "I've come to ascertain whether you would accept me as your partner, if I purchase Elijah's interest." [13]

They looked each other in the eye, according to Long's published recollections, and had immediate rapport. The deal was made.

Governor Brown promptly brought his brother Jackson into the enterprise. Long managed Wewoka, where Jackson and the Governor also took a strong hand, while continuing to build up their Sasakwa store.

And a few months later Governor Brown's life underwent another significant change. Among the young women he knew in Sasakwa was a full blood Creek named Elizabeth Alexander, pretty and cheerful, from a prominent family. On some occasion Elizabeth complimented the chief on the style of his ruffled shirt, or the neatness of his mustache, or perhaps on some humorous riposte he had tossed off. At any rate, he took notice—and took action.

They were married in Sasakwa. He was almost forty-four. His new bride Elizabeth was a little over twenty.

8

Saying 'No' to Senator Dawes

IN LATE AFTERNOON on Wednesday, November 8, 1893, Governor Brown was engaged in spirited and serious discussion at his Sasakwa trading post with his brother Jackson and his father-in-law, G.A. Alexander.

The men were agitated and angry, and with considerable cause. The powers in Washington had enacted laws intended to force the Indians to abandon their traditional way of life, to abolish their tribal governments, and surrender great chunks of their land to white settlers. News had just come that President Grover Cleveland had appointed retiring Senator Henry L. Dawes as his hatchet man. [1]

Alexander, a member of the Creek Nation Council, had traveled to Washington with Governor Brown to lobby against these preposterous changes. Their trips were futile. Brown on this afternoon was lamenting that Washington would push, push and push until the Seminoles, Creeks, Cherokees, Choctaws and Chickasaws were hammered down, robbed of their independence and coerced into becoming part of a new state.

Dusk was closing. Under a cloudy sky, the air turned nippy.

As their conversation rose in intensity, the trading post door opened and two men came in. They stood silent for a long moment, looking around. Neither appeared out of the ordinary—just young white men, tall, leathery, dressed in boots, big hats, the rough garments of farmers or cowboys. [2]

No one else was in the store except two of Governor Brown's sons working as clerks—John W., twenty-two, and Solomon, twenty-one.

One of the men stepped up and asked for a box of .45 calbre bullets. Solomon took a box off the ammunition shelf and handed it over the counter. The customer, smoking a sleazy hand-rolled cigaret, dug two dollars out of his pocket and paid.

For a couple more minutes, the men swept the store with squinted eyes. They went out. Almost immediately they burst in again, accompanied by two other rough looking young men.

"Hands up! All ya! Pronto!"   That barked command caught Governor Brown in mid-sentence continuing his execration of dire misdeeds being concocted in faraway Washington. The store people all fell silent, and stared at the intruders.

The lead cowboy threw aside his cigaret and aimed his revolver at Governor Brown's head. All four men held guns. Five pairs of hands shot up.

"Everybody outside!" The outlaws jabbed pistols at their victims and herded them out the door, lining them up at the hitching rail where four sorry-looking horses were tied.

While two robbers covered the Brown people, the other two searched them for valuables. They took three gold watches, two silver watches and $300 in bills.

"We don't wanna hurt you," the cigaret bandit said. "Don't get scared. It's hard times. We gotta do this!" He repeated his words a time or two.

The outlaws whispered together. The five victims remained lined up, glancing at each other but not talking, their hands still raised. The bandit chief turned to them. "Somebody's gotta open the safe."

Governor Brown caught Solomon's eye and nodded toward him. Solomon marched inside and went to the big iron safe. The leader and a youngish, nervous robber accompanied him. Solomon stood, his arms upraised, giving a quizzical look. "Okay," said the main bandit. "Put your hands down. Open 'er up!"

They found another $1,000.

As they escorted Solomon back outside, the nervous robber's elbow banged something on the counter. His six-gun roared! His leader started and whirled on him. "Quit bein' so goddamned jittery!"

Solomon shivered. On a shelf behind his head a gallon tin bucket spewed him with gooey syrup from a fresh bullet hole.

Two thieves held guns on the Brown people outside. The other robbers went back inside and looted the store. They carried out bolts of flannel, women's and men's shoes, two expensive new saddles, jewelry, muslin and an assortment of clothing. Unfortunately, the Sasakwa streets were empty and provided no witnesses, no help.

The robbers lashed their loot in haphazard bundles to their saddles. They mounted and lined up their victims single file, Governor Brown in front.

"Now march! Head west." For a mile and a half the Brown people walked along the westward wagon road.

"Stop!" The robbers holstered their pistols, and turned their mounts south. "Goodbye," one shouted. They galloped off.

At first light Governor Brown had a posse led by his Seminole Light-horse in pursuit. They tracked the thieves ten miles southwest to the banks of the South Canadian River and there lost the trail.

The robbery was never solved, though it created a stir throughout the Seminole Nation. It made news 100 miles to the west, featured on page one of *The Purcell Register* at Purcell, Chickasaw Nation.

The newspaper quoted Governor Brown: "We believe they were farmers because they were shabbily dressed, rode pony horses, and seemed to be after goods as much as money." [3]

HAVING A PISTOL HELD to his head and being robbed in his own trading post filled Governor Brown with indignation. Even so, that resentment was small compared to his growing anger against the cruel "war" Washington had just launched.

Ex-Senator Dawes was coming to Indian Territory to count heads and give every Indian a smallish piece of their own 20,000,000 acres, and then open all leftover land to white settlers. The mere thought made Governor Brown gnash his teeth. Dawes would be in for a fight! Brown would never let the Seminoles submit or surrender!

134

Brown had several times since the 1880s visited Dawes in his office at the Senate, and argued against the various sly schemes Congress invented to destroy the Seminoles' way of life. Dawes was misguided; he seemed infected by the proverbial stereotype *"The only good Indian is a dead Indian."* [4] The senator, a Yale-educated politician, had been also a Massachusetts editor and lawyer. He was powerful, a man to be feared. Now seventy-seven, Dawes served thirty-six years in Congress, half of that in the Senate. Having been chairman of the Senate Indian Affairs Committee, he had a lot of knowledge about Native Americans. Could President Cleveland's hatchet man come among the Seminoles and look into their wistful and dreamy dark eyes, listen to their musical speech whose language is so full of poetry, and yet hopelessly degrade and doom the tribe to extinction? The likely answer made Governor Brown's heart sink. [5]

Moving quickly, Dawes sent from Washington letters to each of the Five Civilized Tribes explaining his mission and asking appointment of delegates to confer with him. In January 1894, he arrived in Muskogee and opened an office with his two fellow commissioners, plus secretaries, stenographers, interpreters, and a land surveying team. President Cleveland had appointed Meredith H. Kidd of Indiana and Archibald S. McKennon of Arkansas to serve with him. Dawes, paid $5000 a year, hired his daughter Anna, an author and journalist, as his secretary. Congress appropriated $50,000 for expenses.

Dawes' letter to the Seminoles reached Governor Brown at the Council House in Wewoka. Brown opened the envelope and looked at the missive. He felt disgust. A few minutes later he threw away the letter. He did not acknowledge, or reply to it.[6] He intended to ignore the Dawes Commission.

From the Civil War to 1885, the population of the United States had doubled to nearly sixty million. Brown understood the significance of that fact. The only large areas of arable land still unsettled had been traded to the Indians. Pressure was on Congress to take back much of it. The demanding howl came from railroads, white farmers, speculators, and politicians. In the end, Congress attempted in the Dawes Act to satisfy the pro-settlement forces and at the same time protect Indian interests.

Between January and March 1894, the Dawes Commissioners managed to confer with delegates from the Creek, Cherokee, Choctaw and Chickasaw tribes. The Seminoles continued to remain aloof, even from a three-day "international" conference of the four other tribes with Dawes.

The commission was making enemies, not headway. The Creek chief in his own tongue told his tribe the government allotment would give each Creek a tract of ground four feet wide and eight feet long. [7] The Choctaw chief sent three men to trail the Washington officials and at each stop urge their native audience to oppose allotment. [8]

Governor Brown's sagacity finally took hold. In a turnabout, the Seminoles invited the Dawes commission to appear before their General Council in Wewoka on April 6, 1894. After that session, the Seminole Council voted to have nothing further to do with the Dawes commission.[9]

Unhappily, Dawes went the extra step of writing fully what Congress proposed and sent letters to each of the Five Tribes, requesting a response October 1, 1894. Governor Brown received his letter—and again threw it away.

It could be, Dawes came to realize, leaders of the tribes were nefarious in rebuffing him. The most likely reason: crooks and skulduggery. Dawes was startled to discover that in one tribe sixty-one members had control of 1,237,000 acres of the tribe's 3,040,000. A favored few and white intruders held minerals and town sites. [10] Moreover, he ascertained that Indian Territory was lawless; in one tribe there were 53 murders in 54 days and no one punished. Trains were robbed almost in sight of towns, and nothing done, either. That was the report Dawes got.

Aware of the widespread confusion and discontent, Governor Brown sent Dawes a long letter, dated May 9 giving the Seminoles' reasons for defying the government—and at the same time drawing a line in the sand.[11] The Seminole chief explained that his Council "seriously considered" the basic Dawes propositions, which he characterized as requiring the Five Tribes "to agree to a survey and pro rata distribution of all their lands," as well as creation of a territorial government, and for the Indians to become citizens of the United States. His letter continued:

Among some of the advantages it is thought that might be derived by an early agreement with the Commission, rather than trust entirely to action by Congress in this all-important question, mention is made of the following by the Commission:

To protect the Indians in their homes; the lands when allotted them, be made inalienable for a long term of years; that none but these land-owners could be allowed to vote at elections. By which plan or agreement the Indians would be permitted to control all the political affairs of the country thus organized as at present, although representing but little more than one-fifth of its population, including both whites and Indians.

All money held in trust by the United States government, upon which the interest only is now paid annually or semi-annually to the nations to which they belong, and applied by them to the use and maintenance of their tribal governments and to the operation of their educational systems, might be paid out to the Indians in such amounts and at such times as might be agreed upon with the Commission. The sources of supply to maintain the new order of government could be easily obtained, and would have to be—by taxation—in which the lands only would be exempted for the time being. These and many other questions might be presented and adjusted to an advantage to the Indian, perhaps, to a degree far beyond any that could be hoped for if left entirely to the will of Congress, and the present opportunity be allowed to pass and go unheeded by the people. . .

Public meetings have been held at every accessible point in the nation . . . The reply, without exception, has been a firm declination to agree to any of the propositions . . . Nothing remains, then, for us [but] . . . to give expressions to these conclusions . . .[and] some of the reasons that impel our people to this course. . .in this hour of gloom and great trial. . . The various treaties existing between the Five Tribes and the United States . . . have been vouched for by the United States, and relied upon by the Indians. [Meanwhile] . . . various bills in Congress tended to disrupt us as a nation and finally destroy us as a people. If these solemn pledges are to be broken at last, with or without the Indians' consent . . . then, indeed, we are lost.

Governor Brown's letter went on to assert that Indians receiving 130 acres would find only one third suitable for farming, another

137

third for pasture and the remainder "worthless." Reimbursement for tribesmen "who have improved their homes" on land they would not be allotted would heavily cost the Seminole Nation. Thrifty farmers would be hurt and herdsmen would have such "narrow limits" they might be forced to keep their hogs, cattle and horses "at the end of a rope."

"Under the present system," the chief explained, "there is room for all, with no monopolies, either, to breed discontent or cause complaint among our people."

Restrictions on the sale of land to prevent fraud, he wrote, "would be no real advantage" because in a "short time" non-citizens and "the sharp speculator, with money and friends" would find ways to fleece the Indian, leading him to "the gutter, into moral degradation and financial ruin." If paid out immediately on a proactive basis, Brown predicted, trust funds "would be spent in advance, and absolutely squandered." Likewise, the Indian would be unable to pay taxes, and eventually the U.S. would seize "the property itself. . . [and] the household effects."

If U.S. deputy marshals and the Indian police had proved unable to halt "the whiskey traffic wielding such powerful influence for evil . . . we are at a loss to know how we are to be relieved when left alone, as citizens of the United States, to cope with this monster. We feel unequal to the task, and would shun the responsibility." Governor Brown's letter continued:

> We have uniformly suffered in changing a treaty, or making a new one—no more than a mere skeleton of former rights have ever remained—and in this way our progress has been hindered and retarded. . . We have struggled hard to recover our loss, until today we feel not ashamed to invite an inspection of some of our institutions of learning . . . where our young are being educated and Christianized . . .
>
> From this source, more than any other, have we relied to emerge from the surrounding darkness and entanglements to emerge into the broad daylight of knowledge that would place our posterity upon a lasting foundation—the equal of his white brother. Nothing is more certain than unless we are prepared and equipped, we cannot maintain an equal contest with him in life's

race. It is cruel to blast our hopes and destroy the good work so well begun . . . by fencing us into closer relationship with him than at present.

It is alleged that in the Territory the laws are not enforced, and that the local judiciary is a farce. So far as the Seminoles are concerned, we know this is not true, and believe it is slanderous of the other Nations, as well; we challenge truthful contradiction and invite the closest inspection.

We have merely touched upon the outcropping of . . . this new system of government. . . We shall only remark that we see no good reason why there should be any due haste or rashness in dealing with our people, who are wards of the United States Government, and as such are surely entitled to its protection, and may the Great Ruler of all mankind guide us all and give us the wisdom and power to do right in order that even-handed justice be meted out to all alike.

In addition to Governor Brown's signature, the letter was signed "Nath. Cap Harjo, President Council," and bore the attest of "Wm. Danzan, Clerk, approved May 9, 1894."

In telling Dawes that Seminole children were being led "out of the darkness and entanglements" into "the broad daylight of knowledge," Governor Brown spoke factually, and with pride. At his insistence, the National Council had willingly taken $120,000 from annuities coming from the Government and spent the money to erect two handsome boarding schools, Mekusukey Mission and Emahaka Mission.

Mekusukey, built in 1901, was fifteen miles west of Wewoka. It was an impressive brick and stone structure, four floors high in the center section, with two triple storied wings flanked by spacious porches nearly sixty feet long. Large turrets rose to a height of over fifty feet above the two front corners of the building.

On the second or main floor were located the primary classroom, the superintendent's office and living quarters. Also on that floor was the assembly hall, which doubled as the older students' classroom, as well as the intermediate and music classrooms. The kitchen, laundry, and dining room were in the basement, which was half above ground permitting windows to give light and ventilation. The dining

139

room had long wooden tables, chairs and benches, and a piano. The infirmary was on the third floor, and teachers and students roomed on the third and fourth floors. Each of these floors had centrally-located identical lavatory/bath rooms. Unusually modern for its time, each floor had hot and cold running water, with steam heat to each room, plus a number of fireplaces. A huge wooden water tank was located in one turret. Nearby was an engine and boiler house. Barns and sheds were also being built to enable the academy students and staff to raise hogs, cattle and horses, as well as crops and fruit on the surrounding 100 acres.

Enrollment was 112 boarding students, with additional day students. The staff included the superintendent and eight instructors, and the farm foreman and several cowboys and field hands.

Two years later Emahaka, an identical structure, was erected five miles south of Wewoka.

Initially both schools were to be co-ed, but the concept was soon changed, and boys were sent to Mekusukey, girls to Emahaka. Consequently, Emahaka's music room was equipped with a dozen pianos. A strong effort was exerted to give the girls a solid grounding in singing and piano, as well as an appreciation of art and poetry, along with training in sewing and cooking. The Emahaka sewing machines hummed daylong.

Learning to read and write and cipher was the main instruction for boys. They were also carefully taught the white man's tongue and his customs. With that also came lessons on how to make practical and profitable use of their hands—in carpentry, masonry, farm and ranch work.

A high iron fence enclosed each academy. Primarily these were to keep out stray livestock, but also protection against unwanted intruders. Emahaka records, for instance, show that on one night "several Indian boys came up on horses, yelling and shooting off their six-guns, showing off for the girls at the school." [12] Eight-year-old Byron Blake, nephew of the superintendent, Rev. William P. Blake, was hauling a five-gallon can of water in his little "hand" wagon. Frightened by the noise, the boy ducked behind a large post-oak tree. When he emerged, water was spurting from a bullet hole in his water can.

At each school capable professionals were in charge. Discipline was strict, etiquette was enforced, and the students were Christianized and kept in line. The boys and girls who completed their courses emerged well educated. Not much was said or written about the fact these schools made only a dent in the horde of other juvenile Seminoles who continued to live in the shadow of the tribe's aboriginal past.

Emahaka and Mekusukey also were fated to be caught up in the continuing struggle between the Seminole Nation to conduct its own affairs and the efforts of the President and the Congress to effect drastic changes.

In the end, the Brown family would be right in the middle of this desperate and losing battle over schools, especially Alice.

COPING WITH DEMANDS of the Dawes Commission required hours of work and study, but Governor Brown still attended day-to-day routine necessary to keep 3,000 Seminoles united as a nation.

At times it was up to him whether an Indian lived or died.

On July 21, 1894, the National Council held a busy session in Wewoka. First order of business was putting on trial one Coucharty for the killing of a Indian named Ben Brooks. The verdict was guilty.

Governor Brown ordered Coucharty to stand.

"You are hereby sentenced to be executed by Light-Horse on August 24, 1894 at eleven o'clock in the morning. Go now, make your arrangements at home, and return here at the appointed time to be shot to death." [13]

Coucharty, his face a stoic mask, walked silent and erect out of the Council House.

At that same meeting, the Council, according to the minutes that its clerk K. N. Kinkebee provided *The Muskogee Phoenix,* also ordered one Negro whipped for stealing.

The Council then re-elected forty-two officers for four-year terms, including ex-Chief John Jumper as school superintendent; Jackson Brown as treasurer; Este Larney and Couchartochee as Light-Horse captains. A vote was taken to designate the Seminoles' boarding schools, Mekusukey Mission for boy students and Emahaka Mission for girls.

The newspaper quoted Governor Brown as saying: "We are satisfied that during this first term of Council it has done things according to the law of our Nation. And approved. So therefore we leave the Nation in the hands of Providence to bless us." [14]

Second Chief Hulputta-Che Micco addressed the council, *The Muskogee Phoenix* also reported, "in strong words, to try and persuade children of the Nation to do right, and to avoid themselves from drinking, and to try to make an example to their people."

That prompted Governor Brown, the clerk wrote, to stand up again and make Hulputta's words "tougher." The minutes read:

> That was the first time he [Brown] ever spoke strong. And he further said that the day has come when everybody should look out for themselves, telling of the allotment and how bad it would be.
>
> And for that reason, even a Christian, should try to be good so that Jehovah might not send a curse upon the Nation. [15]

During a growing wave of banditry, Governor Brown was twice a victim. Barely six months after the Sasakwa robbery, one of the Territory's most notorious murdering badmen, twenty-year-old Crawford Goldsby known as "Cherokee Bill," struck his Wewoka Trading Post.

Cherokee Bill was on a rampage robbing a bank, stores, farmers, and Katy trains, putting at least two new notches on his sixgun—"not counting Indians and niggers." [16] Teamed up with two Creek Nation killers, Jim and Bill Cook, Cherokee Bill rode up to the Wewoka store, drew his pistol, and barged in.

The scenario was similar to the Sasakwa holdup.

Governor Brown was not at the Wewoka store, but his brother Jackson was, along with Courtland L. Long, their partner.

Cherokee Bill and his pals took all the money they could find, some cheese and crackers, other convenient odds and ends, including two fancy bridles.

They ordered Jackson, Courtland Long and three clerks to hit the road with their hands up. The men from the store were marched on foot three miles north of Wewoka, followed by the mounted outlaws.

"Far enough," said Cherokee Bill. "Stay put. Don't yell."

The bandits galloped away.

If captured, the bandits would have faced trial before Federal Judge Isaac Parker, the legendary "Hanging Judge" at Fort Smith. Since 1875 he had been "law and order" for every person on the Indian frontier, with the exception of members of the Five Tribes. Their crimes and disputes—Indian vs. Indian—were handled by tribal courts. Judge Parker and 200 deputy U. S. marshals held sway over 70,000 square miles of lawless prairies and hills rife with hideouts for outlaws.

Cherokee Bill, though hounded by Parker's deputies, was hard to catch. Finally, with intricate scheming, the lure of a whore, and the bribe of an outlaw turncoat, caught unawares in a rustic hideout he was cold-cocked with a piece of stove wood and hauled off to the Fort Smith jail.

Brought before Judge Parker or shot down by marshals were scores of notorious outlaws—among them Belle Starr, the Verdigris Kid, the Buck Gang, Henry Starr, the Doolins, the Jennings—a grisly collection murderers, robbers and rapists whose exploits provided fodder for hundreds of books, newspaper stories and a number of movies on the outrages, and heroism, of the West.

Judge Parker, who took his job at thirty-seven, was tireless. He opened court at eight in the morning and sat till dark. His rule was harsh, but off the bench he was witty, a school board member, active in church. He ordered 168 killers to the gallows, and hanged as many as six at a time.

In a ten-year period, juries in Judge Parker's court convicted 7,419 criminals—305 for murder, 466 for assault with intent to kill, 1,910 for selling liquor to Indians, 2,860 for sending liquor to Indian Territory, 97 for illicit stills, 124 for violating whiskey revenue laws, 65 for postal law violations, 50 for counterfeiting, 24 for arson, 48 for perjury, 32 for bigamy, 27 for conspiracy, 59 for stealing government timber, 24 for resisting arrest, and 149 for lesser crimes.

Judge Parker was not without his critics— getting roughed up even by Senator Dawes's family. The senator's daughter Anna

143

Dawes, as a journalist from Massachusetts, inspected Judge Parker's overcrowded and filthy jail in Fort Smith. Anna Dawes was outraged. She launched a newspaper exposé that was reprinted in the *Congressional Record.* [17] Money for a new jail was promptly authorized.

Miss Dawes yelled, too, about Parker locking up women criminals and their children. A prisoner named Anna Jones went behind bars at Fort Smith accompanied by her four-year-old daughter. A pregnant woman, Mrs. Arena Howe, was locked up for manslaughter, along with her son, five years old. Her baby was born in jail. The mother and two children later were shipped off to the Detroit House of Corrections where she would serve her ten-year sentence. [18]

Even Governor Brown's sister Alice and two brothers-in-law, George Rollin Davis and Alexander Wills Crain (married to Sukey), all wound up on the other side of the law.

The Indian Chieftain at Vinita, I.T., told the story in its Thursday, November 15, 1894 issue:

> Alex W. Crain, H.G. Malot, George R. Davis and Mrs. Alice B. Davis were tried last week for conspiracy to defraud the government, forgery and presenting false claims, and were acquitted.
>
> Davis lives in Arbeka and his wife is a sister of John Brown, chief of the Seminole Nation. Crain was a United States commissioner and made out a number of pension applications for Seminole and Creek soldiers.
>
> When the pension examiners went down to investigate the claims, the applicants denied having made the claims, signed them or sworn to them.
>
> Some of the would-be pensioners swore that they went to Mrs. Davis and that she filled out the blank application and that Crain afterwards signed their names and fixed his jurat.
>
> There were seven cases against Crain but he was convicted in only two. He filed a motion for a stay of execution.

This edition of Vinita's weekly newspaper was jammed with lively items. [19] For instance this one-paragrapher:

> Amos McIntosh, prosecuting attorney for the Creek Nation, shot Len Atkins, the tax collector, at Checotah Saturday night. It was the outgrowth of a horse race.

144

And this report involving the gang that had held up the Wewoka Trading Post:

> Elmer Lucas, member of the Cook gang, was convicted of train robbery Saturday in the U.S. Court. He held the horses while Cook, Crawford Goldsby, alias Cherokee Bill, Henry Munson, alias Jack Starr, Melbourne Baldwin, alias Skeeter, and Curtis Daysen robbed the Frisco train at Red Fork July 18, 1894.
>
> Cook had been informed there was a big lot of money on the train but they failed to get it. The express messenger saved a packet containing $4,000 by placing it in a book which he carried in his hand.
>
> Lucas was known as "Chicken" and got only ninety cents as his share. Cook, Goldsby and Baldwin are the only three now at large. This was Cook's first train robbery.

On her trip back home to Arbeka, Alice may have given a few thoughts to the tick of the clock. Time seemed to be whizzing by. She had just turned forty-two. Her tenth child, John Frippo Davis, had one month ago celebrated his first birthday. And now her first-born son, George Lytle Davis, eighteen years old, had gotten married last December. Good heavens! She might be a grandmother before Christmas! [20]

9

Magic in a Child's Heart

S WALLOW A RAW chicken heart and you can marry anyone
you want."

Myrtle Davis, twelve years old, huddled expectantly with sisters
Maye, ten, and Maude, eight, watching for any reaction from the sulky
pinched face and guileless stare of their little sister, six-year-old Bess.

"Run around the house seven times and your wish will come
true!" Maye abruptly threw in. [1]

This was one of those glorious days of childhood innocence, a
time to believe in loveliness, to believe in belief, to be so little that
elves can reach to whisper in your ears, as the poets say, that pump-
kins turn into coaches and mice into horses, that a fairy godmother
may appear at any moment.

Maye and Maude were still flushed and breathless from their
latest adventure—trying to set the blacksmith's mustache on fire. He
was wicked—he cussed! He should be punished. Mother wouldn't
let them go near him. But they sneaked up to the window by his
forge with matches. They looked at each other and nodded. They
struck their matches, leaned in and poked them toward the long ends
of his red mustache.

The blacksmith flung down his hammer and swatted away the tiny
flames. He whirled on the window with furious eyes. The sisters fled.

These four girls, sometimes deigning to let tag along baby sister and brother—Irene, three, and John Frippo, two—gloriously romped in their own wonderland. They could wade the North Canadian River below the gurgling falls. They swam in it five months a year. Stealthily, they explored Robber's Cave, eyes alert for rattlesnakes. Jackrabbits darted out of the knee-high grass every time they ventured into the prairie that stretched to the west as far as they could see.

This was their most magic time—the middle of the 1890s. Their mother, Alice, and their father, George Rollin, had developed magnificently the Bar X Bar Ranch and the Arbeka Trading Post. Seven thousand cattle grazed on the open range under the guardianship of twenty cowboys. Across the store's counters merchandise and money or script exchanged themselves at a rewarding pace. Next door stood a white storybook house with green trim, a picket fence, a welcoming latch for visitors, barns, smokehouse, tenant homes and other outbuildings, servants, and the aura of ultimate happiness.

Eldest sister Kitt already was gone from home. At age seventeen on April 24, 1894 she had married Charles Barricklow, twenty-three, a Kansan. The two oldest Davis boys, both Bar X Bar cowboys, were still on the home place. Jesse Edwin, a tall lanky sixteen, was developing into a champion rodeo rider and roper, and courting a neighbor girl, Ella Knight, fifteen. George Lytle at age seventeen had married on December 18, 1893 a Czechoslovakian farmer's daughter from nearby Prague, Julia Banash, eighteen. Their baby girl, Pearl Aliene Davis, was born at Arbeka July 29, 1894. They lived in one of the ranch tenant houses.

Arbeka, on the extreme northern edge of the Seminole Nation, was isolated and in rough country. In her adult memoirs, Maye gave a child's impression of the landscape, recalling a daylong wagon trip:

> We made roads, forded streams by just driving into them and out of them. I had a feeling of being lost in the woods, but strangely thrilling instead of being in any way alarming.
>
> The country in a thirty or so-mile radius of Arbeka was quite broken and sharply so. For two or three miles a prairie that seemed

endless even behind fast trotting horses. Then abrupt change to heavy wooded areas. And steep hills with great rocks sticking up and out in grotesque shapes, or great flat slabs that seemed smoothly cemented to the earth.

We drove over and around everything. [2]

Though remote, Arbeka was not cut off from the outside world; it was a stop on the stage route from Okmulgee to Shawnee. When the six-horse coach pulled up out would step travelers of all ilk and stripe, especially drummers from the wholesale houses.

Alice and Roll welcomed the traveling salesmen, gladly bought their wares, always fed and entertained them, and often kept them as house guests a day or two. This provided a chance to hear news from the East and the latest gossip from elsewhere on the frontier.

Mutual admiration developed between the children and the drummers. After his departure, one sent the Sunday edition of *The Washington Post* which became known as "the David L. Gitt Funny Paper."

Maye stood in awe of the "nattily dressed" Mr. Webber, perhaps "the most frequent drummer," and who called all the children by name. He was a squattist, blond man with a mustache, and full of jokes. [3] He "ate with enjoyment, and with compliments on the good butter, cream, fried chicken, and always freshly-baked light bread."

He brought along a hammock, his "sample." Maye had never seen a hammock except in catalogs. What happened next is related in her memoirs:

> I didn't swoon but he must have seen the worshipful long-ing in my eyes. Anyway he gave me the hammock. He put it up between two cherry trees. It was such a preponderous event there wasn't any envy in the hearts of my brothers and sisters. Just holy deference, a respectful awe for me who had come by such glory.
>
> But there was stark tragedy lurking. After my first few swings I couldn't swing! It made me very ill. It seemed a sacrilege. I couldn't expose myself. My escape was through generosity. I got out and with great and solemn demeanor—with my poor stomach working up to my throat—I said to one by one, "You try it."

Later, her secret safe, Maye would lie in the stationary hammock and make it her dream world. "Any bit of romantic fancy that crossed the lips of anybody went into my hammock dreams. The true Hammock Princess—with a great unknown world at her feet—all because a drummer selling his wares saw into the heart of a little girl." [4]

Fun and games, pranks and adventure dominated the days of these happy youngsters. Holidays, and even routine events, were made festive. On April Fool's Day the cowboys were their targets—salt in the sugar bowl, cream-colored lye soap in the butter dish, pins in chairs, water in their hats left on the porch while dining inside.

"I can't recall mother reproving us for any April Fool trick," recalled Maye. "It must have been because she was safe from our misdeeds. It never would have occurred to us to 'April-Fool' mother. She withdrew behind her closed door, but she knew everything that happened."

They tried to outdo each other, even in eating pecans and peppermint candy, filched from Daddy's store. As Maye tells it: "We would crack pecans, pick out the nuts and fill one cheek, and then in the other stuff candy. As much as our mouths could hold. Then look at each other. One was delegated to say 'ready.' The one who finished eating first won. No prize. Just acknowledged the best."

One tenant woman dipped snuff. This fascinated the girls. They filled little empty cans with cinnamon from the store, and then made tiny dipsticks from dogwood twigs. "How we would dip and spit... all day long!" [5]

Alice demanded orderliness and discipline. She never had to punish her children; a stern look was sufficient. The cowboys were not permitted to swear, play cards, drink, gamble or dance. (This somewhat confused her daughters to whom Alice had confided that as a girl she went to band concerts and dances at Fort Gibson, with a red feather stuck in her hair.) Also Alice forbade the cowboys riding with their feet in the stirrups; their horse might bolt and drag them with a boot caught in the stirrup. Once out of her sight, the riders ignored the order.

Arising at daybreak, Alice made up her "great beautiful feather bed." The sleeping pillows were stored in a closet; the square daytime pillows had embroidery ruffles and tucks. Alice ran a broom handle across the heavy white Marseilles spread to take out the tiniest wrinkle. No one could touch the bed; babies were rigidly taught that fact as they took their first steps.

She then read the Bible. In the kitchen she saw that a large pot of chicken and rice was started on the stove to feed anyone who showed up—and many did. [6] From all over, Seminoles, Creeks and other Indians trooped in seeking her sage counsel on all manner of personal and business problems. She understood their worries, usually had good answers, and could communicate in their tongue. Her counsel was free, and was admired and respected. Whites came, too.

"Mama was not demonstrative," Myrtle wrote. "She kissed us when we went away to boarding school in the fall and she kissed us when we came home in the spring. That was all. But each of us knew her tenderness. Always when the littlest one fell down and lost his mitten and would come in crying from the cold, Mama would say, 'Come here and give me your little hand.' And she would take the little cold hand in hers and hold it close to her body and the world would be warm and right."

In a larger sense, Myrtle felt, "our mother dedicated herself to the Seminoles with the same devotion she lavished upon her children. She was the natural leader of her people. . ."

Their father was almost six feet tall, a little more than two hundred pounds, reddish hair and mustache, and a fair florid complexion —and "beautiful hands," as Maye remembers. "The hands of an aristocrat. Blue laughing eyes, and the happiest manner of mingling with people." The girls found him the "fun-loving partner" in their vigorous happy lives, "always making an old game seem new." To the family he was "Roll." The Indians called him *Davie-thloco*—"Big-Davis." He could mingle as "hail fellow well met" with the Indians, making "store talk" on any article and the price. The Indians knew precisely what they came to buy and paid the price without question. He told humorous stories and evoked laughter from the red men, which is extraordinary. When one Indian bought a new hat, Big Davis slapped it atop the customer's old one with a grand flourish. Ever after, all hat-buyers left the store wanting new stacked on old.

"He had the art of story-telling," says Maye, "that gave him the near-talent of showmanship. He told endless stories on each of us children, giving rich humor to them. He did chew tobacco, and the bright shining spittoons set about for his use—his careful use, scrubbed each day—I can still see."

Maye remembers: "I was still very young when he established a second store at Arlington in Oklahoma Territory, twelve or thirteen miles from Arbeka. He spent weekdays there and came home for Saturday and Sunday. He always brought gifts for everyone, and made quite a ceremony of presenting them, filling us to overflowing with the joy of a party."

The Arbeka store seemed to the children just an extension of their home. Maye recalls:

> We played there much of the time. But we were as observant of restrictions in the store as we were of not disturbing the beds, running through the house, slamming the doors. . .
>
> At the counter nearest the store entrance was a square glass case that had pins, large safety pins for the Indians' shawls, needles and the ribbons. How beautiful those colored ribbons looked through the glass. Combs and large shell hairpins and breast pins that were ornate jewels. The showcases of embroidery, lace handkerchiefs, and other small wares.

Boxes of felt hats—tan, gray or black—were stacked in the Arbeka store. Indians always added a braided hatband with a red tassel. Tubs, dishpans and pots were piled on a counter, with bars of soap underneath. Other showcases held candy, soda crackers and ginger snaps. The children slapped a soft, chewy ginger snap between two soda crackers for a "delicious sandwich." Arbuckle and Lion coffee beans came in one-pound packages and if clerks were busy the youngsters were permitted the turn the big grinder. They were in awe of the warehouse connected to the back of the store. Maye recalls:

> It was the most curious place in the world! In the winter the first thing to greet the eye was the ceiling covered with hanging skins, principally skunk and possum hides. And were they smelly! Stacked sacks of flour, slabs of meat, all neat. Barrels and barrels

151

of pecans. Coal oil in galvanized barrels. If the boys placed a can of coal oil near a sack of flour when they brought provisions into the house, Mama would really bless them out.

There were cots for the cowboys. Poor fellows during the "hide" season! In the summer they slept on the store's long porch. They sang into the night and played the French harp and Jew's harp. In the early morning they had wrestling matches.

In the frontier's alluvial soil, cotton—both long and short staple—flourished enormously, and Alice was one of the first to see to it that her farm hands put in a crop. It was planted in long rows next to their excellent orchard.

In late August when the boles popped open, the children begged to join the farm hands that were assigned to the job of picking the cotton. Alice knew how desperately the youngsters yearned to join in "the terrible excitement" of this new adventure. [7] Cotton-pickers must trudge down the rows of low-hanging plants, dragging the appropriate receptacle, a long canvas sack by a shoulder strap.

Their mother had individual sacks sewn up, proportioned to the children's sizes—a yard wide and four feet long for Myrtle, Maude and Maye, down to "baby" sacks for Bess, Irene and John Frippo.

After an early breakfast, the children started. The sky was blue and clear, the sun bright, and soon blazing. The three little ones lost interest and simply quit. Not Maude and Maye—they were dueling. They had been dedicated adversaries since about age four or five. Maye was older, but Maude was now bigger.

They were trying to outdo each other. They struggled down their rows, snatching boles and popping them into their sacks. Maude picked hard, and was ahead until noon. They ate lunch. On the afternoon start Maude led by thirty minutes.

Maye recalls:

> At two o'clock I caught up with her—under an apple tree in the orchard, sound asleep. I passed and passed her until my sack was full. It must have been four in the afternoon. So hot, so hot! I touched Maude; she was so hot, so hot! I tried to rouse her. I couldn't. Then in alarm I ran to Mama. She sent a ranch hand to carry Maude to the house.

She was delirious with fever. A cowboy was dispatched to Wewoka to bring the doctor. Not until daylight did the doctor arrive; it was a twenty-five mile ride.

That day I had a chill with a great fever following. Maude recovered fairly quickly. But my chill and fever came—hot and cold—every other day. For two months I missed school.

It was near disgraceful. Mama's children did not have chills and fever. Only unhealthy Arkansas travelers and drifters. I was never reduced to a state of embarrassment. Maude and I were only having a distinguishing experience, a strange glorifying cotton malady.

The Arbeka children called their outdoor privy *chokogee*—Little House. It was a long trek, a beaten path to the back of the orchard. It was a three-holer—one large, next a little smaller and the third lower and much smaller for the littlest ones. In winter Alice dressed them as warmly as if going to Muskogee or Wewoka. There were usually four or five in the trouping cavalcade. A big child lent a hand to the smaller. [8]

The children played with dolls—beautiful with white kid bodies and bisque heads and hands. And read Grimm's Fairy Tales and Hans Christian Andersen. On walks they were "madcaps," dashing about to gather berries, collect beautiful stones, pick wild flowers, chase butterflies... But their special spot was Robber's Cave. As Maye remembered it:

> It was beautiful in the side of a high hill. To reach the entrance we half-slid half-walked down the steep hillside. The entrance was halfway down; a great stone extended about two yards over the top of it. The entrance was wide, flat hard dirt over stone.
>
> The entrance was about forty feet high but sloped back about the same distance to an opening just wide enough to crawl through. Then the great round "room" had slick hard rock walls.
>
> In the center there was a ray of light, straight through to the sky. We wrote with "keel," a hard red mineral of some kind, everything we could think of. With hard rock we made our initials deep in the walls. I'm sure they are still there.
>
> There was a tiny stream of ice-cold water that ran in the bottom of the cave on to a spring that overflowed. An iron pipe ran

from that spring outside to a big trough where cattle and horses drank all day long.

Everyone watched for rattlesnakes. Even the Indian dogs; they would rouse when one slithered across the store porch, pounce, get a bite-hold and shake it to death in their teeth. Bess ran in to tell her mother two rattlesnakes were crawling by the smokehouse door. One escaped but Alice pinned the other with a pitchfork. Cowboys and Indians were alert, quicker killers.

For the grownups, life at Arbeka and the Bar X Bar emulated the action and color of the Old West. The cowboys mostly were young and eager and daring. They came and went. Most were taciturn and modest.

"Are you a good rider?" "Wal, jest passable." [9] If a braggart showed up, he was promptly given an ornery stallion called "Rocket" which he wouldn't know bucked fiercely. The new man would try to get seated and about a minute and a half later would be pitched halfway across the corral, amid hurrahs. All the children rode horses. Maye had a hairy little Shetland-Indian pony named "Pet." When she fell off, the pony would stand indifferently until she remounted and then resume a lazy trot. Myrtle trained her horse to run around her in a circle so she could leap on him bareback. He was one of the white fast-trotting buggy team named "Thunder" and "Lightning." Once Maye rode "Thunder" four or five miles accompanying cowboys rounding up strayed hogs. "The horses climbed straight up and down ravine banks," Maye recalls. "Wouldn't have bothered Myrtle or Maude, but it put everlasting fear in me."

Kitt's horse was a beauty—a black mare named "Victoria" with a mane that almost touched the ground and a tail that did. The eldest sister mounted a lovely sidesaddle in an extremely long black riding skirt, with black dress hat tied with a long black veil. "She paced off in style," Maye says, "a far cry from our scrambling little horses." The summer Kitt was almost seventeen she returned from school a little flirtatious and singing light opera songs she had learned in drama class. The clerks and cowboys were struck numb and dumb in admiration.

Secretly the ranch hands would play cards, gambling. When Alice found their decks, she burned them. One lone, busy woman could not change the natural-born mores of frontier men. There were many hints of secret lives of which she was ignorant, or at least never acknowledged. Of whiskey, of gunplay, of dastardly deeds, without overt confirmation of any of the gossip.

Even her two eldest sons—one-quarter Seminoles—were the subjects of demeaning talk in this wild country. Some said both George Lytle and Jesse Edwin had "notches" on the pistols they carried. [10] (There are no records of that.) George, it was said, fathered an Indian baby before he married Julia. (Not shown in any census or tribal roll.)

In the mid and later 1890s, Arbeka was in the heart of outlaw country. One who showed up claiming to be a cowpuncher and got a ride on the bucking bronc "Rocket" was believed to be Cherokee Bill. When thrown, he left meekly, whoever he was.

Not the case with quixotic desperado Al Jennings. Born in Virginia in 1863, Alphonso Jennings came west and was a lawyer in Woodward, Oklahoma Territory until a rival lawyer, Temple Houston, killed his brother Ed Jennings in a shootout, and went free. [11] That apparently sent Al Jennings a little off his rocker. He moved to Creek County and became a cowboy. In time he joined an outlaw gang that spent the summer and fall of 1897 robbing trains, general stores, and a post office, with little monetary success.

The Al Jennings gang galloped into Arbeka in the summer of 1897. As Maye recalls:

> They rode up to the house. My brother George saw them through the window. He ran to the barn and rode out a back gate, to spread the news, I suppose. He was seventeen.
>
> Al Jennings came in and asked for George. My mother said he was not at home. Anyway, not finding him, they ate and stayed all night. Al Jennings was the most gallant, courteous man I remember from the early times. His intelligent conversation with my mother was something even as a little girl I could appreciate, if not fully understand.
>
> The discussion was on the baptism of babies. I remember him saying, "They come out of the water looking like drowned

rats, and not understanding any more." Those words haunted me for years.

(Wounded in the fall of 1897 and captured, Al Jennings was given life in prison. Pardoned in 1907, he starred in a movie of his life, ran for Governor of Oklahoma in 1914, and lost[12])

When he campaigned for Governor, Mama went to Wewoka for one of his rallies just to meet him again. When introduced to her, he said with great reverence, "You are Mrs. Arbeka Davis—Many years, many changes since I last saw you."

Even the genuinely and widely admired "Rollicking Roll" or "Old Man Davis" was hit by opprobrious scuttlebutt. He at times accompanied other ranchers to Kansas City aboard the cattle train taking their stock to market. On the train back, with his pockets loaded with thousands from the sale, he drank and gambled. So the tales went. He was reputed to occasionally lose heavily. (Nothing found in family diaries or memoirs, or Oklahoma history confirms these yarns. However, subsequent developments in George Rollin Davis's life caused some family members to make use of those very rumors to shield them from an unexpected scandal.[13])

An Indian woman named Mahale and her daughters Winey and Liddy occasionally lived in a log cabin at Arbeka and helped with housework. Mahale was small and thin, with a protruding stomach. She would become ill, lie facedown and call Winey, a tiny girl, to walk on her back.

The Davis girls were fascinated. "Come watch," Maude would cry. "This time her back's got to crack. Any minute!" [14] It didn't. Liddy disappointed Alice, who wore an heirloom, high square-cut amethyst ring with a gold flower in the center. When Alice kneaded light bread, she hung the ring on a nail in the kitchen. It disappeared. In the end only Liddy could have taken it. Alice said nothing to the girl. "Indians usually are not known to steal," she told her girls, sadly. [15]

With a couple dozen cowpunchers, as well as the family, to feed three times a day, one of the most essential Arbeka jobs was cook. They came and went, too.

The newest was Victoria Banash, sister of George Lytle's wife Julia. [16] Though Czech, Victoria looked Swedish, having long blonde hair, a taut, energetic slender body, tiny waist, merry eyes

156

that glistened, and unblemished peaches and cream complexion. She was engaging listener and a head-bobbing conversationalist. The cowboys flocked around, but largely bashful, blushing and mute. Victoria looked everybody in the eye and didn't blush.

She was an excellent cook. She quickly mastered the technique of preparing the children's favorite—milk toast, that is *special Arbeka milk toast.* [17] After New Year's 1895 Alice had to slow down a little. She was large and ungainly with what would be her eleventh child, due within a couple of months.

In her rocking chair, she frequently pored over her books for poems to read to her children.[18] Most of them sat transfixed when she recited:

> A child her wayward pencil drew
> On margins of her book:
> Garlands of flowers, dancing elves,
> Bird, butterfly and brook.
> Lessons undone, and play forgot,
> Seeking with hand and heart
> The teacher whom she learned to love
> Before she knew 'twas Art.

Quietly to herself she read: "Land of Heart's Desire/Where beauty has no ebb, decay no flood/ But joy is wisdom, Time an endless song." For some reason she could not explain, an aura of pessimism had crept up on her. Never had she experienced a difficult pregnancy; but now she began inwardly fretting that something might be wrong with her unborn baby. [19]

To cheer herself up, she hugged some children, patted some on the head, and opened her poetry book and read a new verse:

> Get up; for when all things are merry and glad,
> Good children should never be lazy and sad;
> For God gives us daylight, dear sister, that we
> May rejoice like the lark and may work like the bee.

On February 28, 1895, all the children were rounded up, loaded into buggies and taken on an excursion. It was always so when the midwife came. In the summertime it would always be a picnic.

157

When they returned, their mother was holding a little baby brother in her arms. "This is Andrew Jackson Davis," she announced. "Named for his uncle Jackson Brown." [20]

Roll, beaming, freely handed out cigars to everyone who came into the trading post. Within a couple of weeks he was plucking little Andy Jack out of his flowery crib, tossing him up in the air and catching him, while Alice gasped.

The household settled down to its old routine. But not quite.

One morning Alice suddenly began to wonder if she was missing something. Something significant. She thought she detected rather miniscule shifts in the atmosphere in her home. She scrutinized her relationship with the children; it was suitable and unchanged as far as she knew. And she pondered the demeanor of the children toward each other. Nothing there seemed amiss.

Still her disquiet continued; in fact, grew and began to fester somewhat. The milieu of her Arbeka home was undergoing a steady transformation. One day she felt certain of that; the next she chided herself for being a suspicious busybody.[21]

Since April or May, Victoria Banash had started neglecting her kitchen work. She lost her glittering personality. She turned secretive, at times red-eyed as if she had been crying. Alice thought she might be ill, and offered to call the doctor. Victoria refused, snappishly.

When she first became cook, the girl had bounced around as gay as a lark. She chatted with Roll about the weather, business, livestock; when she passed the biscuits she put extras on his plate. They laughed together. Alice saw Victoria, when passing the meat tray, leaning so far over the table that her pretty cheek touched the tip of his mustache.

That was one definite change. Victoria now seemed to deliberately avoid Roll. She didn't favor him anymore at the table; she didn't speak to him, and very little to anyone else.

Alice happened on Victoria and her husband in the kitchen, in conspiratorial-looking conversation. The girl's face was twisted in concern or anger. Alice's sudden entry flustered them. They abruptly quit talking. Victoria hurried outside. [22]

In the middle of the night, Alice awoke suddenly with a horrible thought. No, it couldn't be true! Roll was a steady man, forty-six years

158

old, settled, dependable, honorable. But Victoria was nineteen, beautiful, vibrant, and— Actually not as comely as before. Her slender figure had begun to vanish; she had started wearing a loose apron, but she could not long hide her swelling belly. She had been sick many mornings. Victoria Banash was pregnant!

Perhaps, oh perhaps, she had been seduced by one of the cowboys. Alice grabbed helplessly for some alternative to what she knew was going to turn out to be the sorry truth. [23]

Alice confronted them privately but directly. There was no denial. Victoria was with child—by George Rollin Davis. She had been pregnant since some time in March or April, and expected to deliver in December.

Alice, dazed, crushed, surprised, felt like doom had struck. But she steeled herself, dug deep into her soul for resolve and courage. In quiet control, she told Roll they no longer were husband and wife. She turned, and retreated to her bedroom. In a moment through the closed door came wrenching sobs, and finally shrieks. [24]

Roll hitched up a buggy, filled a suitcase and collected his shaving gear, took Victoria by the arm, and they drove away.

Alice, of course, immediately consulted her brother John. They decided to not announce, nor recognize, the end of the marriage. To hide the scandal, they would spread false word that would confirm the old rumors that Roll drank and gambled on the cattle train. Their story would be that in a poker game Roll had not only been cleaned out but also killed and his body dumped where no one could find it. [25]

(In family papers, one daughter scribbled: "Papa played the man and did the right thing and married Victoria." True. But apparently Alice was upset enough to deliberately delay the formality of getting a quiet divorce. In December 1895, Victoria gave birth to a boy, Edward Earl Davis. But Alice's delay in going to court kept the lovers in limbo, and they were unable to get legally married until December 27, 1897 at Tecumseh, Indian Territory, when their son was two years old.) [26]

10

Whiskey and Human Torches

THE STAGECOACH carrying Governor Brown and a few other passengers clattered off the river ferry, whizzed north about a mile and jolted to a halt in Keokuk Falls. He had just crossed over the Seminole Nation border into the most infamous "whiskey town" in the new lawless Oklahoma Territory.

The driver hopped down and threw open the door. "It's a quick stop," he announced. "You've got only twenty minutes," he added, impishly, "to see a man killed!" [1]

Governor Brown grimaced. He was not seeking booze; he had come to find out what kind of lumber he could buy from the new Keokuk Falls sawmill. He stepped out onto the main street boardwalk in front of the Black Dog Saloon.

The driver was not entirely jesting. Gunplay went along with liquor. Keokuk Falls was known for both. This raw new town had thirteen saloons, three distilleries, ten doctors, three hotels and a coffin factory, but no sheriff of any kind. Owners of the Black Dog regularly blasted across the street at the rival Red Front Saloon. And vice versa. Fights over whiskey, gambling and whores killed about fifty people a year. [2]

Governor Brown resented this whiskey town, just north of the North Canadian River, his nation's boundary, and about a mile west of the Creek Nation line. The saloons were deliberately situated to prey on Indians' known weakness for firewater.

About 100 such bawdy hamlets had sprouted wherever new Oklahoma Territory touched a "dry" Indian border. The slapped-together dives were the single most disgraceful result of the April 22, 1889 land rush, when the Government threw open for white settlement the "unassigned lands" taken from the Seminoles and Creeks as their Civil War punishment.

Congress foolishly had neglected to provide any sort of laws or government for newborn Oklahoma Territory. Land speculators, outlaws, shysters took advantage of the gaffe. Decent settlers established temporary vigilante authority that kept things somewhat in check until Congress fixed the problem. There were 367 wild and wooly days and nights before a legal system was established to bring order to Oklahoma Territory.

Governor Brown had strung a five-strand barbed wire fence the entire length of the Seminoles' western boundary, with gates every five miles. This principally was to keep Seminole cattle and horses grazing the open range from straying. Just beyond one gate sprang up what was doubtless Oklahoma Territory's most dangerous and notorious whiskey town. It was Violet Springs, located in Pottawatomie County. Eight men were killed there in a single day. Andy Morrison, the town's first saloonkeeper, was shot while asleep. [3]

At the extreme south end of Governor Brown's fence came together the borders of the Chickasaw Nation and the Seminole Nation. At that corner, in briar-entangled bottomland, broken by river bluffs and blackjack barrens, a saloon was set up in a secluded rawhide house. The town, called Corners, became a magnet for gamblers, robbers, rough and tumble cowboys, Indians and drovers.

Corners developed a reputation for lawlessness and violence unsurpassed in Oklahoma Territory. Dr. Jesse Mooney, who lived ten miles away, was called to treat "knifings, shootings, lacerations, gouged eyes, fingers bitten off. . ." [4] Even the peaceful farm towns of Prague and Stroud opened saloons that gravely troubled the Seminole Nation. (Statehood in 1907 would make Oklahoma "dry" and the worst of the whiskey towns would become "ghost towns.")

After placing a lumber order at the Keokuk Falls sawmill, Governor Brown waited in the hotel lobby to depart on the afternoon stage. The desk clerk was chatty. "Say, you should have been here last week. Feller who's an auctioneer came to town. Had an ostrich with a saddle. He'd wager fifty bucks he could outrun any horse at one hundred yards. Never lost one dang bet!" [5]

The clerk seemed happy in the whiskey town. Governor Brown was not. He fidgeted in his chair. He could barely wait to leave Keokuk Falls. [6]

BEGINNING WITH THE YEAR 1896, Senator Dawes slowed down. Now eighty years old, the ex-senator started skipping some of the Commission's negotiating trips to Indian Territory, putting in charge an acting chairman. Dawes remained either in Washington or at his home in Pittsfield, Massachusetts. His health obviously was failing. But, hardheaded, he wasn't giving up.

Governor Brown and other Five Tribes chiefs parried for better understanding with their Great Father. Proposals and counter offers flew back and forth. Nothing changed. The standoff held. Surprisingly, Governor Brown found some of his convictions doing somersaults. He had been dead-set against the iron horse. But it was now clear railroads were inevitable. He had to switch, even though trains would bring white settlers. Even Wewoka was getting a railroad—the Choctaw, Oklahoma & Gulf Railway Company. It would connect Atoka with Oklahoma City and El Reno. Already tracks had been laid from the west and met at Wewoka in 1895 with rails coming up from Calvin and McAlester. (In 1902 this would become part of the Rock Island system.)

At Shawnee a group of businessmen decided to organize a new railway company called the St. Louis, Oklahoma & Southern. Governor Brown was invited to be a director; he accepted and was elected vice-president. No route had been settled on. A line down on the Red River near Denison, Texas was being considered. The president of the fledgling railroad, C. N. Points, agreed for five dollars a

162

day to take his team and wagon, a hand level and a wind gauge, and explore the area being considered. That trip was unsuccessful. Not until December 1, 1896 did the St. Louis, Oklahoma & Southern hit on a route—Claremore, I. T. to Wewoka, and on south. By horseback, the line's engineer rode from Wewoka to Whitesboro, Texas, seeking the most feasible route.

Governor Brown kept advocating the scheme. Not much happened until St. Louis capitalists put in money, and the line was completed in March 1901 from Sapulpa direct to Denison, bypassing Shawnee and Wewoka. (Both towns by then already had a different rail line.) In June 1901 the St. Louis, Oklahoma & Southern track, equipment, franchise and other property passed to the Frisco. That railroad, incidentally, turned out to be no friend of John Franklin Brown.

Needing white men with management skills, Governor Brown hired in Wewoka Arthur M. Seran, a twenty-five-year-old Kansan, after learning he had fenced a sixty mile pasture, cut walnut gunstocks, and driven his sweetheart fifty miles in a four-mule wagon to find a preacher to marry them. [7] At an Ardmore business school Governor Brown asked for the brightest student and thus got young James Fleet for the Sasakwa store. Fleet later married the Governor's daughter Alice, and eventually became wealthy as banker and oilman.

An experienced man was needed to operate the cotton gin at the Wewoka Trading Company. Courtland Long was dispatched to Eufaula to recruit A. P. Shaw, thirty-five, who had learned gin operation in Missouri. Long hired him for a month's trial. By buggy, Shaw came to Wewoka.[8]

"Long warned me," Shaw would recall, "that the Browns were Indians. Working for them would be different than working for white men. He told me, 'Do what I tell you.'"[9]

Shaw showed up for work Monday. "Long told me 'Get on the porch and start whittling.' I didn't understand. He repeated, 'Do as I said.'" Shaw sat down and opened his pocketknife.

"A fine looking Indian came riding up on a beautiful horse. He went into the store. I knew that was Jack Brown. But I had to sit on a wooden box and whittle for six days before they would let me have the keys to the gin."

Shaw cleaned up the gin machinery, and then was sent to Sa-sakwa to repair the gin there. "In a few days the Browns told me to bring my family to Wewoka. I had passed my test. We were only the fourth white family in Wewoka. I ginned something like 20,000 bales for the Wewoka Trading Company. But I never did find out what whittling for a week had to do with it!"[10]

Jackson Brown came up with a wrinkle that facilitated trading at the Brown stores. Wewoka Trading Company script was issued in five-dollar, one-dollar and fifty-cent denominations. The Indians called it *Chokasatke*—White Paper. The script essentially was "loaned" to the Indians and redeemed when the Indians received Government annuity payments.

On the Dawes Commission front, talk continued. No progress was apparent. The Congressional group was reorganized to retain Dawes and McKennon, and add Frank C. Armstrong of Washington, D.C., Thomas B. Cabaniss of Georgia, and Alexander B. Montgomery of Kentucky. Everybody was chafing with impatience. Indians grew more bitter. The Choctaws voted a $10,000 fine or summary execution for anyone trying to overthrow the tribe in favor of the Government, but quickly cancelled that edict.[11] Along with the Chickasaws, the Choctaws kept struggling to resolve the allotment dispute. Governor Brown sat on his hands. The Choctaws began to see dollar signs. They wanted $500 each in exchange for giving up tribal rights; they offered to send three delegates to Washington if paid $3,500 each, plus $1,500 expenses for their chief.[12]

The Cherokees, weary of the long wrangle and fearing a dire outcome, considered just leaving Indian Territory. The chief's brother proposed selling all their lands, except mineral tracts and town lots, for five dollars an acre and using the money to buy the nation a new homeland in Mexico or South America.[13]

At length the "victims" on the Indian frontier could clearly read the handwriting on the wall in Washington. Nothing was going to erase it. The red man realized how decisively the Great Father had lost patience. Congress, it was now unmistakable, would not settle for anything less than forcing individual land allotments on the Five Tribes, extinguishing tribal governments, making the Indians accept citizenship and become subject to white man's laws. The aim of

164

the political powers was to eventually combine Indian Territory and Oklahoma Territory into the state of Oklahoma.

While Brown agonized and vacillated, the united opposition of the Five Tribes was broken. First to cave in were the Choctaws and Chickasaws. On April 23, 1897 they signed a treaty, which became known as the Atoka Agreement that essentially accepted the Dawes Commission terms.[14] Governor Brown still refused to surrender. The summer came and went, torrid and drying. On an afternoon ride across his burnt Sasakwa pastureland, he came to the sad realization that this was an omen.[15] The Seminoles' cherished freedom to live in the ancient way was just as dead as his grass.

On September 16, 1897, he did a flip-flop and accepted for the Seminoles the Government's scheme in full.[16] Other tribal officials who signed with Governor Brown were Okchan Harjo, Wilburn Cully, K. N. Kinkehee, Thomas West and Thomas Factor. The treaty divided Seminole land into three classes, to be appraised at $5, $2.50, or $1.25 an acre. Each tribe member could try to select his allotment to include his own improvements, and fertile soil and location on an equal basis. The Dawes Commission would make allotments, aided by a Seminole official. Mineral lease revenue would be split between the tribe as a whole and the individual allottee.[17] The Senate confirmed the Seminole treaty in June 1898, effective immediately. The Seminoles thus were first of the Five Civilized Tribes to surrender.[18]

The Creeks and the Cherokees continued to hold out. It was an Indian Comgressman, part-Kaw Charles Curtis of Kansas, chairman of the House Indian Affairs sub-committee, who ended the stalemate. Curtis had written uncompromising legislation imposing the full scope of the allotment changes on the Five Tribes, whether they were willing or not. His Act was titled: "For the protection of the people of the Indian Territory, providing for the laying out of towns, the leasing of coal and other mineral, timber farming and grazing lands, and for other purposes." [19] The Indians were fearful of the phrase "for other purposes."

Governor Brown, despite being Curtis's close friend, could not get the Congressman to ease up in the least. Though too harsh and penalizing, the Curtis Act inexorably moved toward passage.

Not even the outbreak of the Spanish-American War, which was on the immediate horizon, would be cataclysmic enough to delay it.

165

ON THE WEWOKA SCENE more white homesteaders arrived. They found it too risky to build permanent businesses or homes. Whites could not acquire title to the land, only an "exclusive lease" from an Indian.

Governor Brown envisioned "progress" the white man would bring. He had traveled and had lived through the advance from wagon road to railroad, to the first experimental automobiles; he was well read enough to comprehend how aggressively and successfully science and industry were smashing civilization's old limits and barriers.

A forward step would be to convert the Seminole Nation's capital, Wewoka, into an organized town and actively recruit settlers. He wrote a brochure pointing out advantages, including railway connection. The railroad would gladly distribute them, inviting more passengers and freight. Brown's idea was to earmark perhaps 640 acres around the Council House, the depot, his trading post, and other commercial structures. This town site would be surveyed and divided into lots, blocks, streets and alleys. The Nation would be empowered to sell or lease portions of this property to Seminole citizens, except that title would not be granted unless a building or improvements were erected within six months. Proceeds of the lot sales would go to the Seminole Nation. When the population reached 200, elections would be held for city marshal, city attorney and police judge.

The Seminole Council adopted this plan on April 23, 1897 and appointed as commissioners the chief's brother, Andrew Jackson Brown, the tribe's treasurer; and four close associates, Thomas McGeisey, Thomas Factor, W. L. Joseph, and Dorsey Fife. The act was signed by the Council president, Nath. Cap Harjo, and secretary, Thomas McGeisey. It was approved by Governor Brown.[20]

Unfortunately, only a few Wewoka town lots were sold. Prospective buyers were turned off primarily by the restriction that required building on the land or improving the site in a big way within six months. Three years later, Governor Brown would step up with an offer to buy all the unsold land as a personal investment. His offer was $12,000—and that would set off fireworks!

ON THURSDAY, DECEMBER 30, 1897 an Indian on a bay pony with a roached mane rode up to the gate of the farm that Julius Leard, a white man, had under lease from Thomas McGeisey, the full blood Seminole Nation school superintendent and confidant of Governor Brown.[21]

It was almost sunset. Mrs. Leard, young mother of four, looked up as the Indian, a big man with a scar on his cheek, dismounted and came toward her. He was a stranger. She was home alone with her children. She was not frightened; living her whole life on the frontier had schooled her for situations demanding poise and courage.

The Indian looked pleasant, harmless. In English, he asked if she had a saddle he could borrow.

"I don't know you." Mrs. Leard, taken aback, gave him a sharp look. He lived three miles away on Salt Creek, he said. She stood firm. "I can't lend you a saddle. Mr. Leard is away from home. The answer is no."[22]

The Leard place was about three miles east of the Pottawatomie County line, which also was the western border of the Seminole Nation. Just across that boundary to the west lay the notorious whiskey towns and their ruffians. It paid to stay alert.

Earlier in the day Julius Leard had driven off in their wagon to his brother Herschel's place to help harvest corn. That was six miles away in Pottawatomie County, across the line in Oklahoma Territory. His wife expected him to return by dark, unaware he had decided to remain away overnight.

Watching his mother's encounter with the Indian was the oldest Leard child, Frank, eight, who was playing in the yard. The Indian asked for a drink of water and went into the kitchen, a building twenty feet from the main house. Something made Mrs. Leard suspicious. She turned loose the family bulldog and tried to sic it on the intruder; instead the dog chased hogs running loose in the yard. Mrs. Leard went in the house and came out with a rifle. The Indian mounted his horse and rode off.[23]

Her other children paid no heed. Sudie, six, and Nannie, five, were chasing chickens in the yard. The baby Cora was in her crib in the house.

167

Thirty minutes later Frank, helping his mother carry their supper from the kitchen into the big house, alerted his mother "the Indian boy is back."[24]

The Indian came in the east door. Mrs. Leard picked up the baby and fled out the south door. The Indian grabbed the rifle leaning in the corner and tried to shoot her. The rifle just snapped; it was not loaded. He chased her around the yard and smashed her head with the rifle. She fell unconscious atop her baby.

The Indian threw the rifle into the house, pulled Cora by one arm from beneath her dying mother and threw the baby onto the floor of the house. The Indian then demanded money futilely from Frank, who had none, and then walked away, apparently alone.

Why eight-year-old Frank, who must have been hardened to the rigors of life in Indian country, did not go for help is mystifying. At his age he could easily run to the McGeisey farm, just one mile away. Other farmhouses also were within a mile or two.

Instead he tried to drag his mother into the house. It was too much for him. He left her in the farmyard, and spent a harrowing night in the bedroom with his siblings. During the dark, pigs, attracted by the blood, ate on Mrs. Leard's body, destroying most of her head.

Next morning, Friday, December 31, the boy Frank Leard walked to the nearest town, Maud, carrying the seriously injured Cora (who would die a few months later), leading his sisters. About 10 o'clock he reached the post office and revealed his mother's murder. [25]

Julius Leard was notified. He rushed home, bringing friends. Little Frank told how an Indian stranger killed his mother. Everyone vowed to hunt down the murderer, and get revenge.

What happened next goes down as one of the greatest outrages in the Seminole Nation history, laid out in graphic and chilling detail in Dr. Daniel F. Littlefield's book, *Seminole Burning: A Story of Racial Vengeance.*

Julius Leard's friends formed a posse. They raced up and down the countryside seizing any Indian boy they saw. Many captives did not speak English and were unaware of what was going on. By dark the posse had twenty prisoners. One of these was Lincoln McGeisey, son of Thomas McGeisey. All suspects were taken to the Leard's leased farm and trooped before little Frank to see if he could identify anyone as the killer.

This process took a couple of hours. Present was Lincoln McGeisey's father; he had been summoned by Julius Leard, and remained until near midnight.

The Leard boy did not identify any of the captives. They were released.

When Thomas McGeisey left to return home, Julius Leard thanked him for coming over. "If we don't find my wife's murderer," he added, grimly, "for revenge I'll just kill two or three Indian boys! . . .I may have to kill the whole tribe!" [26]

The posse set up headquarters at the site of the murder. Frustrated and angry, they had second thoughts about the young men who had stood in their lineup. Maybe little Frank was nervous, and needed to take another look at the Indians. The posse mounted horses and went out to round up for the second time some boys, including Lincoln McGeisey. They vowed to get a confession! Back at the farmhouse, they began torturing prisoners. Nobody confessed to the murder.

But after being strung up by a rope until unconscious, Lincoln McGeisey confessed to stealing some items from another farm. Julius Leard and other possemen took him on horseback to his father's farm to retrieve stolen goods hidden in the smokehouse unknown to his father. Julius Leard kept Lincoln captive, and took him away. Alarmed by the vigilantes' second seizure of his son, Thomas McGeisey rushed into Wewoka on Sunday, January 2, 1898, and told United States Commissioner W. S. Fears he wanted his son arrested on the theft charge and put in jail for protection from the mob. Fears signed a warrant and handed it to Deputy United States Marshal Nelson Jones.

Jones, a burnt-out lawman in his fifties, who had been at times accused of both theft and murder, and was a known whiskey-head, was the pivotal person who could have halted the mob's rage. He made two or three trips to the Leard place, but was too cowardly to arrest the McGeisey boy, and loaned his handcuffs and leg irons to the posse to use on their captives. Jones witnessed possemen beating and threatening to shoot several of their Indian captives. He came and went over a period of five or six days, drank whiskey with the posse, and indicated he would look the other way if they took revenge.

However, taking a prisoner by wagon to jail in Wewoka, Marshal Jones went by way of Sasakwa, Dr. Littlefield writes, "to ask Chief John F. Brown's advice in the Leard case," adding:

> According to Jones, Brown told him to use "his best judg-ment in protecting innocent people." Whether Jones made clear to the chief exactly what was taking place at Leard's is uncertain, for Brown seemed unconcerned. Any lack of concern may have sprung from two sources. First, Brown was preparing to go to Washington to make the final Seminole allotment agreement with the Dawes Commission, and he may have been distracted from the domestic scene. Second, the murder fell clearly under federal jurisdiction, and Jones was the responsible law enforcement of-ficial in the district. However, any trust he placed in Jones was misplaced. [27]

Finally on Monday, January 3, 1898, Jones reached Wewoka, and told Commissioner Fears about the Leard developments. Thomas Mc-Geisey came in that afternoon and pleaded with Fears to get his son Lincoln out of Leard's custody, by arresting him on the burglary charge. The commissioner gave warrants to Jones, who said he would go make the arrest. Feeling assured, McGeisey went ahead with his plan to leave on Wednesday, January 5, for Washington with Governor Brown and the other Seminole delegates, and serve as the group's secretary.[28]

When Jones arrived at the Leard place late Monday night a mob of about forty milled around a log fire in the yard, and held twenty suspects. Jones was too frightened to reveal he had warrants to ar-rest Lincoln and another posse captive, George Harjo, also charged in the burglary. Instead he helped shackle some captives, and spent the night. [29]

Next morning, Jones had the two brought outside to the log fire and read the warrants to them. Lincoln McGeisey said his father knew nothing of his burglary. Frank again couldn't identify either as the killer, Julius Leard told Jones he believed them innocent. Jones, however, left Lincoln and the Harjo boy chained up at the farm and left saying he would return Wednesday with his wagon and take them to Wewoka. [30]

On his return, however, the mob was "still riled up." Word had gone out that the mob leaders had decided to *burn* someone to revenge Mary Leard's murder. [31] Jones left with Julius Leard to ride around all day checking Lincoln McGeisey's alibi. When Jones attempted at the end of the day to leave with the McGeisey and Harjo boys, fifteen guns were drawn on him. Finally he persuaded the mob to "give" him one prisoner, Harjo, and left.

The mob remained at Leard's place and finally hit on the plan of seizing a young Indian at Wewoka named Palmer Sampson, who was just out of prison after serving a year for horse stealing. Julius Leard and several others smashed in his cabin door and took him. Sampson's mother ran futilely to Commissioner Fears for help. He did nothing. The Leards fabricated a "confession" and announced it to the mob; Julius Leard stated that Sampson admitted the murder and said Lincoln McGeisey helped him, and that both raped Mrs. Leard.

In another wrong-headed move, Marshal Jones sent his handyman-nephew Jim Jones to get Lincoln McGeisey and Sampson. Jim Jones was rebuffed by 125 armed men. Before escaping, he suggested if "they were going to do anything" to their captives they should go across into Oklahoma Territory, leaving the impression the message came from Nelson Jones.[32]

The mob, milling around their bonfire, waited until two o'clock Friday morning, January 7, to take action. Lincoln McGeisey and Palmer Sampson, locked by the neck on the ends of a long chain, were loaded into a surrey and taken to an Indian "tabernacle" half a mile south of the Maud post office in Oklahoma Territory. Before leaving, the mob set afire the house on the Leard place.

Nearly 200 lynchers and spectators, including a few women and children, assembled at the tabernacle. In the cold under a bright moon, the captives were forced to wind their chain around a jackoak tree, until they stood about eight feet apart.

Mobsters gathered broken tree limbs and brush and piled it around their captives' feet. The mob taunted them. A "preacher" knelt and prayed. Matches were struck and the wood and brush pile was set aflame. The boys were going to be burned alive. Flames leaped up but Lincoln McGeisey stood stoically —even when burning flesh started dropping off his right arm and right thigh. Then he lifted one hand almost as casual as if brushing off a fly. He dropped his head, and died silently.[33] Palmer Sampson fought death, kicking furiously at the burning brush. Some of these flaming faggots flew twenty-five feet into the killer mob.

Someone called Dr. C. P. Linn, Government physician for the Seminoles. He found the charred corpses still chained to the tree, heads and limbs burned off. He summoned Second Chief Hulputta-Che, in charge during Governor Brown's absence. Hulputta arrived in the dark, but recovered the bodies, and buried them in a common grave at Thomas McGeisey's place.

Subsequent episodes in this horrific Seminole burning are virtually useless anticlimax.

Governor Brown and others demanded immediate punitive action. The area around the farm and in the Maud area remained aflame with tension, and racial anger. But it was all against "Injuns," and loudly sympathetic for the Leard family and its bloody loss. Dr. Linn reported some mob members had gathered bones of the burning victims and were displaying them as vengeance souvenirs. Threats were made against the physician. He resigned, and left Wewoka. When Government investigators came to the area, they were rebuffed and hassled as outsiders, and told to mind their own business; locals would not sell them feed for their horses.

It took two years of investigations to gather enough evidence to indict sixty-nine men as being involved in the tragedy. Many were convicted in Federal Court at Muskogee and sent to prison, including Marshal Jones, who was given twenty-one years.[34] Meting out any punishment at all was frowned on by white homesteaders. When Mont Ballard, who served seven years in Leavenworth penitentiary, returned home to Maud, the town threw him a party. And one Oklahoma Territory newspaper, *The Mangum Star,* paid him this tribute: "No one present felt he was extending a welcome to a criminal, but regarded him as a martyr who gave up his liberty in defense of American womanhood."[35]

In Washington, Governor Brown complained that the burning was a violation of Seminoles' treaty rights. He demanded compensation for all victims—and got it. The McGeisey and Sampson families were paid $5,000 each; some damage claims were as low

172

as twenty-five dollars. In recounting the outrage, Historian Edwin C. McReynolds wrote this: "Chief John F. Brown of the Seminole Nation deserves great credit for his calm reliance upon legal remedies, and for his insistence on the treaty rights of the Seminole people."[36]

The real murderer was never caught. Governor Brown speculated he might have been an Indian not of his tribe, or whiskey town outlaws. He said: "Our nation is a small one.... People are crossing it all the time. On the border where Oklahoma joins, there is a long line of doggerel saloons patronized by the worst elements of the population."[37]

Even Senator Dawes was struck by the injustice of the mob's rage, and spoke about it. "If the Seminoles had burned two white boys," he said, "the white inhabitants of Oklahoma would have exterminated the whole tribe within ten days. But when the white inhabitants of Oklahoma burn two young Indians, one of whom is known to be innocent and the guilt of the other greatly in doubt, the Indians remained quietly at home, and appealed to the Great Father for justice."[38]

TOPICS DOMINATING Washington's Capitol Hill scene at the beginning of 1898 were the threat of war with Spain and the Curtis Act. Governor Brown was in the national capital to make his voice heard on the Indian Territory legislation. So were other Five Tribes spokesmen. It was generally agreed Congressman Curtis's bill would pass, and would drastically alter the Indian frontier.

As reported January 20, 1898 by *The Claremore Progress:*

> Governor Brown with other delegates from his nation are in Washington to urge Congress to ratify the treaty recently made with that nation by the Dawes Commission. Opinion as to the ratification of this treaty is divided.
>
> It is pretty generally conceded that this nation should be allowed to close up its own affairs, provision for which was voluntarily made in this treaty, but the objection to its ratification is, that should it become operative, it would create confusion, in that the manner of settling the affairs of the Seminoles, from that to be arranged for the other nations.

173

The Curtis Act moved steadily forward. Congressman Curtis predicted passage, telling the Washington reporter for *The Claremore Progress*: "The passage of this bill will be the beginning of a new era for Indian Territory. When its provisions are executed I expect to see the natural result speedily follow; its formation with Oklahoma [Territory] and the formation of one of the greatest and grandest states of the union."[39]

Just then center stage in Congress was grabbed by the explosion and sinking of the U.S. battleship *Maine* in Havana's harbor on February 15, 1898, with loss of 258 American sailors and two officers. Spain declared war against the United States April 24, and next day President McKinley took up the challenge. On May 1 American Commodore Dewey invaded Manila harbor and sank ten Spanish warships with 381 sailors. Colonel Teddy Roosevelt resigned as assistant Secretary of the Navy and recruited his Rough Riders.

Even before the Rough Riders had time to storm San Juan Hill and cinch America's victory in the war, Congress was again trying to settle the nagging Indian problem. By a lopsided vote on March 28, the Curtis Bill was enacted.

The credit belonged to Governor Brown, proclaimed *The Claremore Progress*. On July 9, 1898, the newspaper said: "The Seminoles trusted in one man, and he was all worthy of their confidence, and measured by the great good he has done his people, and the statesmanship he has shown, John Brown will live in the memory of his people. He will leave a record of noble deeds of which his people will be proud."

America lost 1,460 soldiers and 112 officers killed in conquering Spanish troops in Cuba, but by December 10 the war was over. Spain set Cuba free and to the United States ceded Puerto Rico, Guam and the Philippines, the latter for $20,000,000.

Back in Indian Territory, the Government started moving into high gear to assign the Five Tribes individual plots of land, and bring these red men under the laws of the United States. With its chairman failing in health, the Dawes Commission was revamped under a new leader, Tams Bixby, a Minnesota newspaper editor. Ahead lay a mountain of field and paper work; Bixby leaped to the task with impressive enthusiasm.

174

ON A SUMMER NIGHT in 1898 a banging on his door in We-woka roused Dr. Virgil Berry, the Seminoles' Government physician. Standing there was Jackson Brown.[40]

"Come with me, Doc. Stanton's bad hurt!"

In a buggy, they started for Holdenville, ten miles to the east. Dr. Berry had vaguely followed the career of Stanton Brown, Governor Brown's youngest brother. Now thirty-three, Stanton had married Julia Tuttle, the half-Creek daughter of a Government agent. Stanton was known to have a hot temper. He had worked in the Sasakwa trading company, been a teacher, and was now talked of as a candidate to become superintendent of Seminole tribal schools.

At the scene of the fight, they found Stanton in a small house lying on a pine table spread with a quilt, with most of his intestines in a pile outside his body. His abdomen had been slashed open, and he had lost a great deal of blood.

"Stanton, I'm Dr. Berry. What happened?"

"Just a damn fracas, Doc. I don't rightly remember ..." The injured man's voice trailed off.

"Well, son, just about every inch of gut you own is lying here on this quilt. This is not good!" [41]

By lantern light, Dr. Berry washed his hands in soap and water, poured alcohol over them, and flung them dry. Then he gently picked up the intestines and painstakingly examined them inch by inch.

"No perforations that I can see," he told Jackson. "Not even a scratch or nick."

That both surprised and gratified Dr. Berry. He turned and said to Jackson: "All I know to do is take a chance. I'll mix up a bucket of warm salt water and wash off the intestines best I can. Then I'll put them back. And sew him up."

It took a while to do that. If the knife went a quarter-inch deeper, Dr. Berry saw, the wound would have been fatal. Stanton Brown recovered. The doctor asked no details. Anybody who knew about the fracas kept his mouth shut.

TRIBAL ELECTIONS in the Seminole Nation had their own unique style, color and substance. They were a far cry from modern day poli-

175

tics. Candidates did not campaign nor make speeches. There were no endorsements; no back room deals.

When Governor Brown decided to stand for re-election in 1898 for another four-year term, he merely informed the Council that he wanted to keep the job. And let it go at that. Word would get around.

He drew one opponent, a full blood named Okchan Harjo. Running for second chief were Gilber Johnson and Nutchup Harjo.

The election was held on Saturday, August 6, 1898 out in the open on the wind-swept main street of Wewoka. All the Indians who wanted to vote arrived as early as mid-morning and stood around. At 11 A.M. the election would be conducted in simple fashion. All Seminoles in favor of re-electing Governor Brown stood along the west side of the street. Those for Okchan Harjo lined up along the east side.

Awaiting the final hour, Indians from one camp or the other did a little physical campaigning. Ardent rivals favoring either Brown or Harjo crossed the street and argued with their opponents to switch sides. Some men were pulled across the street, but usually went back. There was some horseplay between friends, but all took the election seriously.

Three Seminole officials went out at 11 and counted noses. Two hundred and fifty-one Seminole tribesmen stood on Governor Brown's west side of the street. The lineup for Okchan Harjo totaled one hundred forty-six.[42] Nath. Cap Harjo, a former president of the council, was elected second chief, 275 to 61.

Reporting the election, *The South McAlester Capital* threw the winner a bouquet. "In the election of their chief," said the newspaper, "the Seminoles displayed good judgment in re-electing Gov. Brown. During his many years in the executive chair his dealings with his people have in the point of ability and honesty been in marked contrast with that of other chiefs of the territory in Washington, and this is a great item when it is considered that the seat of the Indian government is now practically in Washington."[43]

11

Stringing Up a Horse Thief

EWSPAPERS PRAISED Governor Brown for his genius
and integrity, and did so with great frequency. But possible
secret flaws in his reputation came under suspicion in the
late 1890s. The very points for which his character was lauded—
honesty and fair dealing—were challenged. And not only from his
fellow Seminole Indians, but also, and quite seriously, from the
United States Government.

When editors in Indian Territory wrote up the Seminole chief's official acts they usually tacked on some personal encomium. *The South
McAlester (I.T.) Capital* called him "one of the best chiefs the Seminoles
ever had." Those words were repeated by the *Weleetka (Creek Nation,
I. T.) American.* [1] One leading Indian Territory newspaper observed:
"Governor Brown is very dear to his people who have learned to love
him for his wise and judicious management of their affairs." [2]

Extant files of old newspapers, pages tattered, yellow, and
crumbling, or microfilmed in archival reels, carry scores of similar
favorable comments. The *Holdenville (I.T.) Tribune* topped some
rival sheets with a page one write-up that proclaimed:

> Perhaps no man living has left a more lasting impress on
> the lives and character of his people than Governor John F.

Brown. . . These were fortunate years for the Seminole tribe. During that time they had a man of great ability and honor at the head of their affairs. He is the ablest Indian in the Territory, and a statesman of remarkable capacity. He met the strongest men at Washington and convinced them that his course was wise, comprehensive and just. [3]

It was money and land that catapulted the easy-going chief of the Seminoles into a different kind of spotlight and onto the griddle to face accusations of avarice and greed. The money was a total of three or four million dollars owed to the tribe as overdue Government payments. And the land was the extraordinary transaction by which he acquired for $12,000 all unsold lots in Wewoka.

That was perceived as entirely too heavy-handed. It broke open simmering resentment of dictatorial tribal rule. One hundred angry Seminoles gathered in protest at Mekusukey Mission and fired off a hot letter of protest to Washington.

When the Interior Department and Congress started to look into the town site controversy their eyes opened, and they suddenly came up with a question of their own. Just how much tribal money was going into the pockets of the Brown family, and why?

No one seemed to doubt that it was noble and appropriate to lay out the town site of Wewoka. The "catch" that no title would be provided unless "a building or other valuable improvement" was erected within six months proved to be a big obstacle. At the end of three years, largely because of the "catch" just a few lots had been sold.

That's when Governor Brown stepped in and offered to buy up all unsold lots. On February 12, 1900 he made his $12,000 offer to the Seminole Council. In a special session two months later, on April 18, the Seminole Council "accepted and ratified" the deal. [4] But the Council made a significant change in the sale to their chief. The "catch," which had largely stymied sale of lots was eliminated.[5]

This uprising against their chief was partially also triggered by his rush in making the Seminoles the first tribe to agree to terms with the Dawes Commission. That agreement was reached December 16, 1897, and Governor Brown sped away to Washington to seek quick ratification by Congress.

178

While he bustled around the Capitol, the Indian families out in the Nation were stewing in unhappiness over their really sorry life. Led by a full blood named Okkuskey Miller, the 100 protesters gathered at Mekusukey Mission on January 22, 1898 to write their long list of grievances. Already on January 12 Interior Secretary C. N. Bliss had transmitted the December 16 treaty to the Senate. Now on January 29, with the protest on his desk, he asked that ratification be held up until the letter of complaint could be considered.

The jeremiad from the outraged Okkuskey Miller people was couched in their best "tough talk." First, those protesters asserted the Seminole Council had not legally approved the treaty. Although requiring a two-thirds vote of the forty-two town kings, the treaty "was passed with only 23 favoring, 10 opposing, and 9 absentees." The Dawes treaty, said the letter, should be submitted to a popular vote; if not, the Okkuskey Miller group should be invited to Washington to give its views.

Without naming the chief, the protest struck at him by asserting that the "personal interest of some Seminoles hurried this matter" not allowing the tribe time to "reflect, consider, and understand the treaty."

More directly, the letter said: "The national funds are absorbed by only a few of their citizens who have grown rich at the public expense, and we firmly believe that these few persons are oppressing the poorer ones."

The letter brought up missing money. Of the $1,912,942.02 the tribe received for giving up land, $1,500,000 was left with the Government to draw 5 percent interest. The tribe withdrew $221,647.80 to spend on various tribal projects. That left $191,294.20 not accounted for.[6]

When Indians like Okkuskey Miller asked in Wewoka what happened to the money, they were told it was paid as a fee to the lawyer who negotiated the money deal. "The name of the lawyer was never mentioned, and no receipt of the alleged deal was ever shown. . . We ask you to take note of the town-site laws of Wewoka and see to whom only these laws are beneficial and whom they oppress."[7]

Also it was pointed out that the Seminole chief and treasurer were not bonded, were not subject to audit, and that no matter could

179

be brought before the National Council without the chief's approval. "Our people are entirely ignorant of our finances."

Twelve Seminoles signed the letter to the Interior Secretary, five with their X mark.

The protest hit a nerve in Washington. Officials acted a little humbled, conceding they had long known of dishonesty in Indian country but had failed to stop it. One Government report was harshly candid, saying Indian agents had earlier informed Washington:

> . . . that the Seminole tribal officers were misappropriating the Seminole tribal funds entrusted to them, and robbing the members of the tribe of an equal share of the tribal income.
>
> That the reports of the Dawes Commission show conclusively that the governments of the Five Civilized Tribes were notoriously and incurably corrupt, that every branch of the service was infested with favoritism, graft and crookedness, and that by such methods the tribal officers acquired large fortunes, while other members entitled to share in the tribal income received little benefit there from.
>
> . . . There are ample indications in the record before us that the Seminole General Council was mulcting the Nation. . .

The Dawes Commission, it became clear during this inquiry, had in its annual reports to the Secretary of the Interior and Congress pointedly described "the unbridled corruption of the various tribal governments, without singling out any particular government for unenviable distinction." The first annual Dawes Commission report in November 1894 noted:

> Corruption of the grossest kind, openly and unblushingly practiced, has found its way into every service of the tribal governments. All branches of the government are reeking with it, and so common has it become that no attempt at concealment is thought necessary.
>
> The governments have fallen into the hands of a few able and energetic Indian citizens, nearly all mixed blood and adopted whites, who have so administered their affairs and have enacted such laws that they are enabled to appropriate to their own exclusive use almost the entire property of the Territory of any kind that can be rendered profitable and available.

180

The author of the Dawes report could not conceal his disgust with frontier conditions, writing:

> The Commission is compelled by the evidence forced upon them during their examination into the administration of the so-called governments in this Territory to report that these governments in all their branches are wholly corrupt, irresponsible, and unworthy to be longer trusted with the care and control of the money and other property of the Indian citizens, much less their lives, which they scarcely pretend to protect.

There was no way Governor Brown and his brother Jackson could escape the Congressional spotlight in these scandals. Both were attacked on the floor by members of the House and of the Senate in 1897 and 1898.

"These two half-breed brothers were the principal chief and treasurer, respectively, of the Seminole Nation," asserted one Congressman. "Together they ran a trading store in the Seminole country and extended credit by giving due bills, good only in trade at their store, to individual Seminoles in the amount of annuities or other payments owing to those individuals. . .

"All this tends to show that the Seminole tribal officers might have been faithless to their trust . . . and that the Government officials administering Indian affairs and disbursing Seminole funds might have been aware of that faithlessness at the time payments were made to the Seminole treasurer."

Listening to attacks on his integrity obviously wounded Governor Brown; but he held his head high. He would not concede any misbehavior in his official capacity. He felt he retained the trust of important people in the capital. One Washington newspaper even speculated that he might become Senator after the anticipated statehood merged the Indian and Oklahoma Territories.

These accusations of wrongdoing did not, in the end, result in any charges being brought against Governor Brown. He would be essentially cleared after investigations in both the Seminole Council and in the Department of Interior in Washington.

The U. S. Attorney was asked to rule on the legality of the townsite purchase. In a ten-page opinion, Frank L. Campbell, assistant

181

attorney general, held that the advisability of selling the lots to the principal chief and his brother was questionable, and the Council had no legal right to make the sale, and certainly none to waive the "catch." [8] But the wrangle had a aftermath that continued for half a century. In 1903 the Seminole Council would conduct an investigation and on December 17 that year pass an act ratifying the transaction. On March 3, 1905, Congress would ratify and confirm the Seminole Council's action. But later the townsite sale was challenged in the United States Court of Claims, which held that no fraud was shown. It continued to be argued and re-argued, and finally washed out in 1952 in the Indian Claims Commission.

Historian McReynolds observes: "Many persons seemed to be pleased that a man of Indian blood had been able to recognize the possibilities of the unearned increment; and to consider that the choice lay between a handsome profit for the beloved chief of the Seminoles, John F. Brown and his associates, and the same or a larger profit for a noncitizen corporation." [9]

THE DARK ANGEL hovered at Governor Brown's doorstep throughout 1899. His offspring were unable to escape the scourge of tuberculosis, which had come from his marriage into the Chief John Jumper family.

His thirteenth child, named Zara, was born in April 1899 and died before the next Christmas. This was a sentimental family; he had named her for the earlier Zara, the twin born with Alice in 1852 at Park Hill, and did not survive.

His second son, John W., married to a teacher at Emahaka Mission, also died, at age twenty-eight. Death took his No. 3 son, Solomon, who was twenty-seven. His daughter Ruth died at twenty-five, as well as her four-year-old daughter, likewise named Ruth.

That left him, at age fifty-six, six surviving children: Henrietta, twenty-six; Jennie, twenty-five; Martha, twenty; Josephine, seventeen; Alice, fifteen; Andrew, ten; and Louis C. called Tob, seven.

His business affairs were bright and flourishing. He was operating trading posts in both Sasakwa and Wewoka, cotton gins in both towns, and running cattle ranches on a large scale. His newest enterprise was selling real estate. He printed thousands of copies of an attractive and aggressive booklet fronted by the sketch of a bison and emblazoned with a large We-wo-ka—"the only town in Ind. Ter. where warranty deed can be secured." [10] The Rock Island Railroad distributed these pamphlets up and down its lines, and joined the boosterism bandwagon by publishing a pitch of its own. The Rock Island booklet predicted the Seminole Nation capital would have 5,000 residents within two years, asserting that annuity payments of $105,000 were made there annually, and $2,000,000 in cash would be distributed to the Indians when land allotments were wound up. "This is a fine opportunity to purchase a lot cheap in the best town in Indian Territory. Forty dollars buys one business lot or two residence lots."[11]

Gossip in tribal homes and stories in the newspapers were correct; Governor Brown was definitely the richest man in the Seminole Nation.

His glorious dream of a mansion fit for a monarch had finally come through. Across from his Sasakwa trading post he had built a seventeen-room house with ornate galleries on both floors, and two third-floor towers. He had a copper bathtub, heating stoves in virtually every room, bookshelves with space for his two to three thousand volumes. One library section was lined with plate glass wall mirrors, before which he placed the ornate vases he had given his two wives as wedding presents. Prominent in the parlor was a large and gleaming grand piano. [12]

His laundry house contained a "new-fangled" mechanical washing machine purchased from Chicago. Other outbuildings were numerous—to house the horses, swine, poultry, storage, buggies, wagons, and farming implements. His tack room for saddles and harness was elaborate; he bought fine draft teams and the sleekest and most well bred buggy and riding horses in the territory.

Few plantations could be better staffed with servants for the house plus hands for the fields and cowboys for the livestock in the pastures. He took enormous pride in his extensive orchard, which offered bountiful harvests. His front yard fence was white and pristine. The concrete walk to the entry was kept swept of leaves and debris.

183

Despite its grandeur and size, some children found the mansion spooky. On climbing the stairs into the tower rooms, they found that a struck match flickered out almost at once. They whispered about ghosts and fled, too young to understand the whimsy of drafts.[13]

FROM UPSTAIRS in her Arbeka home, Alice Brown Davis could lean on a windowsill and watch dazzling sunsets. The sheer beauty of the dreamlike theatrics of clouds dying in flames ordinarily lifted her spirits. That was not the case on this day in early November 1899; she was too depressed.

Overwhelming sadness had come with realization that the Indians' way of life was once again battered and changing. The Dawes Commissioners were making a tribal roll, a list of each person in the Seminole Nation whose Indian blood entitled them to a plot of land. That was not easy; old folks died and babies were born. When to fix a deadline was debated. The cutoff date for the Grim Reaper and for the Stork was set as August 23, 1900.

Making a survey of Indian Territory, a critical step, began in 1894. Geological engineers were sent from Washington to supervise. They sent out several twenty-man crews with solar compasses, transits, plane tables, chains, rods, pins etc. They camped out in tents and traveled in wagons, buggies, and buckboards drawn by mules. The starting point was at the Indian Base and Meridian, Township 1 North, Range 8 East, 13 miles south-southeast of Calvin, in the Choctaw Nation. [14]

The surveyors first laid out 24-mile square quadrangles, then townships six miles square, and finally sections one-mile square. At each township corner a four-inch iron pipe four feet long was driven into the ground, topped by a brass plate stamped with Township, Section, and Range. Where trees were available they were marked with numbers using a special woodcarving tool.

Indians, superstitious or resentful, occasionally dug up markers, but the task was so successful overall that twenty years later one surveyor was able to find a mark he had carved on a post-oak tree in 1905 hidden beneath new-growth bark. [15]

What perhaps upset Alice the most was that the open range was no more. Under Government edict, ranchers had been forced into a

184

final roundup of cattle that had roamed the pastureland held by the tribe in common. That was no more. Now Indians would have to fence their individual acreage. That this rule would apply in all Five Civilized Tribes did little to ameliorate the hurt.

Her Bar X Bar ranch had been hit a deathblow by the loss of the open range. But the Arbeka Trading Post kept on a steady course, with a modest business upsurge. That was something worth smiling about.

Alice's girls were in boarding school, but four boys remained on the home place. John Frippo and Andrew Jackson, her "babies," were six and four, respectively. Her second son Jesse, twenty, had married his sweetheart Ella Knight a few months previously, May 12, 1899. First-born George Lytle, twenty-three, was her right-hand man, wrangler of the last of the Bar X Bar livestock. He still lived in a tenant house close to the Arbeka store with his wife Julia and precocious five-year-old daughter Pearl. [16]

In November 1899 George Lytle heard that a traveling photographer had arrived in Wewoka and set up a tent "studio." He urgently wanted a picture taken of his little girl. The family piled into a buggy and drove to town.

Pearl was seated on the photographer's bench and the man was focusing his camera.[17]

"Daddy, I want Beauty in the picture!"

George Lytle looked at Julia, and then at Pearl's red curly-haired dog, which had accompanied them. Beauty was muddy. The parents shook their heads, until they saw their daughter start working up a tantrum.

"I wouldn't without Beauty," Pearl recalled in a her memoir. "So they sat her on a chair. Me with a whole package of gum in my mouth, standing beside her with my arm around her neck, happy as could be. . . I got all muddy from the dog, but I didn't care."

A few days later, Sunday, November 19, George Lytle arose at daybreak, ate a quick breakfast, kissed his wife and daughter, and rode off. He had to go over toward Keokuk Falls, he told Julia, to check on some livestock.

The day wore on. The sky was a brilliant sunny blue, laced with occasional wispy clouds. The wind had subsided to a gentle breeze

185

that barely jostled the tops of the tall dry prairie grass. Anybody in the Territory would have been hard put to remember a more glorious Indian summer day.

Late in the afternoon a lone horseman galloped up to Alice's house.[18] She opened the door as he came up the steps.

He was a young Indian she had seen around the Arbeka area. "Mrs. Davis—" he began, and choked up. Finally he managed to blurt: "Wagon is comin' bringin' George. Foun' him this afternoon, strung up. Men claim your boy had some stolen hosses." [19]

Alice was thunderstruck. This beautiful day suddenly exploding into disaster. George Lytle dead, and in disgrace as a horse thief! The news crushed his wife and little Pearl. George was quietly buried in the family plot at Arbeka. Their grief was private; no need to broadcast that another scandal had hit the most prominent family in the Seminole Nation. That concealment effort succeeded. News of the lynching did not travel very far in Indian Territory. The Anti-Horse Thief Association was strong, active, and effective; but it did no public bragging about making use of the gallows. The death of George Lytle Davis was not mentioned in any newspaper of that period. This was unusual because the editors in Wewoka, Purcell, Oklahoma City, Claremore, Holdenville, Muskogee, Eufaula and South McAlester customarily closely followed events in the Seminole chief's family. It has to be assumed none of these editors learned of the lynching, because news of any rustler swinging at the end of a rope almost always was published.

Kitt, in Fort Smith with her Katy railroader husband, heard about her brother's lynching by mail from her mother and Julia. In reply to a letter from Alice that arrived at breakfast time December 8, she wrote:

> Mama, what can I say to comfort you and Julia. It seems almost unbearable at times. Still we know we must become reconciled. Time alone can heal the wound.
>
> Julia's letter was heart-rending. I never read such a pitiful letter. How she loved that dear boy. It seems like a terrible dream to me. I never will think of him as dead. The children said he did not look natural and they could not believe it was brother George.

No mother could have been any more self-sacrificing than you have been to us . . . . I believe the old maxim "Indulgence begats ingratitude" is true. The more you do the more you are expected to do. . . .I often sit and think and wonder if the time will come when I can help and repay you for the expense I have been.

Many, many days and nights I have thought and hoped the time would come to let me prove my love to you and all at home. If that time never comes it will always be a thorn in my heart . . . [20]

CLATTER FROM THE STREETS of St. Louis dinned against the windows of the corporate office where Governor Brown pleaded with executives of the Frisco Railroad.

Spread on the conference table were maps and documents showing how the Frisco intended to extend its tracks across the southeast corner of the Seminole Nation.

The Frisco men exchanged solemn looks, and kept shaking their heads. They declined to make the change the Seminole chieftain requested. [21]

This was 1901, and Governor Brown was still dogged by his long spell of unexpected trouble and disappointment. He was upset because the route for the Frisco branch line from Holdenville in the Creek Nation to Ada in the Chickasaw Nation did not run through Sasakwa, but bypassed his "personal capital," crossing the prairie two miles east of his trading post.

That was to the disadvantage of all his business interests, including his cotton gins, and his cattle ranching. Having been vice-president of the branch line out of Shawnee that had been taken over by the Frisco, Governor Brown felt he understood the mentality of railroad men and could convince Frisco to run the new line through Sasakwa.

He could not. He got a flat no.

On his trip home, Governor Brown put his creative powers to work. How could he solve the dilemma? Could he make a silk purse out of a sow's ear?

As the train rattled south, his answer came magically. Once back home, he tried out his decision on brother Jackson and Courtland Long. Their eyes popped and they smiled broadly and slapped him on the back. [22]

187

Within days Governor Brown had sawyers clearing a grove of trees, men with teams scraping out a main street, and others laying out lots for "new" Sasakwa. If the railroad wouldn't come to him, he would go to the railroad! He began at once putting up a two-story brick building just east of the railroad tracks into which to move his trading post. He picked sites for a new cotton gin—which he would call "The Red Gin," and paint it that color—and a black-smith shop.

Back in "old" Sasakwa he kept intact his mansion and plantation. Everything else moved two miles east to the railroad. Governor Brown expected the iron horse would bring settlers and commerce. He foresaw rapid growth for "new" Sasakwa.

Possibilities of new business ventures intrigued his busy mind. His latest was liquid gold. Oil slicks had for years bubbled up in a few streams and marshes. People convinced him the Seminole Nation sat atop a submerged sea of petroleum. He had to find out. The Wewoka Trading Company moved a drilling derrick onto the B.F. Davis farm west of Wewoka and spudded in. [23] Cable tools only were available, and they were slow. The heavy bit hammered a twelve-inch hole down, down, down . . . Everyone crossed their fingers. At 700 feet a geyser exploded from the hole. The expectant driller shouted hooray—and then sourly clamped his mouth. It was only water! "Keep going," said Governor Brown. "Maybe we're not deep enough yet."[24]

As did many wildcat wells, this Wewoka Trading Company test would soon shut down as a failure. Governor Brown's hunch was correct; he just failed to drill deep enough. Down about five or six thousand feet lay one of the world's greatest petroleum pools, large enough to produce hundreds of thousand barrels of crude a day, and an unimaginable volume of natural gas. Two decades later this underground petroleum pool would be discovered, bringing on a madcap drilling spree that overnight turned Oklahoma crossroads hamlets into raucous boom-towns. And for leasing drilling rights on their often near-worthless farms, the oil play would turn several hundred Indians into overnight millionaires. (The Seminole chief would not witness this historic spectacle; it would come four years after he had gone to his grave.)

188

Early in 1902 scurrilous gossip intensified about Governor Brown's integrity. Still hanging fire were questions about his handling of tribal money and the Wewoka town site. At that point both matters were still in a muddle; they remained under review in Congress and in the Interior Department. Mention of the chief's name among the Seminoles began to bring dire mutterings and angry looks.

This was a poor time for him to be under suspicion. The tribal election was just around the corner. He would be seeking his fifth four-year term.

His heart was heavy for another reason. His second wife, Elizabeth, died late in March. She was buried in the family plot near his mansion just one week before the Seminoles held their nominating convention in Wewoka on Friday, April 4, 1902. Governor Brown was nominated for re-election, opposed by the well-known full blood Hulputta Micco, who had served one term as principal chief and several as second chief.

"There is little doubt of Governor Brown's election," predicted *The Holdenville Times* on April 12. "He has been chief for the last sixteen years, and has, by wise, conservative management, avoided all entanglements and complications both among his people and with the United States government."

Election day—Thursday, June 3, 1902—was sunny and warm. A light breeze followed the Indians converging on Wewoka by wagon, buggy, horseback and on foot. About 500 men would take part in the voting, which was set for 10 o'clock in the morning. To cast their votes, the Seminole men assembled in the middle of Wewoka, and began lining up to face each other across the main street. Those in favor of re-electing Governor Brown stood on the east side; Hulputta Micco's voters on the west. There was some jostling, a few Indians were induced to change sides; but it was a somber occasion.

Three tellers stepped forward and announced that the tally would begin; no further changing sides was allowed. The vote counters walked the length of the street, taking notes. Then they went inside the Council House to add up the votes. Milling about outside were many Indian women (who were not permitted to vote)

189

and children along for the spectacle. Some sought shade under the broad pecan branches of whipping tree. The execution tree was gone. Not used after federal courts took jurisdiction, it had been cut down to clear a site for a business building.

At length the clerk came out and announced the election results. Hulpatta Micco had 340 votes, and John Franklin Brown 173 votes. He was now ex-Governor Brown, defeated about two-to-one. The scurrilous gossip about the chief's integrity had obviously damaged public confidence in his leadership.

His defeat was a "misfortune," said *The Holdenville Times* in its next edition, explaining:

> The trouble with the Seminoles is their system, rather than the man. By. . . Indian custom. . . their government is paternal, and the important functions are centered in the chief. A man of less honesty and ability would have squandered the properties of the people and so entangled their affairs as to require years of litigation to undo.
>
> Governor Brown deserves great credit for what he has not done, as well as for what he has done. To fill the place. . . surrounded by such temptations and at last come out with the cleanest reputation for efficiency and integrity of any chiefs during the time, should have endeared him to a more intelligent people.
>
> Hulputta is a good man with lots of horse sense, and would have made an ideal chief half a century ago, when the function of government was to administer primitive justice to a primitive people. But now it is different. Something more than horse sense is needed. . .
>
> The new chief will probably be beset with. . . hidden entangling schemes. He will have to pass on all leases in the nation, and there is danger he will be illiberal and a hindrance to development. Beyond this, his power to harm is small. [25]

Thus it appeared that John Franklin Brown, private citizen of the Seminole Nation, would now have much more time to pursue his business interests, rapidly growing in number and scope. And that he did for a time—and then sudden disaster threatened to strike him blind. The story is told in the *St. Louis Globe Democrat*'s August 3, 1902 issue:

190

A box of eye salve, whose contents he thoughtlessly rubbed into instead of around his optics, has caused ex-Gov. John F. Brown of Sasakwa, I.T., two months of suffering and for a time threatened the loss of his eyesight.

Gov. Brown reached the city yesterday with his physician, Dr. A. S. Riddle of South McAlester, I. T., and they are stopping at the Southern Hotel. The former still wears a bandage over one of his eyes and is here for the purpose of consulting a specialist and undergoing treatment. He will remain several weeks and hopes to return to his home completely cured.

Some weeks ago Gov. Brown was troubled with his eyesight, and someone suggested he might find relief in the use of a certain eye salve which was carried in stock by one of his stores. He paid but slight attention to the directions, which were to the effect that the preparation should be rubbed on the eyelids and temples, and put a supply of it on the eyes themselves.

As the trouble did not disappear he put on some more of the salve in the same way, and then it began to get serious.

Dr. Riddle thinks his eyes were poisoned by something in the preparation. The St. Louis specialist assured Gov. Brown that he would not lose his eyesight.

HOWEVER MUCH HATE was directed at the Dawes Commission by the unhappy Indians, Alice Brown Davis had to somewhat temper her disenchantment. The commissioners gave her a job—interpreter. The pay was reasonable and the work easy. The employment came at a juncture in her life when her income was dwindling and the family expenses were on the increase. Somehow money burdens seemed to fall on Alice—and, sadly, would for the remainder of her life.

Another surge of depression had struck her. She was saddened in August when son Jesse's second child, a boy named Lewis, died at age six months. That seems to have brought up terrible memories of George Lytle swinging at the end of a lynch rope; Jesse heard her muttering his brother's name as she broke into sobs. [26] Another day when undertaking her daily ritual of reading the Bible she had happened on Proverbs 5:22-23, and mentioned the incident in her diary. [27] She must have shuddered at the words condemning adultery:

191

The evil deeds of a wicked man ensnare him;
The cords of his sin hold him fast.
He will die for lack of discipline,
Led astray by his own great folly.

For a moment, perhaps, she could recall Roll's tenderness and chivalry in the days he helped her into the buggy for romantic rides along the Canadian river at Sasakwa. Those memories might have brought tears, too, having to relive the anguish that came with discovering her husband's unfaithfulness.

In any event, she brightened up when an unexpected proposition came that promised her both lively adventure and foreign travel.

THREE HUNDRED MILES south of San Antonio, the Mexican stagecoach struggled slowly up the steep Santa Rosa Mountain trail drawn by six burros. Reaching the pass near the 3000-foot summit, the driver stomped the brake lever into lock, and hopped down. Shaking dust from his sombrero, he opened the door and invited his passengers to emerge for a breather.

Alice stepped out followed by four other Seminoles—Chief Hulputta Micco, who only a few months earlier had succeeded her brother as principal chief of the tribe, and three members of the Seminole National Council.

The driver shaded his eyes and pointed to a cluster of tawny buildings far off in the valley below, and they could see their destination, the village of Nacimiento de Kikapoo, Coahuila, Mexico.

This was an oddball mission—and about fifty years late at that. But Hulputta Micco was dead-set on this quest. Since he could neither read nor write English, he had commissioned Alice to come along as interpreter. The Spanish language was beyond all of them, but Alice expected to somehow manage to communicate.

Chief Hulputta Micco carried in a soft deerskin pouch, securely pinned within his coat pocket, the priceless talisman that had inspired this journey of adventure. It was a tarnished and curious copper medal, not very large, at least five decades old. [28] It had been cast by the government of Mexico as a "deed" conveying a tract of many hundred acres of Mexican land to a band of Seminole Indians. Embossed on the copper disk was the seal of Mexico, the peace pipe of the Seminoles and two clasped hands, "emblematic of peace and harmony ensuing from this treaty which granted to the Seminoles, a large body of land to be theirs forever in fee." [29]

A wily and daring Seminole malcontent and outcast named Wild Cat had been given this "deed" as a reward by Mexico. Unhappy in Indian Territory, Wild Cat in 1849 led a band of 300, including Negro freedmen, south of the Rio Grande to try to recreate their traditional way of life. The Mexicans near the border were then being raided by Apaches and Comanches who murdered farmers, kidnapped women and children, and stole horses.

Wild Cat leaped in and aggressively defended the beleaguered Mexicans, sending out war parties from his colony to kill or drive off the wild plains Indians. In gratitude, the *jefes* welcomed Wild Cat and his expatriates, established them in a large region near Coahuila, and cast the "deed" medal. In 1857, Wild Cat died in a smallpox epidemic and most of his followers drifted back to Indian Territory.

But Mexico had deeded the Seminoles the land "forever," and Hulpatta Micco was now en route by stage to reclaim Wild Cat's acreage.

Alice remembered all she had read and heard of Wild Cat, starting with his killing many American soldiers in the Florida wars, his dramatic escape from a U. S. prison, his eventual coming to the new Indian Territory. Nothing about Wild Cat, whose Indian name was *Coacoochee*, was ordinary. He was recklessly brave, smart and imaginative, with a trait of cruelty. To punish offenders, he was wont to cut off ears—using a dull knife to intensify pain.

His foray from the Seminole Nation to Mexico began in a fit of pique at being passed over for the position he felt he deserved—chief. He was joined by Gopher John, "chief" of the Wewoka freedmen, who were still harassed by plantation bounty hunters.

Not unexpectedly trouble erupted in Wild Cat's Mexican colony. Officials became jealous of Wild Cat; some freedmen became unhappy and went back home. After Wild Cat's death the colony disbanded, and the Mexican land was abandoned. However, Hulpatta Micco possessed the "deed" disk, and was determined to regain the land. Further, he wanted to carefully check out the Mexican countryside. Some Seminoles still had a yen to just pull up stakes in America and move elsewhere. This might be the place; the chief told Alice he would keep sharp watch for good omens.

When Alice and Hulputta Micco's party arrived in this beautiful valley, in the shadow of the Sierra Madre Mountains, and about 400 miles northwest of Monterrey, Mexico, they were greeted enthusiastically. The Mexicans fed them heaping plates of spicy food, called out musicians and a bevy of nimble dancers in billowing petticoats to serenade them. The *alcade* of Nacimiento proclaimed he was ready to help the visitors' quest. It turned out otherwise. For one reason after another, the Mexicans were unable to honor the medal "deed."

This stalemate continued for three frustrating months. In the end Hulputta Micco, Alice and the other three gave up and boarded the stagecoach to start back home. Though empty-handed, the Seminole's new chief did not intend to abandon his quest.

"Next time," he told Alice, "we must go to make 'talk' with big chief. We go to the City of Mexico." [30]

ON THE CLOUDY MORNING of Monday, April 4, 1904 Ex-Governor Brown sat in his room at the American Hotel in St. Louis scratching out a brief letter to grandson Charlie Brown back in Sasakwa. [31]

"We had a hard rain yesterday afternoon," he wrote, "and today the weather is so cloudy we have not gone to the Fair but may go in the afternoon."

That they did—all thirteen of the Seminoles. And they got knocked for a loop by the stunning splendor and magnificence, the expanse and scope, the inventions and world wonders of the Louisiana Purchase Exposition—the 1904 St. Louis World's Fair.

Alice was there with her six daughters: Kitt, Myrtle, Maye, Maude, Bess and Irene. Also in the party were Jackson Brown and his wife Manie, and the Brown sister Lucy.

They brought along a rarity that would attract macabre attention during the St. Louis Fair's eight-month run, playing to nearly

20,000,000 visitors. In the Indian Territory pavilion was displayed a three-foot section sawed out of the old Wewoka execution tree, studded with slugs and bullet-holes. [32]

The two Brown brothers, publicized by *The St. Louis Republic* as "among the wealthiest Indians" in the territory, had contributed handsomely to sponsor the Indian Territory pavilion, and hence received a sheaf of VIP passes.

"We are located at the entrance," Governor Brown's letter continued, "and every day convinces me that we are very fortunate in securing such convenient quarters." He referred to streetcars that were so crowded half the riders had to stand.

"Manie and Lucy are getting along fine. (The family was worried about sister Lucy, who was showing first signs of her eventual mental breakdown.) I expect you to look after the place and see that nothing goes to waste. I hope our section of the country will escape the floods and washouts which seem to be going the rounds."

The Fair was truly an enlightening experience for the entire Brown coterie, coming as it did just one year after the Wright Brothers' famous flight. Gasoline-powered automobiles, motion pictures and the wonder drug aspirin were only ten years old. Electric lights and telephones were still a novelty but horse-drawn ice wagons remained a familiar sight.

The Brown party saw the public debut of air conditioning, were able to skate on a summer ice rink, speak by wireless telegraph to cities 1,500 miles away. Within the 1,240 acres of the fair they could "see the world": from the Tyrolean Alps to the jungles of the Philippines; from the gardens of Japan to the holy sites of Jerusalem; from Southwestern pueblos to Arctic villages set up in St. Louis with real Eskimos and seals.

The girls gawked and their eyes bugged in astonishment at the sensational sights. Even though coming from the barely-tamed frontier, they fit right in the cosmopolitan St. Louis scene. *The St. Louis Republic* said: "The Indians of the Brown party are all highly educated. The young women are pupils and alumnae of Indian schools, and their clothes are as fashionable as those of St. Louis girls. The party attracted a great deal of attention at the World's Fair yesterday." [33]

195

In their two-weeks stay, the Browns could not begin to take in all the exhibits, which made up a large city surrounding the 600-foot wide Plaza of St. Louis. They were awed by Festival Hall that was crowned by a gold-leaf dome larger than St. Peter's Basilica in Rome. Festival Hall seated 3,500 and had the world's largest organ, with 10,159 pipes. At the hall's entrance was an ornate fountain with water flowing 110 feet wide at the base.

Thomas Edison came to set up the Palace of Electricity, where an electric broiler turned out a steak in six minutes. The transportation exhibit included four miles of railway tracks, working locomotives, turntables, and 140 automobiles that had been driven to the Fair from as far away as Boston, Philadelphia, and Chicago.

The girls went wild watching elephants climb a ramp and scoot down a special slide into a pool of water, the pachyderms seeming to enjoy the stunt. The Brown/Davis females went home humming the classic "St. Louis Rag," the Fair theme song written and played by pianist Tom Turpin, a black saloon owner in St. Louis.

Alice and her youngest were living at Sasakwa, the trading post at Arbeka having been given up. In her memoir, Maye, seventeen at the time of the Fair, wrote: "We had to sell some things to get money for the trip. I'm so glad." [34]

12

Feuding Over Emahaka

FATE THRUST John Franklin Brown back as chief of the Seminoles in early 1905 just as the federal government stepped up relentless efforts to force the Five Tribes to accept statehood jointly with Oklahoma Territory.

Chief Hulputta Micco died on March 24, 1905. The second chief, a full blood named Jacob Harrison, was automatically elevated as his successor. That proved a mistake. Harrison, an illiterate, botched most of his duties as headman.

Worried tribal elders considered impeaching Harrison and asking Brown to again take charge. At Sasakwa, in his mansion, he was active in business and ranching. He continued also as pastor of the Spring Baptist Church. At sixty-two he had just married for the third time. His bride was Sarah Cully, twenty-seven, an attractive full blood Creek who could neither read nor write English. She would bear him two sons and two daughters, between 1906 and 1913, making him the father ultimately of seventeen.

The elders had to wait to approach him. At that time Brown was on the road as one of the Indian Territory dignitaries welcoming President Theodore Roosevelt who was on a hunting trip in the west and southwest. Back on March 4, 1905 in his inaugural address Roosevelt had not mentioned the statehood controversy. But arriving in Indian Territory aboard a Katy train in early April, he spoke out directly and loudly, making clear his administration's intention.

In a speech in Muskogee, he said: "Your Territory, remember, in conjunction with Oklahoma, will soon be one of the greatest states in the Union."

Those remarks and in Congress a continuing onslaught of bills aimed at combining the two territories into one state stirred new resistance by the Five Tribes. These developments occurred just at the time the Seminoles were confronted with their need for a new chief. John Franklin Brown answered their SOS with no hesitation. So on May 5, 1905, the Seminole National Council impeached Jacob Harrison on grounds of incompetence, and installed Governor Brown to replace him. As a result Governor Brown was destined to play a prominent official role in the Five Tribes' battle against single statehood.

The Indians insisted Washington had agreed in recent treaties to give them separate statehood. They did not want to be lumped in with Oklahoma Territory as a single new state; one fear was loss of tribal clout against the influx of whites who now outnumbered the Five Tribes six to one on their own land.

Chief Green McCurtain of the Choctaws and two or three others hatched a scheme to beat the Washington politicians to the draw. The Five Tribes should hurriedly create their own new state![1] That would require writing an appropriate constitution, designating counties and their boundaries, appointing delegates to Congress—and getting it all ratified by a popular vote.

Governor Brown and a band of Seminoles gathered in Muskogee August 21, 1905 to join leaders and delegates from the Cherokee, Chickasaw, Creek and Choctaw tribes in a constitutional convention. The Seminole chief helped jump-start the flurry of activity that in five days produced a 35,000-word constitution for their new state, which was named "Sequoyah" by the delegates to honor the famous inventor of the Cherokee alphabet.

The Five Tribes snagged for a time on a variety of small hurdles that popped up. The Indians managed to steer around them and kept their one-state juggernaught rolling. Oklahoma Territory promoters and politicians screamed in protest, with a negative echo also

198

from the majority of newspapers. Even so, the proposed State of Sequoyah was ratified on November 7, 1905 by a popular vote of 56,279 to 9,073.[2]

Governor Brown and the other chiefs thought the State of Sequoyah was on its way. But it wasn't.

Over-confident, the Indians selected four delegates to represent Sequoyah in the Congress. One was Governor Brown's canny Wewoka Trading Post partner, Courtland L. Long. Twenty Indians were designated to hurry to Washington and lobby to legitimize Sequoyah. Opponents of the Indians' proposed state also organized and chartered a special train to the nation's capital. Cleverly, the anti-Sequoyah lobbyists took with them a good-sized hog that bore placards labeling him "Statehood." That trick gave them the most attention and publicity on Capitol Hill.

Unaccountably, the zeal of the Five Tribes one-staters seemed to sag. The twenty Indians designated to go to Washington and lobby for Sequoyah did not show up. What blows Governor Brown was able to strike were quiet and behind the scenes. Courtland Long aggressively did stalk the marble halls, buttonholing Representatives and Senators.

But the State of Sequoyah was a lost cause. The Indians were too small for a big fight. The Great Father always, always won every battle against the Five Tribes. And now President Roosevelt effectively vanquished the Sequoyah scheme by recommending to Congress on November 17, 1905 the admission of Indian Territory and Oklahoma Territory as a single state. That did it.

The Congress, following his lead, enacted the necessary legislation. President Roosevelt would sign the measure on June 16, 1906, bringing in Oklahoma on November 16, 1907 as the forty-sixth state.

IN THE MONTHS just prior to statehood becoming reality, Governor Brown found himself pacing the floor, excited, frustrated, and worried. If it weren't for being a preacher, he might be swearing. He felt hot anger over last-minute dirty tricks pulled by the Government.

199

In usual cavalier fashion, Washington was ripping apart its pledge to treat fairly the Seminoles even though the tribe was bowing down and submitting to Oklahoma law. Back in 1898, a treaty had been signed containing solemn guarantees; spelled out were regulations for allotment of land and distribution of property and funds of the Seminole Nation, notably money for education. Now Congress had arbitrarily rewritten at least six parts of the agreement.

On bright mornings when he gazed out his mansion's windows, breathing in the air perfumed by his peach and cherry trees, Governor Brown felt he had a sense of what had gone wrong. In Washington was a clique of stiff-necked senators, mostly Easterners, who had never once set foot on the grassy prairies and rolling hills that his eyes at this moment found so beautiful. These legislators didn't understand the territory—certainly not Indian life, and knew little of the Seminoles' true dreams and aspirations, nor could truly feel the depth of their chagrin and regret over the loss of their traditional way of life. The Congress, in its blind way, simply was meddling, hurting his people. And for what reason? On his scores of trips to Washington he had seen these men up close. Constantly they played—and selfishly worried about—partisan politics. Right now the Republican Party was afraid the Democrats might seize the new state, and was scrambling to not be out-maneuvered. What better way than to toady to Oklahoma's white citizens who far outnumbered its red men?

Moreover, from his long dealings with the Dawes Commission, Governor Brown realized the Great Father was suspicious of Indians, believed their leaders slick connivers and the majority of tribesmen lazy and backward.

Governor Brown realized, of course, that he was personally responsible for causing some of the Congressional suspicion. Government investigations were still digging into two of his business transactions involving the tribe. No final determinations had yet been made about his $12,000 purchase from the Seminole National Council of the Wewoka town site lots. In the second incident, the Interior Department had taken hundreds of pages of testimony about the way Governor Brown's trading post was handed a lop-sided chunk of the Civil War claims money supposed to go to "loyal"

200

Seminoles. The Justice Department was still debating whether to attempt to reclaim certain payments that went to the Wewoka Trading Company.

In altering the 1898 treaty, Governor Brown asserted in a formal protest filed in Washington, the Congress had overstepped its powers and violated the Constitution of the United States.

One of his objections was that the Government decided to take sole control of the operation and funding of Indian schools.

And why should it require an act of Congress to permit any Indian to sell his homestead land until he had held it for twenty-five years?

Also why should all United States warrants issued after January 1, 1907 be approved by the United States inspector and paid by the Indian agent instead of through the treasurer of the Seminole Nation?

These were the principal complaints raised by the Seminole chief. The Congress and Interior Department did the expected. They referred all questions to the Department of Justice for determination.

Governor Brown was just hollering down the well. He didn't win on a single objection. The United States Attorney General rendered an opinion in the Spring of 1907 that the Congress had acted within its powers on all these matters. [3]

The Seminole chief then either just gave up his fight, or merely became ambivalent about this struggle. In Washington the first week of March 1907, he was interviewed at the Ebbitt House by a reporter for the *Washington Herald*. [4]

"Our people are getting on very well," Governor Brown said. "I do not apprehend that we will suffer by the creation of the new state of Oklahoma, of which the Seminole Country will become a part."

On his own, the reporter reported that talk indicated the Indians should be recognized by "allowing" them one of the new Oklahoma senators, and "friends of Brown hope to see him come to Washington in that capacity."

These so-called "friends" were talking through their hats. Those who really knew Governor Brown fully understood he had such low regard for the United States Senate that he would never willingly sit as a member for a minute.

His major work in this period was making certain the Seminole reservation was divided up in such a way that each tribesman received a fair share. It was not easy. First, the terrain varied widely, ranging from prime pasture prairie to rock-strewn, brush-clogged hills. The land was appraised into three classes, depending on fertility of the soil and location: first, at $5 an acre; second, $2.50; and third, at $1.25.

Each of the 3,049 Seminoles—2,099 of Indian blood and 950 Negro freedmen—was given a forty-acre homestead of the best class, plus a total of 120 additional acres of the poorer land. Of the $5 land, 24,055 acres valued at $120,279 were allotted. Second and third class, respectively, totaled 248,837 acres at $622,094, and 96,961 acres at $121,201.

To this grand total of 369,854 acres worth $863,574 was added 18,993 acres reserved for schools and churches and children born after the rolls were closed. (The Seminoles were by far the smallest of the Five Tribes, the Creeks numbering 12,000 and the Cherokees 50,000.)

Governor Brown went to Muskogee and personally signed each of the Seminole deeds after extinguishment of the tribal government. The homestead forty acres could not be sold or taxed. But the other acreage could be sold or, with the approval of the chief, leased to non-citizens for up to six years.

When it came to assigning acreage to the newborns, a small controversy flared up. How could this be done fairly? Governor Brown solved the dilemma. Paper slips bearing all the babies' names were put in a hat. The tribal stenographer drew them out; it became the luck of the draw.

ALICE BROWN DAVIS, at her desk as the superintendent of Emahaka Academy, set her jaw, squared her shoulders, and got ready for a fight. The Government was trying to take the girls boarding school away from the Seminoles.

She would not stand for it! [5]

This was more of the pre-statehood meddling by higher-ups in Washington. They were determined, she knew in her bones, to unmercifully beat down the Indians.

Her harried brother was staying up nights, and having to dodge, twist, and squirm to resist five or six other injustices to the tribe. He was about whipped. But she was not. Alice had blood in her eye.

Her enemy was just as determined, and far more powerful. Interior Secretary Ethan Allen Hitchcock sent fair warning. He would order police to drag her away from Emahaka, if necessary.

The trouble began shortly after she was hired in May 1906 to succeed the Reverend William Packer Blake, the academy's only superintendent since it opened in 1894. Blake, who had known Alice and the whole Brown family for two decades, had recommended her for the position.

A Pennsylvanian, Blake had come to Indian Territory in 1887 at age thirty as a Baptist missionary to the Indians, and to supervise the Sasakwa girls school, where Alice was briefly a young teacher. He resigned the Emahaka post to resume fulltime Indian missionary work.

Alice had the educator skills and business experience to run the girls school. She was hired by the Seminole National Council; in effect, by her brother. That was not the main conflict. The problem was that Washington "experts" wanted to dumb down the Indian curriculum. To teach the girls less music and poetry and the boys not so much history and art.

With statehood diminishing the tribal government, the Interior Department intended to take over all Indian Territory schools on March 4, 1906. However, two days before that deadline, Congress voted to extend the governments of all the Five Civilized Tribes until the necessary work of signing allotment deeds, etc. could be completed. Governor Brown immediately took the position that this action extended the Seminole Nation's rights, and thus permitted the tribe to retain control of its schools.

Congress resisted, and quickly got an attorney general's opinion confirming that the Interior Secretary could legally take over the Indian schools. That merely intensified the conflict. Alice refused to back down.

The "War Over Emahaka" might never have erupted had someone other than John D. Benedict, a supercilious politician from Illinois, been appointed by President William McKinley as superintendent of schools in Indian Territory. Benedict got the job as a protégé of the powerful House Speaker "Uncle Joe" Cannon, also from Illinois. Benedict was too autocratic and out of touch with frontier life. As historian Edwin C. McReynolds put it, Benedict

> "...was not thoroughly prepared for the task. He could see weaknesses in the educational attainment of the Indian children and adults, but he lacked the imagination to grasp the full extent of the progress made by many of them in the brief period of their contact with books and the process of learning. He found teachers and superintendents in the boarding schools, with many years of service behind them, whom he regarded as incompetent by the standards of the teachers in the schools of his own state.
> He wanted to change the character of the courses offered, with emphasis upon cooking, sewing and housekeeping for girls; farming, carpentry and the care of livestock for boys. He wanted to eliminate nepotism and tribal politics from the choice of teachers and administrators in the schools." [6]

There was nothing wrong, in Alice's opinion, with the way Emahaka Academy was educating Seminole girls. Being a friend of the Blake family, she had often visited the boarding school. Her own daughters had attended Emahaka, and she knew first hand the good effect of the school's broad and balanced studies.

Alice had been in charge six months and already had the boarding school, located five miles south of Wewoka, humming into its winter term with 112 students before the contest over Emahaka control accelerated into a crisis.

On November 3, 1906, Benedict reported to the Interior Secretary that Alice would not surrender the school. Benedict had sent a Government supervisor from Muskogee to Wewoka to explain to Alice and to the Seminole Council "that their schools would have to be conducted in accordance with the new rules and regulations of the Secretary of the Interior." [7]

That meant the federal government would employ and pay all needed teachers and staff. Alice was offered the opportunity to submit a bid for furnishing board, fuel, lights and stationery.

The supervisor might as well have remained in Muskogee. Alice paid him no heed. Benedict lamented: "Mrs. Davis went ahead and appointed all her employees, several of whom were members of her own family, fixed their salaries herself, and went ahead with her school totally regardless of all instructions we had given her."[8]

Instead of submitting a bid, Alice sent Benedict an estimate of the cost of provisions required to maintain her school during the year. This came to $11,500, one thousand dollars of which was her salary. He heard directly nothing further from her, but learned Alice was going ahead "with her school, conducting it in accordance with Seminole customs, buying whatever provisions she thinks are needed and charging the same to the Seminole Nation."[9]

Governor Brown's flagging spirits were revived by his sister's determined stand. The chief directed the Seminole Nation attorneys, Wilmott and Wilhoit of Wewoka, to file a brief in Washington challenging the take-over.

The "war" going on over Emahaka Academy caught the attention of Territory editors. *The Muskogee Times-Democrat* reported on November 12, 1906 that the attorney general had confirmed the Interior Department's authority, and thus "it would be illegal for the Seminoles to keep the school because they would have no right to pay money out of the tribal funds for its support." The newspaper added:

> All other schools but this one have been turned over to the Interior Department. Gov. Brown's sister is principal of it and his brother is tribal treasurer, so it seems to be a family affair, and they don't like to give it up.
>
> Since Supt. Benedict is backed by a decision from the attorney general, the Indian police will be used to take possession of the school forcibly if it isn't given up.

The nepotism criticism was enhanced by *The Purcell Register* in the Chickasaw Nation, which pointed out that a fourth immediate family member was involved. Governor Brown's brother Stanton was tribal superintendent of schools.

"No difficulty," the newspaper said, "has been experienced under the new plan except in the Seminole nation . . . at the Emahaka Academy. All of the schools in the five nations are in session. The

205

government shows a determination to assert its authority in the Seminole Nation, declaring that the tribal authority no longer exists." [10]

Even so, Alice was headstrong and would not bend.

The chief wanted to back her up. But he was wise and far-sighted. His administration was, in the opinion of the *Indian Citizen* newspaper, "the finest illustration of one-man-government the world has ever seen. Nothing was ever attempted in the Seminole Nation without his consent and approbation having been obtained." [11]

In this conflict, the Seminole chief extended himself by making a hurried trip to Washington to intervene directly with Interior Secretary Garfield, but apparently with no success. [12]

Governor Brown sat down with Alice and gently explained why they could not win this battle. She bridled at his decision, but gradually came to see that resistance was hopeless.

The chief promptly dispatched a letter to United States Indian Inspector J. G. Wright at Muskogee with the information that he had advised his sister to surrender Emahaka Academy to Superintendent Benedict. [13]

The Wewoka attorneys followed with a letter assuring Wright that the Seminole Nation would turn over the school "in a peaceable manner."

But Alice took her time about it. Finally, on a sunny afternoon she marched regally through the three floors, noting that the premises were neat, orderly and clean. Then she went out the front door, and stood for a long moment, muttering a prayer. She descended the steps to her buggy and rode away. [14]

In the aftermath, Benedict had to eat a little crow. When Alice submitted her final claim for service at Emahaka, he leaped on it with critical eyes. But he could find nothing to challenge. He scribbled on his O.K., and ordered the bill paid from tribal funds.

However, Benedict got in one final jab. He added a notation that Alice had "purchased provisions and quite a good deal of furniture from the Wewoka Trading Company, a company owned and controlled largely by Seminole officials." [15]

Ultimately Emahaka Academy would be abandoned in 1914. (The imposing but empty building would be destroyed by an accidental fire on June 6, 1927.)

ON SATURDAY, November 16, 1907, in the capital city of Guthrie, thousands paraded and frolicked in the streets to signal statehood. First came a telegram from President Roosevelt. He had officially signed the Oklahoma Constitution. That launched a flurry of festivities. Charles N. Haskell, forty-seven, a turncoat single-stater and "railroad" lawyer from Ohio, was sworn in as governor. A smiling Indian princess wearing a buckskin dress, beaded moccasins, with a feather in her glistening black braids mounted a public stage. A cowboy with a happy grin gently seized her hand. Forward stepped a "preacher" in swallow-tailed coat and "married" them. This elaborate mock ritual was supposed to signify the union of the two territories. Merry-makers cavorted, and didn't cease their hooting and hollering until long past the next sunrise.

All of this Alice learned from afar. She remained quietly at home in Wewoka. It was now, of course, Wewoka, county seat of Seminole County, state of Oklahoma—no longer an Indian territory under tribal control.

In pensive mood, she spent much of statehood day taking stock of the changed order. [16] How would this affect her life? What will happen to her family? Most Indians, she realized, already were mystified by the white man's laws and customs. The intricacies of being citizens of the state of Oklahoma was bound to confuse them all the more. For her own family, Alice could foresee nothing that would be too detrimental.

Alice was now fifty-five years old. Looking back, at times it seemed much longer. Her life was not easy. Since betrayal by her husband a decade ago, she had borne responsibilities too burdensome for one parent, a woman alone in rough country.

When the Arbeka Trading Post and the Bar X Bar ranch flourished, meeting the financial requirements of large family had been no problem. It was different now, and had been for some years. What resources remained after her divorce from Roll had been eaten up; and the demise of the open range had also been the death knell for their cattle ranch and subsequently the Arbeka store. That shut her off from steady income.

To support her family now, Alice operated as a catch-as-catch-can businesswoman. Mainly she capitalized on her strong constitution, her keen understanding of commercial practices, and her superior skill in the back-and-forth interpreting and translating of language and custom differences between the whites and Indians.

She, as her diaries described it, "went to town" every day and counted on having good luck. [17] Her earnings did not sink quite to hardscrabble depths, but they were meager. Most frequently she acted as an interpreter in the courts or for federal bureaucrats. Lawyers called on her regularly for dealing with their Seminole clients. For many small tasks she was paid merely one dollar. There were as well twenty-five dollar fees, but the daily accounts she recorded in her diaries do not show an abundance of the larger payments.

Alice kept a sharp eye on the future. She had experienced an "awakening" at the 1904 St. Louis World's Fair, seeing the new inventions—motorcars, electric broilers, irons, printing equipment, medical instruments, other gadgets that dazzled the insular mind. The Twentieth Century was offering great opportunities, but would demand more of achievers. She was determined that her children would be equipped for the challenge with good health, education, social graces, the development of any latent musical or artistic talent they possessed. [18] Some daughters she sent to North Texas Female College and Kidd-Key Conservatory of Music and Art, a fashionable "finishing school" in Sherman, Texas. From Kansas City, she ordered a $650 grand piano so the girls could learn to play, and squabbled with the dealer for four years over paying for it. [19] Mrs. Kidd-Key threatened to halt one girl's graduation unless Alice kept her promise to pay the long overdue final $280.55 tuition. To square the bill, Alice talked the school ma'am into taking title to piece of her rugged Oklahoma prairie land; Mrs. Kidd-Key complained later the tract was worthless.

In financial emergencies, Alice would trudge to the Wewoka bank and mortgage her cow, her horse, and perhaps a sow to get a $100 short-term loan. The money crises were almost always triggered by her children's needs or problems. Alice spent little on herself. Her diaries rarely contained her private thoughts; mainly they were account books showing her daily income and expenses. One telltale sign of her struggle were notations of receipts for eggs she sold wholesale to the Wewoka Trading Company. (Like other householders, Alice kept a fenced-in hen house.) One day an entry: "eggs 90c" and the next: "eggs 75c."[20] Her brothers, Governor John and Treasurer Jackson, were without doubt the Seminole Nation's wealthiest; but there is no evidence they offered Alice any extraordinary financial assistance. At least nothing monetarily significant is revealed in a search of family correspondence and memoirs. Alice was known for extreme pride as well as being staunchly self-reliant. It might be that she would have resented and rejected excessive bailout from anyone.

In 1907 Alice was saddled with responsibility for only five of the eleven children she had borne; the others were out of the nest. Her first, Katie, had died an infant. George Lytle had been lynched in 1899, leaving his widow Julia and daughter Pearl, a now thirteen-year-old whiz kid who became a favorite of her grandmother. They still lived on part of the old ranch at Arkeba.

Daughter Clara Estella (1877-1956), known as Kitt, about to turn thirty, had just married for the second time. From her marriage to Charles D. Barricklow, she had a son, Clarence. On February 14, 1907 she married Howard Twinam, forty, a rancher and lawman who would serve several terms as Seminole County sheriff. Kitt was destined for a rather mundane life, which would take her to Ardmore and three or four other Oklahoma towns, including Paden, where for a brief time she operated a hat store.

Jesse Edwin (1879-1921) remained a cowboy his entire life and never strayed from his homestead at Arbeka, the allotment he drew as a quarter-blood Seminole. From his marriage to Ella Knight on May 12, 1899 came five sons and one daughter, between 1900 and 1909.

Laura Myrtle (1883-1969), called by her middle name, had on August 27, 1901 married young Eugene Clinton Aldridge (1876-1966), who was destined for a rewarding career as a capitalist, building several Oklahoma hotels. For several years he would be Wewoka's mayor, first elected in 1925.

Ella Maynie (1885-1962), known as Maye, had married just that summer, on July 22. Her husband was Ben Davis Locke of Antlers, brother of Victor M. Locke, chief of the Choctaw tribe. Both men were half blood Choctaws; their mother was an Indian and their father a white pioneer merchant.

Still at home on statehood day were daughters Flora Maude (1887-1932), called Maude; Elizabeth Marguerite (1889-1979), called Bess; and Irene Genevieve (1892-1969); and sons John Frippo (1893-1962) and Andrew Jackson (1898-1972) known as Jackson, or Jack, or his stage name Dennis Thornton.

Maude was in love with a handsome cattle trader, Madison Cocke Jones of Okemah, and they would be married September 20, 1909, and have a daughter, Joycette, in 1911, and two years later a son, Madison Junior. Madison Senior would enter politics and be elected court clerk of Okfuskee County in 1916. Maude was to win attention as a notable soprano, skilled musician and songwriter. She was the most universally talented of the Davis girls. Not only did she serve as translator (with her mother) for the Dawes Commission, she developed into a prolific writer of Indian lore and history. She had become fluent in the Seminole tongue by deliberately getting demerits when attending Emahaka Academy so as punishment she would be detailed to the laundry where she could spend time with the native hired girls working over the tubs, and learn the language from them.

Elizabeth Marguerite, always called Bess, would marry on May 15, 1914, Vernon Lee Kiker, an Alabamian who had come to Wewoka to teach school. Kiker would become deputy treasurer of Seminole County but run afoul of the law in 1916. Indicted for embezzling $807.65 in county funds, he would plead guilty, and be fined $2,000 and sentenced to three years in prison. By 1924 he had reclaimed his good name, becoming a wealthy oil and gas operator, and serving eight years in the Oklahoma Legislature. He and Bess had three sons and a daughter. And of all Alice's sons-in-laws, Vernon seems to have contributed the most to bolster Alice's sagging finances.

Irene Genevieve met William Shaffer Key when he came to Wewoka from Alabama to enter the hardware business. They were married May 5, 1914 when she was twenty-two and he twenty-five. Shooting up from private through the ranks of the Oklahoma National Guard, he became the major general commanding the 45th Infantry Division in World War II. He also was for a few years warden of the Oklahoma Penitentiary. He was a 33rd degree Mason. The Keys had two sons and a daughter.

Alice's two youngest sons made her life miserable. To the day of her death, both drowned her with sad tales of their misfortunes and poverty, and hounded her for money, which she rarely had. This was especially true during the Depression. They also got her involved in their romantic misadventures—fortunately most all of this by mail, but their tragic episodes ripped their mother's sensitive heart.

Worst of the two sons, by far, was John—arguably the most wanton and worthless of all the Davis family. For a time the boys were enrolled in Sacred Heart Boys School near Shawnee, run by Benedictine monks. Hard-up Alice found paying their way a real struggle. The school mailed her Jack's bill for $10.85, with a typed note: "Why do we not hear from you?" [21]

By eighteen, John had left home to wander haphazardly the rest of his life, staying in touch by mail with his mother, but seeing her only a time or two a year. Rarely did he hold a job, and those usually were as dishwasher or something else menial. He was adept at wooing shop girls, sponging off them, and then deserting them, leaving a few pregnant. He stole from friends and strangers, forged checks on his mother, got in scrapes with the law, and stiffed hotels and pawn brokers across a dozen states. When it served his purpose, he could exude charm. In 1914 he was sent to the Oklahoma Hospital for the Insane at Norman. Released after a few weeks, he resumed his wandering and scamming life.

At Sacred Heart, Jack had the good fortune to be taught to play the cornet by a friendly monk. That musical ability was his entrance ticket to a life spent in the world of tent shows traveling the small towns. After a brief stint in a theater orchestra, Jack was on the stage by age eighteen as a leading man. The stage became his life. He hopped from one touring company to another, and married four of his leading ladies. He starred in two or three one-reel western movies shot in Montana, and felt he had a chance at the big time. He adopted the name Dennis Thornton for showbiz fame. But celebrity eluded him; he was never more than a struggling tent-show actor and occasional horn player.

On that historic Saturday morning in November 1907 while the telegraph key was clacking out Teddy Roosevelt's message to go ahead and start Oklahoma's statehood festivities, back in Wewoka

Alice sat down at her table and opened her diary. Her scrawl is difficult to read, especially when she used a blunt pencil.[22] This day she wrote:

Saturday, 16th day of November 1907

Will clean house and make beds if Lizzie comes.
Will go to town today and extend my note at the bank for thirty days.

Paid grocery bill in full	10.00
Collected	1.00
Paid water & light bill	2.00
Got Nokusella out of jail	11.50
Bess	3.00
Eggs	.60
Paid Lizzie for taking things to Kitt	4.00
Will write letters today.	
Balance on hand	21.30

Alice closed her humble little book, and went out the back door to feed and water her chickens. It was a beautiful Indian summer day, an appropriate salute to the birth of the forty-sixth state.

This brown-skinned woman with her hair piled in a bun dipped cracked corn out of a rusty tin pie pan and scattered the grain in the chicken yard. She would have been thunderstruck if she had then the least inkling that Oklahoma history would one day elevate her to a top rung.

Alice Brown Davis knew not. Nor did any other living soul—that she was to become chief of the Seminole tribe. Not when, and really not why.

Jackson Brown (*left*) and Governor Brown set high sartorial standards in their public appearance.

Photographed near the turn of the 19th Century, members of the famed Seminole Lighthorse police line up in the street, with members of the Seminole Council standing on the porch.

Photos courtesy THE SEMINOLE NATION MUSEUM
and Gene and Martha Aldridge

Street scene in Sasakwa in the late 1800s.

Governor Brown's mansion near the old Sasakwa.

215

Mekusukey Academy for boys, south of present Seminole. It was identical to Emahaka, the girls' school.

An atypical scene of a Seminole woman carrying a papoose.

Identical towers used on both Emahaka and Mekusukey.

In one hunting camp, Jackson Brown (*center*) displays his deer kill.

Affluent members of the tribe favored buggies.

Members of the Brown-Davis families enjoy a sunset on a rocky bluff on the western edge of Wewoka. Alice (*front row center*) is shown with (*front row*) Mrs. Andrew Jackson Brown, and Mrs.S. H. Miller, holding Eugene Miller. (*Back row, from left*) Charles Miller, Clarence Borden, Clarence Miller, Donny Morgan, Edith Morgan and Maye Davis.

Stanton Brown (*center*) pictured with his family - wife Julia and children. He served as Superintendent of Seminole Schools under his brother John's administration.

The Frisco railroad station in "new" Sasakwa.

Family members gather for the funeral of Governor Brown's son, John W., shown (*center*) in his casket.

Tribal burial practices included building "houses" atop Seminole graves. This is a scene near Wewoka at the turn of the 19th century.

221

Advent of the railroad brought excitement to Wewoka. Here, presidential candidate William Jennings Bryan (*in doorway of train*) stumps on a whistle-stop tour.

On market days, main streets were clogged with farmers and ranchers and horses and wagons.

The Seminole Nation "whipping tree" still stands on the lawn of the county courthouse in Wewoka. This photo was used as the front cover of *The American Bar Association Journal* issue of April 1972.

Indian tribes played a violent game of "stickball." Females stood on the sideline and often had to nurse and bandage injured players. The games lasted hours. Bones were frequently broken and on occasion players died of their injuries.

Thomas McGeisey (*seated center*) was a Seminole tribal official and confidant of Governor Brown. His son, Lincoln, was burned to death by a white mob in 1898, falsely accused of killing a Seminole county settler's wife. Standing are two members of the Seminole Tribal Council.

224

One fad in the 1920s was to play "dress-up" Indians. Here is Bess (Mrs. Vernon Kiker) on the left, with a friend.

At church camp meetings and ceremonies such as the Green Corn Dance, the Seminoles built outdoor thatched pavilions for protection from the elements.

Governor Brown's trading post at the first Sasakwa, before the Frisco railroad caused him to move and establish a new town.

Postcard image showing the first Wewoka Trading Company built in Wewoka. It was replaced by a larger, more modern structure in 1902.

Under drifting clouds in a somber sky, in the solitude of the vast windy prairie, the intriguing beauty of Governor Brown's mansion could have beckoned the inspired brush of any western landscape artist.

Photos courtesy Gene and Martha Aldridge
and THE SEMINOLE NATION MUSEUM

227

13

Heartbreak in Love and War

THE INDIAN GIRLS smiled and chattered as they piled a thick mat of palmetto leaves on the swampy ground before spreading blankets. That, they explained to Alice, would keep her bed dry. They were straightening up a thatch hut in a village midway between Lake Okeechobee and the Atlantic Coast town of West Jupiter, Florida.

This was the first week of October 1909. Alice had come to Florida with missionaries to enlighten those Seminoles who had refused to leave the Everglades. An odd thought struck her; these natives fixing her living quarters could be kin from her mother's lineage.

"If I wrote all day I could not tell you all the strange things we have seen," she said in a letter to folks back in Wewoka.[1]

Her brother Jackson had organized and financed this expedition of eleven Baptist Seminoles from Oklahoma—and came close to paying a horrible price for his Christian effort. The Florida Indians, who had remained basically hostile to whites, became suspicious because his complexion was light and his speech different. Two braves, Alice wrote, "threatened to cut his tongue out." [2] Wise heads intervened, and friendship was established.

Alice found the Florida tribe "a curiosity," their talk not easy to understand. Going to the Atlantic shore for her first sight of the

228

ocean—"God's handiwork"— enthralled her. She behaved like a tourist, writing that she bought a packet of 200-year-old beads and two buckskin dresses. [3] Hunters killed two deer, and she bought venison at fifteen cents a pound—"very expensive eating."

With Alice was her daughter Irene, seventeen. Jackson brought his wife Manie Lou and their granddaughter Lucy, ten years old. The others, from Wewoka and Sasakwa, were the Rev. Daniel Long, Sissy Long, Mr. and Mrs. George Scott, Lizzie Bruner, and an interpreter *Nokociloght* (John Wesley).

After a month of preaching, the missionary party returned by train to Wewoka, feeling they had made religious inroads. Joe Bowers, a trader who had been their go-between with the Everglades Indians, corresponded frequently with Alice. "Glad you got back okay," Bowers wrote. [4] "After you left the Indians killed a brown bear. Tell me the name of that herb medicine you want and I will try to find it. I saw DeSoto Tiger a few days ago and he said he and Sam Jones wanted to visit you this summer."

A few months later: "We had a severe storm. Water was sixteen inches deep in the house you people stopped in, and eight feet deep in the orange groves where you got grapefruit." [5]

Jackson Brown's interest in religion had intensified. He erected a new Baptist church in Wewoka for his preacher brother-in-law Major James Factor. For his own family he put up the largest house in Wewoka, a two-story mansion that was a junior edition of Governor Brown's Sasakwa palace.

Alice found her brother Stanton, superintendent of tribal schools, going in the opposite direction. She heard tales and sent a letter upbraiding him. He responded with thanks for her "reproof and sound advice," adding:

> I have indeed indulged too much. . . which infected me morally, mentally and physically and had it not been for the strong constitution I was gifted with I could have filled my grave long since.
>
> While I may have lost all honor and respect among relatives and friends, it is great consolation to perceive that the Creator has held watchfulness over me. Before it is too late I resolve to come to him as the Prodigal Son, humbly and repentant of many grievous sins and pleading most urgently for forgiveness. [6]

229

For the remainder of his life, which at times became dangerously aggressive and violent, Stanton would come to rely heavily on Alice as a calming influence and moral compass.

In 1910 Alice went back to Mexico as interpreter for a Seminole Nation delegation once more going south of the border to again try to reclaim the land grants Mexico awarded Wild Cat in 1850. Her party reached Mexico City on the day a revolution erupted. Repressed peons and Indians took up muskets and machetes against President Profirio Diaz and would keep the country in bloody turmoil for six years. Alice's group hastily left the Mexican capital, but vowed to return and pursue their quest after the revolt ended.

Her patient competence and enormous compassion usually thrust Alice into central roles in most "situations" in the Brown family. She proved caring and long suffering. Especially with her sons Jack and John. For more than twenty-five years, her heart, her purse, and her ingenuity would be called on with devastating frequency to overcome, solve, or stave off their struggles and escapades.

In May 1910 Alice got an unexpected letter from her lynched son's widow, Julia. "Please help me sell my heifer. Try for twenty dollars. I have to have an operation." [7] Julia, thirty-five, was admitted to the Oklahoma Methodist Episcopal Hospital and Training School at Guthrie. She looked her surgeon in the eye: "You'll have to bring me through—so I can keep working and pay you."[8] Her room cost ten dollars a week and the operating room three dollars. Her uterus and left ovary and a large tumor were removed, and she recovered.

By coincidence, Julia's sister Victoria wound up in the same hospital for the same surgery a few months later; by propinquity Alice learned of her plight. Even though Victoria had destroyed Alice's marriage to Roll, Alice felt compassion for her. [9] Victoria Davis underwent three drastic surgeries, suffered terribly, and finally died on May 12, 1912, leaving a seventeen-year-old son and her distraught husband Roll, sixty-three.

Another family tragedy that weighed heavily on Alice was the mental breakdown of her sister Lucy, the most beautiful of Dr. Brown's daughters, and known as Sukey, and married to Alexander Wills Crain, one of Governor Brown's business partners in Sasakwa. Because of erratic behavior she was committed at age sixty-three to

230

an institution in Canton, South Dakota known as the Asylum for Insane Indians. Alice stayed in touch by mail. From the asylum on January 4, 1913, Sukey wrote:

> Dear Sister:
> I received your letter of December 12, 1912. Glad to hear from you. I haven't heard from home since September. You tell them to write to me. Tell Mr. Crain to write me and come to see me soon.
> I have numbness in my feet and head, and a sore tightening in my stomach that is very disagreeable. I don't rest at all. There is nothing being done for me here. Do come and take me home. I don't want to die here.

At Alice's urging, Alexander Crain visited his wife, but her pleas to come home went unheeded. Lucy Brown Crain died there April 25, 1915, and was brought back to Wewoka for burial.

Most certainly Alice's son John was born with a mental deficit. His brothers and sisters believed that to be true. The pattern of his adult behavior confirmed his peccancy, instability, and moral corruptness. He left Wewoka at seventeen, and never again truly came home. The sly boots lifestyle he created was astounding, almost unbelievable.

A precursor of John's career as a cheat and con man is clearly visible in a letter Alice received March 27, 1911 from a family friend, Gus G. LeCompte of Holdenville, official district court reporter. In Oklahoma City, LeCompte ran across John, whom he knew, at the Huckins Hotel. While LeCompte was absent, John obtained a key to his room and stole a new pair of patent leather pumps, silk hose, and a necktie, and tried to return them to the store for cash. "I didn't want to cause embarrassment," LeCompte wrote. "But this is a penitentiary offense. Unless I am reimbursed eight dollars, I will file charges." Alice, of course, sent him the money. This was just the first of several hundred scams John would pull.

The handsome boy had easy sway with shop clerks or creatures of the demimonde. When John pursued Inez Womack in Oklahoma City in 1912 his mother was kept informed by the smitten girl's letters. A pattern clerk in a dry goods store, Inez was about John's age, nineteen.

231

When they broke up in early 1913, Inez gave John her last 35 cents and he went to Tulsa where he was arrested for stealing a suitcase and pawning its contents. Inez rushed to Tulsa and wrote Alice:

> If you can't get the $75, I will try to get it. Please let me know. I know I can help him some way. I think he will be a different boy after this. I had to come home. You know I love him and would do anything in the wide world for him. [10]

On May 26, 1913 while visiting sister Maude in Okemah, John stole a man's pants and overcoat. Alice sent the victim $4, and he didn't prosecute. John bummed around from Denver to Kansas City, where on Aug 10, 1913 he wrote his mother:

> Dearest Mother:
> I didn't ask you for any ticket. I ask you for money. Now if you can't send things when I want them, why we can't agree. So I guess you people had better drop me because I don't care about hearing from you.
> I think you owe me money for the land you beat me out of. I just wasn't old enough to know, that was all ...Don't worry about me. I can get along some way and if I get in trouble, that is just my misfortune.

John returned briefly to Oklahoma City, and to Inez. Her trust and affection were poorly placed. On February 5, 1914, Inez wrote Alice:

> I am sick and must have an operation. I haven't as much money as I need. Can you make a loan to me of $25? I will pay it back the first of June. Johnny hurts me awful bad to think he doesn't care enough. He knows I'd give him my last penny, and do without. One day you will understand everything. If you can help me, remember I will pay you back.

On February 11, 1914, Inez again wrote:

> Your letter came this morning. I am sorry you couldn't help me. I guess I will just have to give up. I have worried until I am

just crazy. The operation I must have will save me from disgrace. I can't write it all on paper, but someday I will tell you all. Mother said if we could get $25 she would sell her furniture to get the rest. I would be only one week in a private hospital. My room would cost $25 and the doctor is $25. I hope you don't blame me, for I am a good true and pure girl. You have daughters of your own and if they were deceived, you couldn't turn them down. Pray for me. Please destroy this letter.

Alice heard nothing further from Inez until October 9, 1914. "I wrote you last winter... I have lots to tell that I can't write... I am so blue. I certainly feel sorry for Johnny. I thought maybe he'd change. I'm crazy to see him."

Her "Johnny" did not change. Inez saw him on an Oklahoma City street on December 3 "and he passed like he doesn't know me. Never even spoke. . ."

The nine-month gap in Inez Womack's 1914 correspondence with Alice—from her attempt to raise money for her abortion to early October—covers much of the time John spent in the Oklahoma Hospital for the Insane at Norman and the aftermath.

The available written record of his confinement begins on April 23, 1914, when John grabbed asylum stationery and in pencil wrote Alice:

Dearest Mother:
I arrived here this p.m. and sure am lonesome. I want you to come and see me at once. I have something very important to tell you so please come. And if you can't, please tell sister Irene to come. Mama, you don't know how it is to be in a place like this. So please be sure and come.

As ever, your son,
Jno F. Davis

Alice did not go to Norman. She had pressing matters at home. Her two unmarried daughters had just announced their engagements, Irene to marry William S. Key on May 5, and Bess to marry Vernon Lee Kiker on June 7. "I do hope Bill Key will be good to Irene,"

233

Maye wrote Alice. "She is an unusually deserving girl. She can be all that a good wife means to an ambitious man. . . she will not expect a continuous honeymoon." [11]

Alice mailed John a new suit of clothes. He thanked her in a May 5 letter, begging: "I am not crazy. I don't know why you want to keep me in a place like this. Come and get me out." By July 25 he had been released and had a job at a power plant in Kansas City apparently arranged by Irene's new husband. John was soon fired; he couldn't even hold a job as dishwasher.

By enmeshing Alice in his wretched life, John drowned her in despair, frustration and shame. Alice saved each of his letters, filing them in an empty shoebox. Examining the hundreds written by John over a span of two decades reveals the selfsame dismal scenario. Some years were a little worse than 1914 or a little better, but not by much.

Once Alice even called on Roll to get their son out of a jam. He wrote her March 31, 1915 from Cushing, Oklahoma:

> Dear Alice:
>
> I got here yesterday morning. Found John all OK. Nothing the matter with him only wanting a little money. He claimed his suitcase was held for $1.85 at a hotel here. I paid it out and we will start home this A.M. He says he don't want to go to Wewoka. I will take him to Castle [*where Roll lived*] for a few days. He wants to go to OK City. Write or call us at Castle Thursday.
>
> Yours as ever, G.R. Davis

There was a significant difference between John and Jack in their whining to mother for money. Jack's came less frequently and not as outrageously demanding as his brother's. Even so, Jack felt his mother was obligated to help him. That was demonstrated in this letter written June 15, 1911 while still in his teens yearning to become a musician and actor:

> After paying my debts, I'm still in the hole. If you can send me even $2 it would help. . . If you could give me a start believe I could make some kind of riser. . . If you will send me $50 I will

234

> try to double it in two months, and if I fail to do so I will never ask you for another cent as long as I live. You have let the girls have that amount. Why not trust me once more? It is nothing more than fair. Maybe you would see the boys are not as unworthy as you think.

Playing the cornet, which he learned at Sacred Heart, opened the way for Jack to become a tent show musician. By the summer of 1913 he was in Texas with the Worthen and Allen Shows, whose leading lady was a pretty brunette named Ione McBride. Jack's one-quarter Seminole blood, thick black hair, flashing dark eyes and athletic build did not escape Ione's eye. She suggested he lay aside the horn and try acting. Jack became her leading man, both on and off stage. They were married around Valentine's Day 1914 when he was nineteen.

Jack and Ione jumped from one cheap tent show to another. From Shawnee on January 17, 1915, he wrote his mother he was "down to my last five cents" and asked for a loan. But at the end of the year, he got an unexpected "big break."

Their tent show hit Roundup, Montana, just as a film studio opened there. Answering a casting call, Jack got on at $30 a week to be the cowboy "hero" in one-reel westerns. The director praised his acting; Jack envisioned lifetime "success" in the movies. "Then, Mother, you will never have to work again, and can live with me." [12]

By the middle of January 1916, three or four westerns had been shot. The director went to New York to sell them. Jack stayed in Roundup and wrote two one-reel scenarios—featuring fierce mountain lions, a pretty girl in distress, and evil-looking two-gun desperadoes. But his screen acting bubble burst. The one-reelers didn't make it to the screen. Jack asked his mother for a $30 loan so he and Ione could get out of town and back on the tent show circuit.

FROM EIGHT HUNDRED MILES away, Pancho Villa in 1916 gave Alice something to worry about. Because of him two of her daughters were on the dangerous Rio Grande border. Maye Locke and Irene Key went along when their husbands were dispatched as National Guard commanders of troops sent to protect America from the Mexican insurgent's raids.

President Woodrow Wilson responded to Pancho Villa's deadly border attacks by sending General John J. (Black Jack) Pershing and U.S. soldiers after him. To help guard the Texas border, the Army called up Captain Ben Locke's Choctaw Indian cavalry from Antlers and Captain William S. Key's infantry from Wewoka.

While their husband were busy at nearby Army camps, Irene and Maye found life in rented rooms at San Benito, Texas dull. They learned to enjoy chili and tamales, and found tricks to defeat invasions of giant mosquitoes.

On September 14, 1916, Irene wrote her mother:

> It takes so long for your letters to reach us. Maye went down to Ben's camp and found your latest just laying on the clerk's desk. Thank you for the lovely tablecloth. I need things like that more than anything else. Billy says we will really build a home as soon as we get back. This tablecloth will be my starter. The lady's house where we stay is well supplied and we are near the camp.
>
> What do you think Maye and I did yesterday? We left the children with our Mexican woman and went over to Brownsville between trains and nearly walked our heads off and didn't get a thing. Dead tired from the trip. I don't think much of Brownsville as a place to shop. I prefer Holdenville. Got sunburned to death when I went in the water.

For a year American troops tried to chase down Pancho Villa, and failed. But the country's attention was turning away from the Mexican war, because America was on the verge of World War I.

In the midst of war gloom, Alice was shocked by disaster right in the heart of the family. It involved Bess's husband, Vernon Kiker, deputy treasurer of Seminole County. State auditors had praised his books as among the best. But on February 12, 1916, Kiker was indicted for embezzling county money back in 1914, a total of $807.65. [13] Bess's husband at first fought the charge, but on May 21, 1917, would plead guilty, be fined $2,000 and sentenced to three years in the Oklahoma penitentiary.

Then another hammer blow struck the family. On the afternoon of Wednesday, January 3, 1917, Jackson Brown dropped by for coffee and a chat with Alice. He was lonely; his wife Manie Lou and thirty-eight-year-old married daughter Becky Miller were in San Antonio to spend the winter. He was unusually talkative. Besides the weather, he discussed aging; within two months he would turn sixty-three. On leaving he kissed her cheek, with the familiar brush of his mustache. [14]

Next morning a neighbor discovered Jackson crumpled and sprawled at his gate, stiff and cold. The doctor concluded he had died during the night from a massive heart attack.

The funeral was held in his home the following Sunday. The Reverend Daniel Long of the Wewoka Indian Church, who had gone on Jackson's 1909 mission to the Everglades Indians, conducted the service. Interment was in Wewoka's municipal Oakwood Cemetery, with burial rites by the Wewoka Masonic lodge. On page one, the *Wewoka Capital-Democrat* reported:

> A unusually large crowd attended these services...Hundreds of people of all races and from many different towns were present as a mark of respect to this splendid man. . . The death of Mr. Brown was a decided shock to the people of Seminole County, as he seemed to be in excellent health. . . [15]

War fever was rising all across the country. President Wilson kept promising to keep America out of it. Alice was worried; if the United States did get drawn in, her two vagabond sons surely would be drafted. On April 6, 1917 President Wilson declared war on Germany. He recalled General Pershing from the futile Mexican adventure and ordered him go overseas and smash Kaiser Bill.

But the Davis boys went on bumbling through life, each whining to their hard-pressed mother, and safe from the draft for the time being.

From Kansas City, John wrote Alice that he was broke, but would "starve before I ever ask you for another cent as long as I live."[16] Jack mysteriously disappeared. He left Ione with their six-month-old son, named Andrew Jackson Davis, and no money. Ione retreated to her parents' home in Salt Lake City, and informed Alice on June 30, 1917 of her plight, asking help.

237

Alice did not hear from Jack until six weeks later. From Greensburg, Kansas, where he was with Karl Simpson's Comedians, he wrote:

> I haven't written Ione and baby since I've been with this show. . . Not being able to send them any money, I've been just too ashamed to let them know of my existence. If it were possible for me to go out of their lives without causing them to suffer, I would do it...Something always happens to keep me in debt and absolutely powerless to help them. My thoughts almost drive me insane. What would you advise me to do, Mama? [17]

One week later Alice sent him five dollars he needed to pay his musician union dues.

THE OUTBREAK OF WORLD WAR I triggered a bizarre and dangerous episode at Sasakwa that roused and directly involved Governor Brown. Being warned that a desperate army of night riders was approaching his mansion with flaming torches, he grabbed up his old .45 revolver, and went rushing out to the front gate to confront the mob—one man standing alone.

This trouble erupted suddenly in the summer of 1917, but the armed rebellion had been gradually festering for five or six years. The anger grew out of failed farms, the conflicts between tenants and landlords, mortgages and foreclosures, and poverty.

t took the army's draft call to trigger the uprising.

On a bright and sunny July 27th, an aging farmer named John Spears gathered four hundred distraught and dispirited farmers at his place outside the hamlet of Francis, seven miles south of Sasakwa. Over his roof flew an American Flag and a Socialist flag. Flaming-eyed speakers in worn overalls loudly denounced President Woodrow Wilson. The fired-up men brandished rifles and cursed "Kaiser Wilson." [18]

The rabble at John Spears's place was exhorted to march on Washington, D.C., shooting anyone who tried to stop them, and throw "Kaiser Wilson" out of the White House. On they way they would subsist on roasting ears and barbecued beef—spawning the sobriquet "Green Corn Rebellion." Perhaps they could commandeer a train and ride to the capital. [19]

On Thursday, August 2, 1917, John Spears's night riders made their first attack two miles from his farm at the Frisco railroad bridge over the South Canadian River. They started a fire on the bridge, and blasted part of the trestle with dynamite. [20]

In the county seat of Wewoka, Sheriff Frank Grall was alerted, and reached the scene about dusk with Deputy J. W. Cross to arrest the arsonists, and a gunfight broke out. Twenty-five or thirty shots were fired. A bullet nicked Deputy Cross. The sheriff pulled back to get reinforcements. [21]

In the dark, the rioters set out on foot with flaming torches, heading north and proclaiming they intended to burn down the town of Konawa, and then Governor Brown's mansion, and every building in Sasakwa, after first looting hardware stores for ammunition, before going on to Washington.[22]

Historians attribute the basic unrest to poor people pinched by economic factors they could not control. Land had become too expensive for Oklahoma's 200,000 small farmers. Speculators pushed prices up 246 per cent between 1910 and 1914. Half the farmers couldn't pay their mortgages and got squeezed into becoming sharecropping tenants. Whole families worked too hard and too long to eke out only a hardscrabble life. Because the war curtailed exports, cotton fell from twelve to seven cents a pound. [23] Small Oklahoma farmers bitterly resented having to dip their cattle against the threat of Texas fever; that seemed to them like a trick to benefit the big ranchers. Farmers who balked had their livestock seized by the sheriff, and sold.

Angry farmers joined a new protest group called "Working Class Union," or WCU—wrongly depicted in Oklahoma newspapers as an offshoot of the IWW or "Wobblies." Beginning in 1915 WCU night riders dynamited dipping tanks and burned the barns of county commissioners who authorized the tick program. These raids were known as "sending the Jones Family." [24]

When John Spears organized his WCU chapter, he is reported to have said: "Anyone can join. Dues are twenty-five cents. Once in WCU, you can't quit unless you die or become a millionaire." Members swore an oath with one hand atop both a pistol and a Bible. [25]

Word of the rioting reached Governor Brown at his mansion about sundown Thursday August 2. An Indian boy galloped up to alert him the mob was on a rampage. The Governor shouted instructions, ordering his wife Sarah, the children and the servants to take cover. "Hide in the woods!" [26] To hired man Taylor Shelton, he barked: "Get on the phone and warn the store at Sasakwa!" Shelton did, and then ran and hid in a tree.

Governor Brown took time to check his pistol. When last had he fired it? He couldn't remember. He twirled the cylinder and thumb-tested the hammer. Then, at seventy-four and already losing vigor, he walked to the front gate and stood there ready to defend his home.

Yowling threats and brandishing firebrands, John Spence's insurgents marched from out of the west. Governor Brown could hear their voices and the tramp of their feet on the road. He watched the gleam of their torches come within three hundred feet of the gate where he stood. With pistol in hand, the Seminole chief anxiously watched the marchers, four abreast, come into view. He cocked his .45, he said later, and waited for the mob. [27] But the night riders did not turn in at his place; unaccountably, they kept marching toward Sasakwa, two miles to the east.

By this time one thousand possemen were converging on the region to guard towns and bridges. The rioters, reported *The Oklahoman,* were "terror-stricken at the speed with which hundreds of possemen took up the trail, scurried through dense thickets and fields in the hills in an effort to evade capture." [28] National guardsmen joined the pursuit; the Frisco sent trainloads of armed men to Sasakwa.

A posse surrounded WCU protestors in camp near the Green Corn hill swinging bridge north of Sasakwa, and attacked. Three men were killed and 450 arrested, effectively quashing the rebellion. Wallace Cargill, a WCU secretary, was shot in the abdomen and died within an hour. [29]

Heavy-handed prosecutors made an example out of the WCU by sending Spence and several others to prison. But for all its drama and social significance this was a minor episode in the history of the Seminole Nation.

CONGRESS ENACTED three WWI draft calls, and eventually Alice's two sons would wind up in khaki. On April 8, 1918 John began drilling in Georgia with Company M 59th Infantry, American Expeditionary Force. He begged Alice to get him out, or at least send money. [30] When his unit went overseas May 6, John remained ill at Mineola, New York Base Hospital Number Five, Ward Two. His sweetheart, Gertie Dobson of the Abbey Hotel, Muskogee, kept writing Alice that she would wait for him—faithfully.[31]

Jack reported to Camp Travis, San Antonio, on February 7, 1918. With his cornet skill, he was assigned to the band, and applied for officer candidate school. His sister Irene paid a welcome visit; she was quartered in San Antonio with her husband "Captain Billy" Key. Jack informed his mother that he had taken out $10,000 in GI insurance payable to Ione ,the baby, and Alice.

Both sons went overseas, but by the time they arrived the shooting had already stopped. Alice thanked God for hearing her prayers.[32]

14

The Indian Rope of Love

VERNON KIKER took off his hated prison uniform, hugged and kissed his wife Bess and then made love to her in a private residence at McAlester on a late Spring afternoon in 1918.

He was well along in serving a three-year sentence for embezzlement. But by some trick not known, most likely bribing a guard, he had wangled a perquisite denied other prisoners—to freely walk out of the Oklahoma penitentiary for conjugal relations.

Bess had come down by train from Wewoka. An amiable and understanding couple rented her a bedroom. Every other day Vernon was able to leave "The Walls" and spend a private hour or two with his wife.

Bess elaborated in a letter to her mother on June 23, 1918:

> I received your letter. Verne sent it down by Kilgore. You addressed it to Mrs. Vernon Kiker, care of the warden. That made me pretty shaky. I have never gone to the penitentiary since I have been here.
>
> Verne comes down every other day and stays an hour or more so I am better satisfied than I was at home and I hate to think of leaving here, but I guess I'll have to about July 1 for I'll be out of clothes by then. I only have enough to do me a week longer.

I am not gaining a pound. I weigh just 100. Mr. Morley and Mr. Frye do not even know that I am in town. So my boy and I have had visits and the time seems just half as long when I am here. I have written some poetry, about eighteen poems, to amuse myself.

These are good old people and will do anything for Verne and me. I will send you a check for $5. It will help some. P.S. Do not write me as it might get me in trouble.

In Wewoka, Alice pored over war stories in the Oklahoma City and Tulsa daily newspapers. Her heart thumped in anxiety as the Allies got their 1918 offensives in motion. General Pershing's doughboys take 15,000 German prisoners at Saint-Mihiel and win battles in Belleau Wood north of Château-Thierry, in the Argonnes and Ypres. U.S. Private Alvin York becomes a hero by almost single-handedly capturing 132 Germans and 35 machine guns. The Red Baron is shot out of the sky after killing 80 Allied aviators. Captain Eddie Rickenbacker whips seven German planes in a dogfight, and by war's end destroys 26 enemy aircraft. The tide is turning. German sailors revolt; Wilhelm II abdicates. Alice gets a sense the war is almost over.

But not without cost to her family. Stanton's son James, an Army private, twenty-four, is wounded. The War Department telegram says he is on a hospital ship, heading home to recover.[1]

Germany surrendered and hostilities ended November 11. Soldiers in the trenches put down their rifles. Americans at home celebrated wildly. Maye, in San Antonio with Captain Locke, told Alice the newspapers put out a couple of Extras. "People went crazy. One man drove a mule through the lobby of our biggest hotel. I felt crazy myself." [2] Downtown in Salt Lake City, Ione found streets roped off and jubilant hordes. "I got sick of people pulling my hair and stepping on my feet. I just went back home."[3]

In the first week of January 1919 Alice noted in her diary that Vernon Kiker had been released from the penitentiary. [4] Her boys were still in the Army—in Germany. She expected them back in a few months; John was begging her to help him get out quickly. Jack had shaped up; at least had begun writing Ione, still in Salt Lake with their son.

243

Now sixty-eight, Alice remained in reasonable health, working long hours. But in the Spring of 1919 reading became difficult for her. Kitt offered advice: "Have your eyes examined at once. You use them too much. As you grow older they grow dimmer. Bathe them in salt water." [5] Dr. W. I. Davis, the Wewoka optometrist, determined that Alice was developing cataracts. He prescribed some drops to use daily.

By the end of summer, both John and Jack had been discharged. Alice had expected to be thrilled to have them back home as civilians. Everyone could start fresh, and all have a better life. After the hugs and kisses of welcome, and her handing them the $250 or so allotments they'd sent from military pay, Alice became depressed. [6] Nothing had changed, not really. She realized they were the same old John and Jack.

Indian summer arrived, and lifted Alice's spirits. The sky was blue, endless, and sunny. Wildflowers waltzed in the quickening breeze. The air scattered the prairie's grassy perfume. This fall season of the year 1919 was as beautiful as any she could recall.

Not the slightest inkling did Alice have at that moment of the maelstrom of disaster about to barrel down on her family. Unknown to any, destiny already had poised their clan on the brink of heart-wrenching sorrow. Devastating blows would strike— soon, rapidly, and heavy.

First, Alice's ex-husband became quite ill. So did Governor Brown. And brother Stanton was carrying on a hateful feud with his son-in-law.

In Okemah, Maude took her father Roll into her home and nursed him. She was having trouble of her own; husband Madison Jones was drinking far too much. But Roll was seventy years old, batching alone on a little run-down farm. Maude wouldn't desert him. [7]

Alice went to the Sasakwa mansion in late September and spent a few days checking on her brother's health. He was failing, she could see, and rapidly. Within barely a month, Governor Brown would be seventy-six years old. He had covered a lot of ground, often at a fast clip, and worked long days; that kind of grueling life takes a heavy toll. Alice suggested he cut back on work and slow down, perhaps even quit preaching every Sunday at his Spring Indian Baptist Church.

244

Her brother bristled then relaxed and quietly shook his head. His response did not surprise Alice. She persisted, gently: "At least, get everybody to help you more. Count on me. I certainly will." [8]

The disagreeable situation in the Stanton Brown household was well known to the whole family. For many months Stanton had been openly on the outs with daughter Bertha's husband, Arthur Stroup. Their homes were within a few hundred yards of each other on farms not far south of Wewoka, too close to keep from fraying already raw nerves. Stroup was a farmer, twenty-nine, two years older than Bertha. Stanton, now fifty-four, found his own wife, Julia, forty-nine, often taking up for Stroup in their frequent quarrels about Bertha's marriage.

On the morning of Saturday, October 4, 1919, Stanton showed up at the Stroup home and called Arthur outside. He announced he had come to collect overdue "crop rents." His son-in-law came out and faced him. [9]

"A controversy arose during the conversation," said the *Wewoka Capital-Democrat*, "in which Brown pulled a .38 calibre pistol. Stroup grabbed the gun and a scuffle followed during which a shot was fired, the ball taking effect in Stroup's left side, ranging downward and lodging in the hip."

Wild excitement ensued. Bertha ran out, gasped in horror, and went back to grab up sheets and towels to try to staunch her husband's bleeding. Julia dashed white-faced from her house to the chaotic scene. Stroup was loaded up and hurried to Dr. W. L. Knight's office in Wewoka. The sheriff was summoned.

"An operation was performed Saturday afternoon," continued the story in the *Wewoka Capital-Democrat's* Thursday, October 9 edition. "Mr. Stroup's condition has been very serious and hopes for his ultimate recovery very slim until yesterday when it was stated he is better and may recover.

"Brown was arrested and is being held in the county jail pending the result of Stroup's wounds."

From behind bars, Stanton not unexpectedly turned for help to his moral anchor and mainstay. He summoned Alice to the jail and asked her to get him a lawyer. [10]

245

Bess spread the news by mail to Maye who agonized to her mother about "the awful thing that has happened to the family." Maye's October 18, 1919 letter added:

> I know you are worried almost to death. If people would only learn to think, how much trouble could be averted. I only hope the boy has enough regard for Bertha to lighten the result. He could make the case as hard as possible. Mama, please keep yourself calm.

Arthur Stroup did not die, but the violent incident wrecked Stanton Brown's home and marriage. His wife Julia's love turned to hatred, and daughter Bertha never forgave him. [11]

AS THE MANSION'S pecan, sycamore and oak trees dropped leaves and the mild October days passed pleasantly, Governor Brown withered perceptibly. Now he climbed out of bed with difficulty; his gait became unsteady. He had no appetite, and ate little. His beard seemed grayer than ever, and a trifle unkempt. Wife Sarah hovered watchfully near his door. His son Tob, came to his side as his strong right arm. Now twenty-seven, Tob also was a Baptist preacher, and had at times conducted services at his father's Spring Baptist Church, just across the road from the mansion.

At daybreak on Sunday, October 19, 1919, Tob went to his father's room. The Governor was wan and drowsy. Tob suggested his father remain in bed and permit him to go conduct the church service, which started at 10 o'clock. The Governor stared at the ceiling and then turned to his son. "Thank you, Tob. I have something I want the people to hear. Perhaps they will be kind enough to come to my side and listen." [12]

Into the fluttery shade of a tall sycamore, Tob helped move out of doors his father's black leather couch. Holding his son's arm, the Governor hobbled to the couch. He got comfortable, semi-upright. From their regular pews across the road, the people came—about 100 men, women, children. Over this congregation hung an air of quiet reverence. [13]

246

Straining to make his voice heard, Governor Brown offered up prayers and went through the usual preliminaries. Then he sat up as erect as he could, and delivered his sermon. (Tob made mental notes which he later transcribed.)

It was Governor Brown's intention to recite the Twenty-third Psalm but adapt and alter the Bible's message of eternal hope into words that would have clear and precise meaning in Seminole Indian hearts. Thus he spoke:

THE ROPE OF LOVE

The Great Father above is a Shepherd Chief. I am His and with Him I want not.

He throws out to me a rope, and the name of the rope is LOVE.

He draws me, and He draws me, and He draws me to where the grass is green and the water is not dangerous; and I eat and lie down satisfied.

Sometimes my heart is weak and falls down, but He lifts it up again and draws me into a good road. His name is Wonderful.

Sometime, it may be very soon, it may be longer, it may be a long, long time, He will draw me into a place between the mountains. It is dark there, but I will not draw back. I will not be afraid, for it is there between these mountains that the Shepherd Chief will meet me, and the hunger I have felt in my heart all through this life will be satisfied.

Sometimes He makes the love rope into a whip, but afterwards He gives me a staff to lean on.

He spreads a table before me with all kinds of food. He puts His hands upon my head and all the "tired" is gone. My cup He fills till it runs over.

What I tell you is true, I lie not. These roads that are "away ahead" will stay with me through this life and afterward I will go to live in the "Big Teepee" and sit down with the Shepherd Chief forever.

John 14:1 Verses 1-4
A Comforting Thought

Dr. C.P. Linn came from Wewoka to examine his patient on Sunday evening and did not leave. "How bad is he?" Tob asked. "Pneumonia," said the physician. "Your father is in God's hands."[14]

On Tuesday, October 21, the Governor was too weak to get out of bed. He waved aside food, but a little before 6 o'clock in the afternoon asked for hot tea. Sarah hurriedly brought a cup and held it out. Governor Brown reached for it but groaned and abruptly dropped his hand. Sarah and Tob felt their hearts break. The singular and noble spirit that emerged from White Skunk's accouchement in the Cherokee Nation on October 23, 1843 had come to the end of the trail. The soldier-statesman-merchant-chief had gladly seized the rope of love and been drawn to the "Big Teepee" to hunger no more and to sit down with the Good Shepherd forever.

His funeral was held in the Sasakwa mansion. Mourners came by the hundreds, overflowing the house and spilling out on his front lawn. Business in Wewoka came to a standstill out of respect, stores and offices closing between 3 and 4 o'clock in the afternoon. Governor Brown was buried in the family cemetery about 200 yards west of his mansion. His tombstone is a three-by-six-foot flat piece of granite inscribed:

JOHN F. BROWN
Chief of Seminole Nation
Oct 23 1843
Oct 21 1919
A Servant to His Country

Newspapers across Oklahoma unstintingly sang his praises. In his obituary, the *Wewoka Capital-Democrat,* in part, said:

> He had a most winning personality, was educated and had stored away a wonderful knowledge of the affairs of life generally. He spoke the English language beautifully and his enunciation was surprisingly clear and correct. Socially when not occupied by some of the cares of his trust, he was a companion to be sought after and prized. He had a keen sense of humor and prized a good story. Many stories are told among his friends of his sparkling wit and he was a master of repartee.

He was a great leader and could converse on any subject with interest. He doubtless knew that knowledge is a great comforter in advanced age, so he planted the shoot in his youth so that it might shade him when he grew old. He had mastered the art of how to grow old which Shakespeare says "is one of the most difficult chapters in the art of living."

He was a beloved minister of the Baptist Church. . . He was a personal friend of President Cleveland and President McKinley. . . He has lived well, laughed often, and loved much; he had gained the respect of intelligent men, the trust of pure women, and he loved little children. He has filled his niche and accomplished his task; has left the world better than he found it in that he loved mankind, never lacked appreciation for the beauty of nature or failed to express it. He looked for the best there was in others and gave them the best he had.

His life was an inspiration; let his memory be a benediction. He was a great and good man; he lived a good life. May he rest in peace from the trials and afflictions of this life.

By odd coincidence, just the week before his death, the Wewoka Trading Company had published a large ad in Wewoka's weekly newspaper announcing that after forty years the store was going out of business, with a sale that would be "the sensation of Seminole county."

The ad boasted the Wewoka Trading Company would be disposing of an enormous stock of merchandise ranging from "shoe laces and canned beans to horse collars, buggies and tractors." Sale prices included: Heliotrope flour, 100 pounds, $5.95; $2 men's shirts, $1.59; $5 blankets, $3.95; $120 Hot Blast kitchen ranges, $97.50; and women's $1.25 voile waists, 98 cents.

Two or three weeks after Governor Brown's funeral there was spread in Wewoka some back-fence gossip about Myrtle's husband, Eugene Aldridge. No details are recorded, but the story obviously reached Alice's ears. And she reacted in some fashion that must have been vigorous because John by mail from Hotel Kinkade in Oklahoma City reprimanded her on November 25:

Gene has been the best friend that we have ever had and I don't think you should look into his affairs like you did. You could

249

go to him today and he would do anything for you. I know you are getting old but you must try to control your temper.

Mama, I thought I would write and ask you if you would like to take a trip down to Maye's. If you let me know I will meet you and we can both go and stay down there for a month.

John's next letter, two days later, gave Alice a feeling of *déjà vu*. He had his watch in hock for $100, and couldn't get it out. Her hands trembled as she folded the letter and filed it in one of her shoeboxes. Tears of frustration doubtless stung her eyes. Her mother love was harnessed to the same old treadmill.

The first of December Roll's condition became desperate. Maude telephoned from Okemah almost every day. Alice felt bittersweet memories. [15] Her mind's eye could picture the handsome and witty George Rollin Davis of forty-six years ago. Their business struggles, the children, the Arbeka trading post and the Bar X Bar ranch, and then . . . that girl Victoria!

Alice was aware Roll was lying helpless in Maude's house only thirty miles away, probably in much pain. Maude said his kidneys quit working, and poison turned him yellow. Maude was too sensitive to directly suggest that Alice come see Roll alive; but Alice understood her daughter's urgent hints. Alice steeled herself; part of her heart wanted to forgive, but her wound was deep and still open. She did not go the thirty miles to Roll's sickbed. [16]

In Maude's spare bedroom on Saturday, December 13, 1919, Roll folded his hands across his chest, said "Amen, amen," and died. *The Okemah Ledger* carried his obituary on page one: "Pioneer Citizen of Okfuskee County Dies." The funeral was held at Maude's house and her "Papa" was buried in Okemah's Highland Cemetery. The newspaper listed out-of-town guests: Myrtle and husband Eugene, Maye and husband Ben, Bess and husband Vernon, Jesse and wife Ella, and Kitt. Alice did not go to Roll's funeral.

EMERALD WAVES were cresting with explosions of sparkling white froth on the Florida beach not far from Alice's window. It was January 1920, less than a month after Roll's burial, and she had returned to Florida as a missionary to the Everglades Seminoles.

250

"It was a long, tiresome trip," she wrote from Stuart. "I did not even get off the train to eat for fear of being left behind. I am located with the Fishes who are Indian and I feel right at home with them. They have two daughters, both courteous young women. I am asked to stay the winter but I guess I'll be glad to go home when the time comes." [17]

Committed to remain three months with other Baptist missionaries, Alice brought along plenty of stationery, and chatty correspondence flew back and forth between Stuart and Oklahoma.

Streets in Wewoka then were so muddy Bess had to go by buggy to visit a friend. "But I had a nice time, had fried chicken, corn, gravy, hot biscuits and apple pie. . . Have not gone to church because of my cold, but it is better. . . Sent off for a food chopper, half dozen pure linen ladies handkerchiefs, bottle of toilet water, dental cream, can opener, bath towels and curtain material." [18]

Bess, incidentally, was up to 113 pounds. "I'm getting fat. Verne says if I weigh 120, he will buy me $500 worth of new clothes. So I'm trying to make it."

Maye in Antlers appreciated getting "a nice long letter" from her mother. She responded January 27, 1920: "You will be like a new person when you are home. A change is surely the most beneficial thing in the world. You can just be free from worry. It was exactly what you most needed. Don't let these moonlight escapades make you romantic. You might be tempted in an orange grove. . ."

Maude brought up Roll's death by mentioning that he had willed his hand-carved walking stick to Jesse with instructions to pass it on in the family. Maude wrote that she and Jesse went through a large trunk that had survived the Arbeka shutdown.

> I found a letter to you from Mrs. Kramer written the 21st day of September 1887 congratulating you on your safe delivery and wishing you well, and said the little Miss Davis would be a source of comfort to you in years to come and so forth. That could be none other than me! Hence I have it tucked away with other valuable treasures.
>
> I took all the old letters and things and put them in a tin box. Everything was in a bad state of decay. The mice had destroyed so many old papers. I found one of the old books I am thankful to say is in very good shape. It is "Theodosius Constantia," published in 1762, I believe. [19]

251

"I acted as a midwife yesterday," Maude wrote later. "My neighbor had a hard struggle and I went over and assisted my first case and got a diploma. I could tell you more about it than I can write..."

Jack had returned to his wife and their little boy. They were together and he was working in Portland, Oregon, when "a terrible cloudburst hit us." Ione was in the hospital with scarlet fever. [20] There was more bad news. Jack said his theatre was closing for lack of business. He was keeping little Jack "with me, just like a pardner. He stays in my dressing room until show time. Then I sit him in a front seat and he stays there until I come for him. Everyone thinks he is a very fine child. P.S. Thanks for the $25. Perhaps the time will come when I can repay all you've done for me."

Some untoward incident, the facts of which are not known, marred Alice's missionary work in Florida. It seems to have concerned whiskey-selling. On her return to Wewoka, Alice received a typewritten tirade from Joe Bowers, who had been a friend to the 1909 mission. His letter—furious, ungrammatical, and illiterate—as he sent it:

> I am just in recp of your leter which you tak grat plesur in acusing of ever thing but somthing decen, i know where you got your informason from an the won that mad that statment is not a frend to enyone...i can prove that your statment is folce ...i never saw a still in my life and i dont feel like having eney such as you aquse of any such crime...i am not ashamed of my reckerd neither am i afread of your threts you are at leberty to hand out eny infamson you lik about me this my furst time to ever be aqused of being eny such a out law as this [21]

John had begun romancing a department store clerk in Oklahoma City. Like his other sweethearts, Mae Good began an intimate long-running correspondence with Alice. John was sick, she wrote. "The poor boy suffers so much, and I worry about him...Yes, I know money is hard to come by and I will do all I can for him. I will go down and see about John's watch. The interest is 50 cents a month, so don't let it worry you." [22]

By July 1920 Jack was traveling with the Berkeley Players in Nebraska; Ione and their son, now three and a half, were in Napa, Idaho. Jack was playing leading man opposite Doris Berkeley. He sent a picture of Doris; she was a knockout. Alice dreaded what might be coming—Jack and Doris continuing their love scenes after the curtain rang down. [23]

Alice needed money as badly as her sons. She sent her daughter-in-law Julia Davis a $6 check; it bounced for "insufficient funds." [24] In July John was in Claremore, Oklahoma, taking mineral baths advertised as helping arthritics and syphilitics. "I think the water is helping me. It sure does cost. I have been paying 75 cents for baths every day. My barber bill and laundry cost quite a bit. So my money don't last long." [25]

In a rare instance, he was contrite. He wrote his mother December 3 to say he was sorry for berating her over the phone.

Her nephew Louis C. "Tob" Brown came to question Alice about her efforts to reclaim the Wild Cat land grants in Mexico. With C.C. Patten and others, Tob was leaving for Mexico City on January 8, 1921 to make one more try. They were taking along the mystical copper medal on which the Mexican "deed" was emblazoned, the same talisman carried by Alice and Chief Hulpatta Micco on their journey. One of the Seminole delegates was, as Patten wrote in *The Oklahoman* on January 16, 1921, "Aha-la-ko-chee, an old man who resided on this very land which he is going now to see and who speaks the Spanish language." Tob's emissaries spent two weeks south of the border. But it was another water haul; the Seminole Nation finally totally abandoned pursuit of the Mexican claim.

Alice's son Jesse became critical in early 1921 from chronic respiratory illness. Physicians disagreed whether he had tuberculosis. From his bedside on February 8, 1921 she wrote Jackson Brown's widow Manie:

> In the daytime I feel so encouraged about Jesse, but at night it's the same old thing. He will cough at intervals all night. I want you to come up for company for I get so lonely with no one to sit up with me.

253

Alice became frantic in seeking help. She tried in vain to send him to a government hospital in an arid western state. She asked his siblings for advice. Kitt suggested milk;[26] Maude sent to Wetumka for a curative "calmus root." "Let him eat honey," urged Julia Davis. Mae Good wrote: "Mama says get a bottle of cod liver oil, eat raw eggs with milk, and keep his bowels open." [27]

Julia Davis, widow of her lynched son, visited Jesse and suggested bringing in a Christian Science practitioner. Alice did so; but the man said he couldn't help unless Jesse quit taking any medicine. Julia's mother sent a curative tea.

Night after night Alice sat up with Jesse. On her knees, Alice prayed. [28] In her diary on April 18, Alice wrote: "My heart is broken as I can do nothing to keep him." About 4 o'clock on the morning of Thursday, April 21, 1921, in the little Arbeka ranch house where he had spent his adult life, Jesse's heart stopped while his sobbing mother held his hand. He was forty-one.

Funeral rites in English and Seminole were conducted at the home. Jesse was buried in the family plot at Arbeka, on the summit of a hill. Exhausted and ill, Alice couldn't go to the grave, where his sister Maude recited:

> Goodbye, 'till morning comes again;
> The shadows of death bring thoughts of pain,
> But could we know how short the night
> That falls and hides thee from our sight,
> Our hearts would sing the glad refrain,
> Goodbye, 'till morning comes again.

GOING INTO THE JAIL in Wewoka was nothing new for Alice. Over the years countless Indians had summoned her for help, or lawyers sent for her as interpreter. So she was nonchalant entering through the sheriff's office on Sunday afternoon, August 7, 1921. Looking up, the sheriff merely waved to the jailer to let her behind the bars. [29]

The jail, like all jails, stank mightily—heterogeneity of unwashed bodies, dirty linen, urine, the phenol suds swabbed about by a trusty with a grungy mop. The fetid aroma at times gagged her.

254

Ordinarily the jail dog, a large black hound called Blackie, slunk close to the wall, docile, tail down. In a hundred or so visits, Alice had paid him no attention. Usually her eyes were on the floor, alert for spots slick with vomit or worse. Today was different. Blackie moved deliberately into her path, bared his fangs, and growled. Startled, Alice started to step around him.

The hound sprang, clamped his fierce jaws on her left arm, and jerked her down. Alice screamed as she fell to the floor. The sheriff jumped up, ran over and beat off the dog. Her sleeve was shredded; blood gushed. "Holy cripes!" cried the sheriff. "I can see the bone!" [30]

Alice was hustled to Dr. Guy Van Sandt's office two blocks away. He cleaned the wound, took stitches, and bandaged her arm. "Lucky, lucky, lucky," the doctor murmured. "A hound that big could have taken your arm off." [31]

Lucky was not how Alice felt about the attack. Pain disturbed her sleep for about three weeks. Dr. Van Sandt put on a new dressing every other day. In her diary on Sunday, August 8, Alice made an entry: "Jailed dog is killed today." It was little satisfaction to her that the sheriff took Blackie out in the alley behind the courthouse and shot him, and refused to get another jail dog. Her diary on Wednesday, August 17: "I went to town today and had my arm dressed." On Saturday, August 20, she wrote: "I had my arm dressed and the doctor said it would be OK in a few days and he would wash it."

NOT SURPRISINGLY Alice's trial and tribulations began to exact a toll. Interpreting for the questioning of witnesses in a November 25, 1921 Wewoka murder trial, she fainted but recovered quickly.

"Did you have trouble with your heart?" Maye asked from Antlers, on November 25. "Those trials are hard on you I'm sure. Ben isn't making anything, and the house isn't paid for but I've tried to learn to be cheerful and can do it on mighty little. That is my greatest help. It takes me out of myself and makes the unpleasant things easier. I can see I am never alone in having burdens. Thank you for the electric iron. It is saving my life."

At Christmas, Alice was in the dumps. It had been a year of one heartache after another. She was terribly disappointed in her two vagabond boys. Rather, she was irritated—or perhaps even angry. She felt an urge to get bile out of her system; so at night on December 28 she began a letter to Jack:

My Dear Son:
   I will write you a few lines tonight although I do not know where to send this letter. You can't imagine how distressed I was to know that you was leaving the state without coming to see your mother.
   I thought that you might run down if only for a day and I'm afraid that Mother is not finding any excuse for you but doing so I realize that in these strenuous times we must be on the alert to make a few dollars to keep from starving but with it all I have not neglected my duties.
   I expected you would call me from the city and I was at home all afternoon as I was afraid you might not locate me if I went downtown, even at my expense.
   I have been heartsick all day as I had a very despondent letter from John in not being able to give the Good family gifts and I sometimes wonder why any of you could expect one at my age to do things when those younger are unable to care for ones dependent upon them.
   What would you think if Mother forgot you and you was helpless and perhaps hungry? I have been very sick this Christmas for I was unable to send Ione and baby a thing and I wondered if you would remember baby if not the mother.
   You know we all wrote, your sisters as well, and told you not to marry when you was so young that we all felt you was too young to even know your own mind. In time you may get into serious trouble if Ione wanted to cause you harm. They could claim that you did not provide for baby so before you spend another dollar on a live-in girl, do send him, if it be only a dollar a week, or even a month.
   It is only that I'm fearful for you that I'm writing in this way and it is the love that I have for you that prompts me to even speak of it. I went to John himself and asked him if he ever thought of his mother having the blues, too. When I ask to borrow money and am refused, I am not trying to borrow it for myself. I don't mind

256

how I look in Wewoka but I was ashamed to be seen in the city in such shabby clothes and see those who don't work near as hard as I always do have respectable clothing.

Well I do have some pride left even at my age. I know that you are ambitious and do not even give up when you lose out so often and I'm glad that you are trying to put a few dollars away but I do not want you to neglect your child. God gave him to you and you must love him as I love you. And I do want you to remember that he owes his existence to you.

Had I known in time that you were coming to the city I would have had a box of something to eat to take along with you but as it was I had no time to get it to you. John told in his letter that you was there only between trains.

Although I have been at work all day, I have spent most of the time in tears. A woman brought me two chickens; I was expecting a turkey. I expect that Myrtle will eat dinner with us, she and her family. Billy Jr. has the chicken pox so Irene will not be here. Bart is at home for the holidays. I have had a lot of cards and Pearl sent me some stationery and stamps. I shall have to write often to her.

I had a real blue letter from Julia. The crux of it was that if not for Pearl and the baby, she would just quit trying, but I wrote her that she and I must be faithful to the end.

Well, your mother will only hope that you will get into something that will pay you to work hard. I will be waiting to hear from you before I can send this letter. One of the things that Jesse said to me was, Mama, you always say things that hurt people's feelings, and I may again have done so. But I don't mean it that way, but only because I feel this to be my duty.

I was reading my Bible and saw that God punished Eli because he had not chided his boys and I thought I may be neglecting my duty, too.

oOo

Saturday, 31st December

I had laid this letter aside, thinking I'd not send it but decided that I would, as I do not think I've said anything that you will not feel is right. And remember that I'll miss you tomorrow. Mae and John will be here. I'm sad tonight so take this in the spirit it is written and write to Mother. Remember me kindly to Doris and

257

thank her for her remembrances and good wishes. With a prayer that God will bless you and keep you and enable you to make good resolutions the first, and keep them.

I will close with love from
Mother

Apparently Alice must have had more than second thoughts about chiding her son, notwithstanding God's punishment of Eli. Under the lamp at her modest little table, she could have read the letter over a time or two. She even addressed an envelope to Andrew Jackson Davis, care of Brunk's traveling show, and pasted on a two-cent stamp.

But in the end, she never sent it. Her letter, scrawled on eight pages, and the stamped addressed envelope were found in one of her shoebox files.

15

An Indian 'First' in the West

UNDER A CLOUDLESS Oklahoma sky, the brazen afternoon sun beat down on a goodly throng streaming into the
United States Courthouse in Muskogee. It was late summer—Wednesday, August 16, 1922. Up the wide steps they came,
somber singles, twos and threes amiably chatting, and intent-look-
ing larger clusters—all invited to become eyewitnesses to a rare
and important event, a sensational "first" in Indian history in the
American West.[1]

It was a singular scene and a serious crowd; most faces showed
the significant features of Indian blood. Ladies wore their festive
best, long skirts of delicate material that fell to their ankles, and
wide-brimmed "picture" hats banded with splashy ribbons. Men
were mainly in business suits.

In New York and Chicago, sophisticates were just then atwit-
ter over the birth of the zippy Jazz Age; flappers with bobbed hair
daringly showed their knees and drank twenty-five-dollars-a-bottle
booze in Prohibition-defying speakeasies like Texas Guinan's in
Manhattan. A far cry, of course, from Muskogee. In 1922 this town
was busy, boisterous, and noisy, on the Arkansas River, with three
railroads, large wholesalers, and on a million-dollar building spree
for hotels, Bacone Indian College, and a new Veterans hospital.[2]

Not all vestiges of Oklahoma's pioneer days had disappeared; teams and wagons and men on horseback still moved along the Muskogee streets, now becoming noisy with the clatter of Model T's.

At about 1:30 o'clock up the courthouse steps came a stylish and buxom aristocrat the newspapers genially hailed as "Miss Alice"—Alice Robertson, sixty-eight, a pioneer Indian Territory missionary's daughter who at seventeen went East to college, worked for the government in Washington, came back to Oklahoma to supervise Creek girls schools, became Muskogee postmaster, was the first woman elected to Congress from Oklahoma (for only one term), and in World War I earned fame as the heroine to doughboys in transit who ate free in her railroad canteen and in her downtown cafeteria.[3]

"Miss Alice" wore a lavish dress of dark material with hundreds of white polka dots of two sizes evenly spaced. It fell to the tops of her white shoes, had three-quarter sleeves and three rows of white ribbon about knee high, and dollar-size white buttons down the front. Her hair was concealed beneath a dark, tight beret.

To greet "Miss Alice" at the center door stepped forward a smiling, well-tailored, military-erect man—Major Victor M. Locke Jr., the federal government's No. 1 official in Oklahoma for directing Indian affairs. His title was Superintendent for the Five Civilized Tribes.

Hovering at Locke's elbow was a girl reporter, Frankie Cornelius, with an open notebook. Her assignment was to write several hundred words for a full-page feature for next Sunday's edition of the state's largest newspaper, *The Oklahoman,* of Oklahoma City.

The major directed ushers to escort "Miss Alice" to the U.S. district courtroom on the second floor. He then scanned the other arrivals. It was as if, Frankie Cornelius noted, he was waiting to greet an important personage, perhaps the "star" of the event. The distinguished president of Bacone Indian College, Dr. Benjamin D. Weeks, came up the steps. Major Locke welcomed him with a firm handshake. His name went down in Frankie Cornelius's notebook.[4] In turn Locke warmly greeted, as they arrived, S. Bailey Spring of Hugo, representing the Choctaw tribe; Former Congressman W. W. Hastings of Tahlequah, a member of the Cherokees; and F. W. Farver, another

260

Choctaw, designated for a prominent role in the occasion, and Czarina Conlan, an Indian affairs writer for the Oklahoma Historical Society.

Two touring cars pulled up and a delegation of seven women and two girls alighted. Major Locke rushed down the steps. The ladies held back and differentially permitted their most senior member to step forward and grasp the hand proffered by the grinning Locke.

She leaned forward, a bright smile on her bronze face, and softly uttered a few words to Locke. She was a poised and distinctive personage, seventy years old, dressed in black, a somber attire that fell to her ankles, a banded turban hiding her long coal black hair, wearing lace-up black shoes and black stockings, carrying a gold-banded purse the size of a briefcase, with a small medallion suspended on a black cord around her neck, and an expression that bespoke power, command and stubborn control.

She was Alice Brown Davis!

Standing with her were five daughters [Myrtle was unable to attend], and three granddaughters, one her first, Pearl Davis Dovell, now a widow at 28. The adults wore long black dresses, and picture hats. Reporter Cornelius jotted down that all carried smaller handbags, and a few had brooches similar to their mother's. The younger granddaughters, looking a bit awed, were 13-year-old Aleece Locke, Maye's daughter, and Joycette Jones, 7, Maude's daughter. The girls wore light-colored short-sleeved dresses that barely covered their knees, and black stockings. The whitish picture hat Aleece wore had a crinkled gaudy brim; Joycette's looked heavy, with a thick ribbon hanging over the right side of the black brim.

Major Locke escorted them up into the second floor courtroom, and got dignitaries seated in front of the high judges' bench. "Miss Alice" Robertson unboxed a dozen American Beauty roses, stepped forward and presented them to Alice Brown Davis. "The queen of roses," she said, "for the Queen of the Seminoles."[5]

Major Locke began the proceedings, reading from a typescript:

> By way of explanation as to the occasion of these ceremonies, I wish to make a brief statement:
> Since the arrival of the Dawes Commission back in the year 1893 it has been the intention of the Government to bring the

affairs of the Five Civilized Tribes to an end. What appeared to us at that time to be the work of a few years has stretched into decades, and, using the slogan of the World War, "We are still carrying on."[6]

He turned to look at solemn-faced Alice, seated in the center chair. Everyone present knew what was coming next. The invitation had contained full details.

Major Locke went on, explaining how Indian tribal governments had been abolished in the process of Oklahoma becoming a state in 1907, eliminating the tribes' laws and chiefs. Now an unexpected hitch had developed as the Government deeded away former Seminole tribal property. Some Washington bureaucrat discovered that under U.S. law these deeds required the signature of a Seminole chief, qualified by blood.

"I shall not enter into detail," the major said, "as to why this emergency arose, as it would require too much time."[7]

Major Locke recounted how he had informed Washington on Feb. 20, 1922, that the Seminoles had no chief, and advised that the President appoint one. Commissioner of Indian Affairs Charles Burke gave his approval in a letter dated May 20, 1922. [8] Locke considered candidates, and finally nominated Alice Brown Davis as Principal Chief of the Seminoles. A telegram came on July 28 that President Warren G. Harding had signed her appointment.

Watching and listening, the reporter was already composing in her mind the lead paragraphs that would begin her story in next Sunday's *Oklahoman:*

By Frankie Cornelius

MUSKOGEE, Okla., Aug. 19-(Special)—History was made when Mrs. Alice B. Davis of Wewoka was inaugurated at Musk-ogee Wednesday as chief of the Seminoles, one of the Five Civilized Tribes. It is the first time in the history of the North American Indians that a woman has occupied the leading tribal office. Unlike her predecessors of the early days who were inducted into office with tomtoms and incantations, Mrs. Davis, appointed by President Harding, was inducted with ceremonies quite the contrast.

No Indian ceremony in the past twenty years has been as elaborate as Mrs. Davis's inaugural. The United States courtroom was filled to capacity for the event, and the exercises were fully in keeping with the historical importance of the occasion. Tribal leaders from all parts of the state gathered to bestow honor on the only chieftainess in Indian history. [9]

Frankie Cornelius didn't have her facts exactly right, and likewise in error was *The Oklahoman* headline that read: "America's First Woman Chief." (When Maude Jones, a prolific writer and Indian historian, first learned her mother was to be made chief, she did research. True, Alice Brown Davis was the first female chief since the Five Tribes came west in the early 1830s over the "Trail of Tears." But Maude Jones found that Indian tribes in Virginia as far back as the time of Pocahontas had occasional female chiefs. Earlier in the 1670's, Chief Philip of the Pequot tribe in Canada had two "squaw" war chiefs. "Unfortunately," Maude Jones told her mother, "the British troops caught them asleep, presumably raped the women, tied them to rocks and threw them in the river to drown.") [10]

The fact that Chief Alice was the late Governor Brown's sister had absolutely no bearing on her selection, Major Locke said.

I wish to declare that Mrs. Davis does not attain this high honor through her relationship to the former chief—she is a woman of distinction in her own right, and has demonstrated time and again, by a life of usefulness and hard work, such qualifications as may be required for the attainment of the highest honors authorized in the political schemes of government peculiar to Indian Tribes.

Neither does Mrs. Davis reach this exalted station through hereditary privileges. Regardless of the high sounding passages written by sentimentalists, there is no such thing as hereditary political rights in the social or governmental fabric maintained by Indian Tribes. If it is meant that a person, or persons, belong to ruling families, then there is some justification for the claim; and in this connection, may I here add that Mrs. Davis is an outstanding member of one of the most prominent families in the Five Civilized Tribes.

It is said that back in the early days of these tribes that the qualifications necessary for elevation to honors of this kind were

263

that the person so aspiring had to be trained to "act as a Judge in time of peace, and to be a leader in time of war."

To know Mrs. Davis very well is to become acquainted with a mind full of Indian wisdom and philosophy, and judging from the alacrity with which she dispatched the manpower of her own family to the Army during the late struggle, one would know that she possesses in full measure the spirit and all the qualifications necessary to successful leadership in time of war.[11]

The afternoon wore on. Dr. Weeks, an old friend, came forward and praised Chief Alice, as did all Indian leaders present. Judge Farver administered the oath of office. The *Oklahoman* photographer shot at least fifty pictures—the last in sunlight on the steps of the courthouse with the new Seminole Principal Chief at the center of a lineup of her daughters and the three granddaughters, the youngest perky and cute enough to be dubbed *the bee's knees* if Jazz Age slang ever reached Oklahoma. The long day was exciting and tension-filled for Alice—and quite tiring.

In the evening a reporter from the *Muskogee Daily Phoenix* came to the Hotel Sever to interview her. Having obviously not done his research as thoroughly as Maude Jones, he asked: "How does it feel to be the first Indian woman chief in history?"

"Well," Alice replied, "I did feel a little scared at first, but I went through it all right."

The reporter included that quote in his story, adding that she was "a bright-eyed, alert little woman nearly seventy years old." [12]

THE FINEST TRAITS of Major Victor M. Locke Jr. were his bravery and brainpower, and his worst were reckless use of firearms and firewater. He bragged with brutal candor to newspaper reporters in Oklahoma that he had "the educated brain of a white man and the heart of a savage." [13]

His boast of these disparate emotions of head and heart proved troublesome to him at times, but not at the end of this day.

He felt a deep sense of satisfaction. The investiture had exceeded his brightest hopes; nary a hitch. Alice Brown Davis had rightfully earned this recognition and reward. Nobody could dispute that. [14]

The major, of course, knew Alice well. He had dined and conversed with her often when she visited her daughter Maye and his brother Ben on their farm down in Pushmahata County. Ben once chuckled that Alice was so little she might not outweigh a hundred-pound sack of horse bran. Long talks with her had convinced Major Locke that Chief Alice was studious and brilliant, just as he had proclaimed in his investiture speech.

They had much in common. Both were mixed blood Indians. Locke was a quarter-blood, his mother being a mixed blood Choctaw and his father a young white Confederate soldier from Tennessee. [15] Locke, forty-six years old, also had been chief of one of the Five Civilized Tribes. In 1911 President William Howard Taft had appointed him to fill a vacancy as head of the Choctaw Nation. Locke was the Choctaw chief, amid some political controversy, until 1918 when he resigned to serve in the U.S. Army in World War I. He was fluent in the Choctaw language, as Chief Alice was in the Seminole tongue; both had acted as official interpreters. Each was well liked and respected by the full bloods of their tribes.

Locke in his current role as official mediator between the Government in Washington and the Cherokee, Choctaw, Chickasaw, Creek, and Seminole tribes commanded a large staff that handled Indian affairs in forty counties in Oklahoma. His Muskogee office daily received about 500 letters and mailed out around 700. The superintendent collected and disbursed millions of dollars in tribal and individual funds, approved appraisals, land and mineral leases, and deeds and allotment restrictions, assisted probate attorneys, particularly in regard to minors.

Politicians in Washington and Oklahoma already were looking critically over the major's shoulder. They were apprehensive the Indian spoils system that had existed for a century might be upset. For example, Locke opposed a scheme to dispense pro-rata the $25,000,000 the Choctaw and Chickasaw tribes had accumulated in coal and asphalt leases. Locke wanted to hold the money as a tribal educational trust fund, rather than paying it out to individuals, who might be mulcted by speculators and sharpers who used whiskey and guile. Greedy whites certainly had their eyes fixed on the vast oil pools being increasingly found beneath Indians' land, and worth millions.

ALICE'S ELEVATION to chief initially appeared a successful innovation. The excitement generated by the inaugural gala bubbled a week or two. Oklahomans in general seemed pleased with the unique event. Leaders of other Indian tribes continued to send congratulations, and Major Locke felt he had achieved something worthwhile.

(Appointing Alice as chief started a trend. Within a year, the Kaw tribe had a woman chief, Lucy Tayiah Eads. Much later came others: Wilma Mankiller of the Cherokees; Roberta Jamieson of the Mohawks; G. Anne Richardson of the Rappahannock.)

Alice became national news. Feature stories popped up in newspapers from New York to Los Angeles identifying her as the first "squaw" chief.

On its editorial page, the *Tulsa World* hailed her on August 21, 1922 thusly:

A WOMAN CHIEFTAIN

The wise person who declaimed there is nothing new under the sun was only approximately wise. Mrs. Alice B. Davis has just proved that there is something new; she is the new chief of the Seminole tribe of Indians.

The traditional business of an Indian chief was to fight; he was the war-lord of the tribe, leading its warriors and directing them both in war and in the chase. At one point of our nation's history the Seminoles were a most war-like people. How those old chieftains must now squirm, if from their haunts in the happy hunting ground they can now look back at earth and see a squaw ruling in their places!

And old Geronimo, Spotted Tail, Black Kettle, and others whose names even yet cause a shudder of fear in the hearts of old-time pioneers, what must they think if they can now see a squaw occupying the teepee of authority and honor in the midst of an Indian tribe?

But the day of the chase and the war trail has passed. Of all the myriad throng of plains people who once inhabited this continent and contested the white race inch by inch as it made its way westward, only a mere handful now remains. Some of the most powerful tribes, having been decimated by death, due to an un-

266

natural mode of living, or become assimilated by the conquering race. Those that still preserve their tribal entity are so completely under the jurisdiction of the Great White Father at Washington that the tribal government is merely nominal, as well administered by a squaw as a warrior.

The world moves, it changes, it works wonders before one's eyes. By injustice and oppression, even, it carries humanity on and on to greater heights. But who in this day of idealism, of self-determination, when men self-righteously proclaim the rights of subject people—who of us can contemplate our own vanquishment and destruction of the American Indian without an uneasy blush of shame?

For a brief time Alice remained in Muskogee and obediently carried out the superintendent's instructions. Locke presented her with a stack of allotment documents that had been left incomplete at the time Governor Brown died in 1919. Locke instructed her to sign the papers and affix the chief's seal. [16]

The Government was dealing cautiously and meticulously with the Indians. Congress had executed so many convoluted Indian laws that some shreds of authority possibly remained with the Seminoles under the 1866 treaty. Hence the Superintendent of the Five Tribes was directed to dot every "i" and cross every "t" in all transactions. To sign this series of incomplete deeds appeared to be the chief reason for Alice's appointment. Not called on to perform any other duties, Alice returned to her home in Wewoka. In time she received a Government check for eighty-five dollars for thirty days service as chief. But no further compensation. For all practical purposes, the new chief of the Seminoles , after only one month, had been fired or retired and put on the shelf. Wewoka lawyer-poet Rudolph N. Hill hailed her in this published tribute:

THE INDIAN CHIEFTAINESS

I know a woman with a soft brown face,
A face all wrinkled now with lines of care,
A chief who knew the burdens of her race,
A woman-chief who saw the future's lair

For those she loved, whose race seemed nearly run,
Her kinsmen of the wild, red tribes who go
To tread the pathway of the sinking sun,
Who, proud as monarch pines, fall grandly slow;
She keeps their ancient customs undefiled,
She calmly sees the white men hurry on
To greater works, undreamed of, vast, and wild;
She knows these, too, will some day all be gone,
Yes, gone to sleep with nature's simplest child—
And so I paint her for tomorrow's dawn.

Alice's life went on as usual; she now had become chief of the Seminoles in name only.

But that calm situation would not last long.

THE YEAR 1923 broke open the long-running political quarrel centering on Oklahoma Indian affairs. The controversies stretched from President Harding's own desk, down through Interior, the Indian Commissioner, the Five Tribes office, on to local political cliques and the Governor of Oklahoma. "Chief" Alice was destined to be dragged into the wrangle.

Debate raged over whether Indians were rapidly enough assimilating themselves into the white man's lifestyle. Certainly not as fast as the Interior Department wanted. Don't be so impatient, countered Oklahoma newspaper editors. Their columns frequently deplored and ridiculed the Government's heavy-handed effort to make the tribes abandon their ancient customs and traditions. The *Muskogee Daily Phoenix* fired this salvo:

> Heaven protect Lo, the poor Indian. The greatest curse that has been his is this "government by wireless," this abundance of free advice given by those who believe Lo still builds his fires at night outside his teepee door and dare not adopt the ways of civilization in fear that the moment he learns the English language he will be defrauded of his buffaloes and his head feathers. [17]

Such criticism did not daunt United States Commissioner of Indian Affairs Charles H. Burke. He believed he knew what was best for the red man; he had the support of his boss, new Secretary of the Interior Hubert Work. (A Colorado military surgeon, Work, sixty-three, a lifelong Republican and former Postmaster General, had been appointed by President Harding to replace Albert B. Fall, disgraced in the Teapot Dome scandal.)

Commissioner Burke and Secretary Work conferred with other Interior officials seeking answers to difficulties with the tribes. Burke finally concluded he needed to personally take a whack at practices or customs he believed fed the Indians' laxity and heathenism. Calling in his secretary on February 23, 1923, Burke dictated this circular addressed "To All Indians."

Not long ago I held a meeting of Superintendents, Missionaries and Indians, at which the feeling of those present was strong against Indian dances, as they are usually given, and against so much time as is often spent by the Indians in a display of their old customs at public gatherings held by the whites. I feel that something must be done to stop the neglect of stock, crops, gardens, and home interests caused by these dances or by celebrations, pow-wows, and gatherings of any kind that take the time of Indians for many days.

Now what I want you to think about very seriously is that you must first of all try to make your own living, which you cannot do unless you work faithfully and take care of what comes from your labor, and go to dances or other meetings only when your home work will not suffer by it. I do not want to deprive you of decent amusements or occasional feast days, but you should not do evil or foolish things.

No good comes from your "give-away" custom at dances and it should be stopped. It is not right to torture your body or handle poisonous snakes in your ceremonies. All such extreme things are wrong and should be put away and forgotten.

You do yourselves and your families great injustice when at dances you give away money or other property, perhaps clothing, a cow, a horse or a team and wagon, and then after an absence of several days go home to find everything going to waste and yourselves with less to work with than you had before.

If at the end of one year, reports that I receive show that you reject this plea, then some other course will have to be taken.

269

Secretary Work, new on the job, felt he needed a first-hand look at Indian problems. In May 1923, on a quick trip to Oklahoma, he was shocked to be confronted not by tribal dissent, but by white political intriguers. Rabid and vocal, they had both local and national agendas. Oklahoma's Republican Party expressed to him disappointment with President Harding. They wanted more say in federal patronage, and not such strict oversight of probate courts where rich oil leases usually were handled.

Also complicating Indian affairs were the antics of just-elected Oklahoma Governor Jack Walton, forty-two, a Democrat and former mayor of Oklahoma City. Walton went on the worst tear the state had seen by a chief executive, trying to fire both university presidents, battling the Ku Klux Klan, and eventually clamping martial law on the entire state. Before his impeachment (November 19, 1923), he hammered Indian bureau patronage, setting off an attempt to discharge Major Locke on trumped-up charges of drunkenness.

Locke, always aggressive and outspoken, had offended rivals by some appointments to patronage jobs. More importantly, according to the ubiquitous Oklahoma political newspaper *Harlow's Weekly,* Locke "made some enemies . . . generally speaking . . . by his refusal to permit them to rob the Indians." [18]

Secretary Work was cautious in making any promises, fearing to further alienate Oklahoma support for President Harding. Keeping an eye on his own problems, he left the state with an inspiration. That was to select an advisory commission of about 100 leading citizens "from the four corners of America" to study Indian assimilation. At the same time he summoned tribal officers to Washington for similar discussion, including about thirty from Oklahoma.

Amid this furor, Commissioner Burke once again needed the Seminoles to give him a chief-of-convenience to sign a sale of tribal property. So Alice's name once more was sent up through Interior Department channels to the White House, and for the second time she was appointed chief by President Harding.

As a result, on Wednesday, June 6, 1923, Alice was summoned to the Five Tribes Superintendent's office. (By that time Major Locke was being railroaded out of his job.) In Muskogee, Alice was handed a document to sign, conveying Seminole property which

270

had been auctioned off to a white man. After reading only a few lines, she recoiled in shock. This was abominable! The Government was selling Emahaka—*her* Emahaka Mission Academy where she had been superintendent until it was snatched away in 1906 by the Interior Secretary, and turned over to that hated Government School Superintendent John D. Benedict. She had resisted that transfer until overwhelmed at the bitter end; and she intended to fight now. The Government, she felt, had badly mistreated the Seminoles in taking over tribal education. Not only had the Interior Department seized Emahaka, but had in 1914 closed the school, forcing the girl students into the white public schools which were poorly suited for them.

A senior Muskogee office clerk hovered over Alice as she sat at a table leafing through the several pages of the Emahaka document. The clerk asked her to sign as chief.

Alice looked up dubiously, as she later recounted the incident to her daughters and before a Congressional hearing. "Well, I will have to study this carefully. I will take the deed back to Wewoka and look it over and get back to you. . . . Besides, I did not bring my seal with me." [19]

The clerk said the lack of seal wouldn't make any difference, and again asked her to sign.

Alice set her jaw. "I'm not going to sign today."

The clerk then suggested she take the deed home, look it over, sign it and return it within twenty days. He offered no explanation for setting a time limit. Nor did Alice ask; she already knew she did not intend to sign the deed. [20]

Controversy over Emahaka was not new. It stemmed from errors made by Government surveyors back in the 1840s when they established the border between the Creek and Seminole Nations. It was discovered later that the corrected new line ran right through the middle of Emahaka! At that time Governor Brown had lodged a protest and attempted to resolve the conflict. Nothing was settled and the border dispute had hung in limbo for years. Eventually the Creeks had acted on their claim to one-half the Emahaka land and allotted it to a tribesman. He had died and his heirs had sold it to a Holdenville real estate dealer. That resulted in the current effort of the Interior Department to get a legal conveyance from the Seminole tribe.

Back in Wewoka, Alice painstakingly re-read the document, neatly typed, encased in a blue binder, with a blank space on the last page for the "Principal Chief of The Seminole Tribe" to sign. In Alice's view that would permit the Government to literally rob the Seminoles of property worth at least $40,000. She conferred with tribal elders, who supported her decision. [21] She sent the deed back to the Muskogee office without signing it.

Just then Locke's replacement, a former Vinita postmaster named Shade Wallen, had his hands full and the Emahaka deed was laid aside until July. Secretary Work decided to discuss the quandary with Harding, but the President had just departed Washington to make a tour of western states.

Secretary Work never got to talk to Harding—not about Emahaka or anything else. In San Francisco on August 2, 1923, President Harding was stricken with a thrombosis, a blood clot, and died. Vice President Calvin Coolidge succeeded him, and for a number of weeks the changes in the administration either slowed or sidetracked routine Indian business.

As time passed, Alice went about her own affairs in Wewoka, with no new official word regarding her status as "chief" of the Seminoles. In the Five Tribes office in Muskogee the unsigned deed was still pigeonholed.

One year later the Emahaka controversy was revived. The unsigned deed was forwarded to Secretary Work. Government lawyers advised him that even without a signature of the Seminole chief, the Secretary of the Interior had authority to convey the property. On December 22, 1924, Secretary Work signed the deed. Later the Department of Justice had second thoughts and challenged the legality of the United States government conveying Indian land without specific tribal approval. So the Interior Department sent instructions down to the Muskogee office to nominate another Seminole as chief to get the deed signed.

Thus on October 22, 1925 President Coolidge appointed a Seminole full blood named George Jones as chief of the tribe.

George Jones was educated, an accountant, short, stocky, and fifty years old. He was a distinguished horseman and had the eyes of an eagle. (Grandson Glen Cornelius says Jones once caught sight of something beside the road on an auto trip near Wewoka. "Stop!" he ordered the driver, and got out. He picked up a fifty-dollar bill. It was believed accidentally dropped by a bandit gang then raiding the area.) [22]

The Five Tribes superintendent lost no time in summoning Jones to Muskogee. [23] The new chief was handed three deeds to sign. He looked them over carefully. Then George Jones picked up the pen and signed two of them.

"There is one more," he was told.

"I see that," Jones responded. "I have signed these two—the church deed and the cemetery deed. The school property document I can not sign."

"For what reason?"

"The surveyors made a mistake. That is the Government's problem. Your people ought to fix it. This deed does not provide any compensation for the tribe. We have talked about this; I know that Mrs. Davis would not sign. The Government is bigger and stronger than we are, and you may take our property away. That doesn't make it right. This deed, in our opinion, is not worth the paper it is written on."

His response irritated Superintendent Shade Wallen. "If you don't sign," Wallen said, "we will withdraw your appointment. You no longer will be chief!"

George Jones was not fazed. "That is up to you," he said, mildly. "I never asked to be chief. It makes no difference to me. I didn't know I was chief until I read it in the newspaper."

Unwilling to give up, the Government appointed a third Seminole, a full blood named Harry Tiger, as chief. Called to Muskogee, he, too, refused to sign.

Secretary Work then threw up his hands and let the transaction stand. A group of Seminoles employed an attorney to resist the Emahaka loss. But in the end the courts demonstrated the truism that the Seminoles knew in their hearts from the outset—the Government was bigger and stronger than the Indians, and would always win.

In an aftermath that saddened "Chief" Alice, Victor Locke Jr. met his worst downfall in 1927, but it was in no way related to having served as Five Tribes superintendent. Rather it was a bloody personal tragedy in which, said *The Tulsa World,* Locke's "savage heart" caused him to follow "an antiquated Indian code of honor."

In his hometown of Antlers, the major was informed that a young Choctaw named Abner Battiest had seduced two Indian girls who were Locke's wards, and had also "roughed up" his blind, eighty-six-year-old father, Victor M. Locke Sr.

Witnesses overheard the father and son talking together in the Choctaw tongue. Then, said *The Tulsa World,* they heard Major Locke "give the dreaded Indian turkey gobble. He had reverted to savagery. He had given warning of impending death to an enemy." [24]

Finding Battiest at home, Major Locke shot him dead with a rifle. Then he walked to the sheriff's office and surrendered. The trial in Pushmahata county circuit court was a sensation, reported *The Tulsa World* on November 18, 1927, adding:

> The judge who heard the testimony was a brother of one of the defense attorneys and also a close friend of the defendant. So was the prosecuting attorney. All those factors availed him nothing in court.
>
> The fact remained that Locke had put aside the white man's law in order to conform to an antiquated code of honor. A jury of farmers found him guilty and he received a 10-year prison sentence. The verdict was regarded as a triumph of written law over unwritten law and duty over friendship.

While Locke's conviction was on appeal, Alice and other of his friends worked to get him pardoned. On December 29, 1930, a large delegation of Indian women prominent in Oklahoma political and civic circles accompanied Locke to see Governor W. J. Holloway. In the group were Alice and her daughter, Irene Key.

The governor heard the group's petition and granted Locke a full pardon. The women cheered; Locke cried.

16

Oil Wells, Death and Romance

L AWYER C. GUY CUTLIP was carrying on a vigorous conversation with Alice, a long time friend, in his second-floor office near the Wewoka courthouse. It was mid-afternoon March 17, 1923, a murky Saturday.

Just as he picked up a pencil to scribble a note on the court document they were discussing, the door burst open.

A burly laborer rushed in yelling. Alice recalled later how the noise startled her.[1] Turning, she saw a man in denim shirt and overalls splattered head to foot with big dirty globs that glistened with an oily sheen.

"She blowed!" the intruder screamed, with so much exhilaration he almost strangled. "She blowed, Mister Cutlip! Gawd Amighty— she's a gusher!"

Guy Cutlip leaped to his feet so fast he kicked over his swivel chair. He was stunned, but his face broke into a two-thousand-watt smile.

"Mrs. Davis, come on. Let's go! Let's go see that oil well! I'll drive us in my Ford."

Heading south out of town, Alice knew precisely where the lawyer was going—two miles southeast to wildcatter R. H. Smith's drilling rig, the Betsy Foster No. 1. It had taken months, but Smith

275

punched down to about 3,400 feet. Then he ran out of money. Cutlip could smile secretly. Only three days ago, the wildcatter had come to him. "I'm broke—but I can't quit. There's oil there! If I just had two hundred dollars. . ." [2] Cutlip got Smith the two hundred. And now—boy, what a break!

They found Smith frantically shutting down the gusher. It came in spewing 20,000,000 cubic feet of gas daily and 500 barrels of crude, splattering his crew and the prairie. Smith had no place to store the oil; he needed tanks or pipeline hookup. He'd have to stop the oil flow until he could get storage.

Sightseers flocked to the discovery well. Alice knew Wewoka would go nuts, and it did. Within days the little village exploded into one of Oklahoma's big oil boomtowns, and hardly a single resident, red or white, was ever quite the same again.

The oil boom might have proved a windfall and changed Alice's life, but it did not. By mail from California, Jack earlier had urged her to borrow money and grab oil leases and get rich. "This may be your opportunity to bring your ship in." [3] It was much too late. As early as 1913 when restrictions were lifted on Indian non-homestead land, speculators had leased about every inch of the Seminole Nation, most for as little as 25 cents an acre. One geologic entrepreneur, shoe-salesman O. D. Strother, gobbled up 4,480 acres, but drilled only dry holes or struck dreaded artesian sulfur water. Four months after he died, his men brought in a $7,500,000 gusher. [4] The husbands of Alice daughters Irene, Myrtle, and Bess would cash in on the oil bonanza, but those men already were making money in business. Some of the Sasakwa Browns also got lavish oil royalty.

To Alice came only the drudgery of poking into Seminole tribal lineage and translating the tongue for lawyers checking into bloodlines, heirships, leases and other deals. In million-dollar transactions she got mere nickel-and-dime fees. Most Seminole Indians had already been cheated. Some, by sheer luck, got millions in oil royalties. Few could handle prosperity. Alice heard of some newly rich Indians buying Cadillacs, hauling pigs in the back seat, and abandoning the vehicle if it ran out of gas. Sad but true. Of course many other landowners, speculators and spur-of-the-moment investors like Guy Cutlip pocketed big shares of the unexpected oil millions.

276

Flowing 3,500 barrels a day, Betsy Foster No. 1 set off a drilling stampede that turned the Seminole Nation into a drilling hub above five or six oil pools which in their 1926-36 heyday yielded 702,157,800 barrels of petroleum. Alice and other "old settlers" lived through boom nightmares. As many as 100,000 strangers descended upon the cluster of mushrooming oil towns—chiefly Wewoka, Seminole, Cromwell, Maud, and Bowlegs. Overnight came an influx of men and material. The horde had no place to sleep or eat, until tents and shacks sprang up. Into Wewoka came oil field crews of rig builders, truckers, pipeliners, pushers, muleskinners, and their like. To the sparsely settled area also flocked doctors, lawyers, geologists, teachers and preachers, bankers, newspaper publishers. Also gamblers, dancehall girls, dope dealers, bootleggers, burglars and stickup men.

In the hectic and generally lawless start-up of the boom, it was not unusual for guns or knives to flash and leave about one dead a day—a murder mystery or a killing in plain sight during a brawl. Wewoka escaped some of the woolliest lifestyle but spawned bootleggers and a red-light district one block from the courthouse. The "fix" was in; Wiley Lynn, a federal prohibition agent turned crook, paid off politicians and protected Wewoka brothel queen Rose Lutke.[5] Lynn also in Cromwell gunned down the famous frontier Marshal Bill Tilghman. Surprisingly, Lynn was acquitted, only a short time later to be killed in another gun duel with a lawman.[6]

Ten pairs of Missouri mules had to be hitched to a sixteen-wheel wagon to haul a boiler to a well when rain turned dirt roads into hub-deep mud. But oil riches gave Wewoka and Seminole, and a few of the other towns, paved streets, water and sewer systems, street lights, fine homes, brick offices, thousands of Model T's and other motorcars...

The 1929 Wall Street crash doomed the sudden prosperity. Alice and most everybody else in town soon felt the pinch of the Great Depression. The oil business was severely crippled. Crude that had brought $2.65 a barrel fell to 15 cents. [7] Wewoka's and Seminole's population shrank as the boom played out. Cromwell, the cornfield that was transformed into a rootin'-tootin' hellhole, virtually evaporated; so did Bowlegs.

As far as making Alice's life brighter, easier, or happier, the oil boom could just as well have not happened.

She had reached the age—seventy-two in 1924—where she should have expected to be able to slow down and sit comfortably in her rocker. Life never gave her ease and serenity. Instead, as long as she could breathe and totter around, she had to scrounge stray dollars that her two sons were never too proud to beg for and take. Alice had a heart, too, for Jack's discarded first wife Ione McBride and their boy Jack Jr. For more than ten years Alice kept in touch, and now and then sent checks.

Long suffering and self-sacrificing, Alice finally resented the years when she was put upon and forced to do without and live shabbily. On rare occasions her temper exploded. Not, apparently, too often. Her discouragement seemed to mainly be confided to her diary. " I should send John F. his $3, but so far do not have it," she wrote April 30, 1924. "I feel a bit discouraged but have been reading where we should take no thought of the morrow but only have faith. But do I have it?"

On May 1, she made a collection for a lawyer and sent John three dollars, and congratulated herself, "My body is whole, and I can work yet." Later she complained privately, "I have been home all day and feel like I could scream but I guess this is to be and I'll have to meet the situation. What to be will be." [8]

She noted on October 28, 1925 that she was being "ignored" by grandson Jerry Aldridge, but observed "that's a cross I'll have to bear." Her diary on November 30, 1925 reveals her bank balance was a mere $3.70. She made a bittersweet entry January 20, 1925: "I was married fifty years ago today."

Daughter Maye encouraged Alice to keep striving for happiness, describing her own struggles, contrasting them to the despair of her sister Kitt:

> I am just as full of faults as Kitt is, likely many more. I don't believe at any time her life has been harder than mine, but I simply have to get some happiness out of my life some way. And I do most earnestly try to enjoy thoroughly the best part of it. . . . The embarrassment of poor home, lack of good clothes, etc. is

extremely hard on some people and I for one know how to sympathize with these particular people because a nice home and good clothes mean almost too much to me.

But the lack of them can be supplanted by other things. Often there are times that the effort doesn't seem worthwhile, but it is! Situations and families are the saddest things in the world and make those involved terribly unhappy. You are likely more deeply hurt than any of the others. It would probably be good if you were to kick us out of your mind for a while. [9]

Alice never had a real home of her own in Wewoka until late in life, and then only a modest little white shotgun style bungalow. She was galled by some of her daughters, and made it known at least in her diary. Once she moved into daughter Myrtle Aldridge's palatial home—but within a week left, unhappy with something about the arrangement. At the Kiker's, Alice helped Bess store summer clothes in a trunk. She commented that winter was coming on and suggested putting a wood box next to the stove in her room. Bess rejected the idea. In her diary, Alice lamented:

> Well, I hope before I die there will be some way so I can have a shelter of my own and can have a few things the way I want them. But this may be the cross for me. If it was right for me to have things, I'd have them. So I will have to bear this in silence, adapt myself to conditions, even if not satisfactory and do just the best I can under existing circumstances. [10]

From the back of her mind, Alice recalled one line from Shakespeare's King Lear, Act I: "How sharper than a serpent's tooth it be to have a thankless child." The mother's displeasure with Bess's attitude toward her apparently became a running, rather than occasional, grievance. Her diary for December 25, 1923 says:

> Christmas Day and I always have something to annoy me on these holidays and it always comes from Bessie. She can hardly be civil to me in the presence of her sisters or anyone else. She will reprimand me as if I was a child and then I must cease to feel that I have no home and put up with this kind of treatment and from my own child. I can only wish that I had some other dwelling place,

but. . ."Foxes have holes and the birds of the air have nests, but this son of man hath no place to rest his head."

The years took their toll. She had always been strong and athletic, never fat or slovenly, a strong swimmer even at seventy. She had to have her teeth extracted—an ordeal that required four or five visits to the dentist. "Oh, how I dread it," she told her diary. Unfortunately her upper plate did not fit properly, and pained her. "It was a mistake to pay in advance," Kitt told her mother.[11] Alice's bones and joints flared up with rheumatism and arthritis. She would go to the mineral springs at Sulphur, Oklahoma and "take the baths." She thought the warm water helped.

Heart disease stole up on her slowly, but with unremitting certainty. Her blood pressure became erratic, and gradually elevated. Two physicians—Linn and Van Sandt—instituted the best regimens known at those times, with minimal success.   The common cold knocked her down occasionally. In the mid-twenties her diary recorded she "was in bed all day today. Hope I can go to town tomorrow." [12] Similar entries began to dot the pages, usually followed by "I hate to be sick." Her eyesight continued to diminish, but only rarely was that mentioned.

Her diaries were a story in themselves, being mainly a collection of bound long-paged ledgers intended for bookkeeping and the cheap eight-by-ten ruled composition books used by school children. Either she failed to write for many scattered periods, or the books for a number of years were lost. Her entries were skimpy, some enigmatic, but all helping to delineate her character and on occasion her mood.

Her inclination to stoicism is clear in this brief, but total, account for Sunday January 25, 1925:

> Jack and John came today. Jack has been away 7 years from Wewoka. He is still in the show business. Will go back to the City tomorrow afternoon. Got Indian for sister J (meaning house help for Jennie Factor) today. Still owe 85 cents on the garden.

Next day's entry was just as laconic. Alice got up at 5:30 in the morning, started the fire, and went back to bed. "Jack wants to get some money. Borrowed five hundred dollars from Farmers National Bank. Verne signed note with him for above amt. due in 60 days. Jack gave me for medicine $5.85."

The co-signing outraged John. As soon as he got back to Oklahoma City, he mailed his mother a long tirade against "my rich brothers-in-law," although all of them had been conned by John several times into forking over cash to get him out of jams.

Alice took refuge in her Bible. "I feel discouraged this a.m.," she wrote October 1, 1923, "but will leave all in the hands of Him who doeth all things well." Another time she told of getting up early and reading Psalm 78, being impressed by God showing both anger and mercy:

> They were not faithful to his covenant,
> Yet he was merciful;
> he forgave their inequities
> and did not destroy them.
> Time after time he restrained his anger
> and did not stir up his full wrath,
> He remembered that they were but flesh,
> a passing breeze that does not return.

IN CHOCTAW COUNTRY, incipient tragedy tiptoed into the hillside home of Maye's family in the little town of Hamden south of Antlers. Her husband, Captain Ben Locke, commander of the Indian cavalry company, was stricken with a persistent cough. that led to exploratory lung surgery at the U.S. Veterans Hospital at Muskogee and long confinement there. Maye had a farm home with a cow to be milked, garden tended, stove wood split, chickens fed, soiled clothes boiled in an iron kettle over an open fire, fences repaired, and two innocent, vulnerable daughters, Allece, fifteen, and Benita two years younger.

Alice sent Maye new linen handkerchiefs, prompting this response: "If I were less selfish, I couldn't enjoy your little packages so much for I know I am perhaps taking the things you need.... Mama, I get so sorry for the life you are living. It just makes me sick. I know you would enjoy having your own things and doing as you please so much."[13]

Though infrequent, Alice had managed visits to the Locke place in Hamden. She often related to friends how Benita, at about six, had listened to a family discussion about branding cattle. Benita leaped up, put her arms on her hips, and stuck out her jaw in indignation. "We don't have to brand our cows!" she shrilled. "We can just tie blue ribbons on their horns." [14]

During less desperate days, Captain Locke got access to a hospital typewriter and launched a commendable career as a writer. His poems and short stories dealing with Indian folklore and frontier-days adventure were widely published in newspapers and Indian and military magazines. [15] His poem "Doughboy—Buckskin Ben" was incorporated in a Muskogee World War I memorial statue. Editors commended his work, particularly "The Lonesome Indian Chant," "The Girl With the Rosette Garter," "The Gold Leaf That Withered," and "The Wildcat."

At the end of four years in the Muskogee hospital, Ben Locke died January 3, 1928 at forty-five. Maye, two years younger, had to go to work right away to make a life for her young daughters. She became an attendant at an Oklahoma Indian home at Eufaula, and later held similar jobs with the federal government in Colorado. (Maye died in Oklahoma City on January 24, 1962.)

THE STATE PENITENTIARY at McAlester became a sort of second home to Alice. Her son-in-law William S. Key was appointed warden in 1924 by Governor M. E. Trapp, and served until 1927. It was fifty-mile train ride from Wewoka and Alice visited the warden's quarters frequently, often baby-sitting while Irene was away on a trip with Warden Key.

Alice took pride when he introduced needed prison reforms. Within two years Key had the prison on a self-operating basis needing no state appropriation. [16] From 1928 to 1932, Key became chairman of the State Pardon and Parole Board, and in 1935 again was named warden, by Governor E. W. Marland. Not many months later, Key was drafted to head the Oklahoma WPA which built two hundred fifty schools, fifty-three armories, and twenty libraries. He ran as Democratic candidate for Governor in 1938, losing by 3,000 votes. He had a distinguished career in World War II, and died January 5, 1959 in Oklahoma City. [17]

Myrtle's husband, Eugene C. Aldridge, went into the hotel business. He gave Wewoka its tallest main drag building, opening the four-story Aldridge Hotel one block south of the courthouse on July 5, 1927.

For an opening night gala in the hotel ballroom, Jack came in off the road and assembled a dance orchestra to play the one-night gig. Myrtle and her husband were just then concentrating on a second big event—sending their oldest son, J. Bart (1902-1961), on a honeymoon cruise to Europe. Only a week earlier J. Bart, twenty-five, had married pretty Wewoka schoolteacher Marjory Rose McNemer. The idea of a wedding trip abroad bugged Wewoka eyes; it was a gift the parents could afford from oil boom royalties. Their son's career had already been spectacular. He starred three years at the University of Oklahoma in basketball and baseball, was elected to the State Legislature while still in college, and got his law license at twenty-three. [18]

IN MONTROSE, Colorado, Alice stepped off the train August 17, 1923 and scanned the platform for a tall Seminole Indian sixty-one years old. To help her spot him, William G. Glover had promised he would wear beaded moccasins to the depot. That was a superfluous identity clue; "Billy" Glover was the only Seminole Indian in that part of Colorado.

This rendezvous had taken months to plan, inaugurated by Glover writing Alice after her appointment as Chief. Glover wanted to adopt one or two Seminole Indian boys to live on his 640-acre ranch at Placerville, Colorado. Born in the Everglades in 1862, Glover was orphaned and had been raised by a white woman in New Jersey. He attended Carlisle Indian school in Pennsylvania, before going west with a rancher in 1882.

"The best thing to do is have you come out to see how I am fixed here," he suggested as their correspondence progressed. [19] "I have a large ranch, and saddle horses and cows, and a house in town at Placerville. I will send you a ticket to come and then I can go back with you and get the boy."

283

Alice was leery. She tried to check up in Florida on Glover with little success. Finally, apparently intrigued by the rarity of the invitation, she agreed to visit his ranch if she could bring a companion. That suited Glover; he'd send two round-trip tickets and promised a horseback camping trip into the mountains.

Unable to find another woman as traveling companion, Alice took with her the Aldridges' youngest boy, Gerald called "Jerry," seventeen. Glover greeted them warmly, put them up in the Placerville hotel, toured them over his ranch and nearby mountains. Only vaguely did he talk about adopting an Indian "son." Rain blighted their outdoors activities. Alice found her breathing labored in the mile-high altitude. Jerry was too young not to be restless.

After only a few days, they departed. Glover was disappointed, but expressed a desire to come to Wewoka for a visit. On her return, Alice received a letter telling her to not worry about the expense of the trip. "I'm sorry you didn't get to go to the Ute and Navajo reservations," Glover wrote. "But the little boy wanted to go home to his mama. Did she let him nurse when he got home? Don't tell him I said that. He might get mad and not like me when I come to visit Wewoka." [20]

Glover and Alice kept letters going back and forth from 1923 into the 1930s. He visited Wewoka twice and maintained a sharp interest in events in Alice's life. He admired Maude greatly, and wanted her to teach him to speak Seminole.

Barely five years after accompanying his grandmother to visit Glover's ranch, "Jerry"Aldridge was killed February 15, 1928 when a stunt plane in which he was a passenger crashed in Dallas.

Glover wrote: "Jerry's death must have been terrible for you and his parents. He was a fine young man and it seems sad that he could not have lived to accomplish that which he was striving to do. The only comfort is our Heavenly Father. He cares and loves us all. He has done for us these things that are for our own good, no matter how hard it may seem." [21]

JOHN'S MARRIAGE to Mae Good may have settled him down somewhat. But not a great deal. His basic mental apparatus probably was beyond any corrective adjustment. He remained for his lifetime a sponger and trickster. Just one year before Alice's death, John forged two checks on her pitifully slim Wewoka bank account.

"Received your letter and check yesterday," Mae wrote Alice on February 10, 1924. "Also got a letter from John. He said he had a promise of a job. I hate to see him away from me but he wanted to go to work. He gets so blue doing nothing."

Ten days later, Mae wrote again: "Johnny came home this morning. Today is my birthday. I am 25 years old. My sister in Missouri sent me a birthday cake. It sure was nice."

Any reward Mae Good Davis earned for loving and trying to guide her irresponsible husband, she never collected. The Dark Angel zeroed in on her in the Spring of 1929. After several weeks of anguish, she was taken to an Oklahoma City hospital for exploratory surgery.

On May 4, 1929, John wrote his mother:

> Mae is a very sick girl. She is just coming out of the ether and is doing fine. They found a cancer in her stomach below her right ribs but we won't tell her about that because she wouldn't last long.
>
> The doctor said to tell her he took the tumor out and she will get along fine. I sure hope she gets along all right. The seven years we have been married, she has not missed one night saying her prayers.

On May 24, he told Alice:

> Mae is up and weak. I would go out and get something to do, but I will have to wait. Mrs. Good paid our hospital bill which is $125, but I have to pay for the operation, $150. Mrs. Good has helped all she could.

Alice sent forty dollars. Kitt visited Mae a month after her release from the hospital, and wrote her mother: "Mae looks so pretty and her condition puzzles me....There is such wistful sadness in her big eyes." Mae's mother, hiding their guilty secret, contrived with John to give the doomed girl one last vacation. The three of them spent a couple of weeks in Colorado Springs.

But the cancer continued its secret feasting on Mae's stomach. On December 17, 1929 John sadly told his mother his wife was confined to bed, and had not eaten for a week. The doctor came and gave Mae hypos for pain, and left a nurse with her. Before the end of the year Mae was dead, just thirty years old. Her loss shook up John. He grieved for a while, and then, now thirty-six, moved on with his hapless, vagabond existence.

KISSING HIS LEADING LADY on stage in the glare of footlights was superb training for Andrew Jackson Davis's lifelong passion—romance. He was married four times; and over the years his amorous misadventures on the meandering tent show circuit left numerous naive maidens with broken hearts. Jack fathered six children, always initially showing them a burst of intense love, but was so willing to discard them and their mothers that his first son would turn desperate and commit suicide.

Jack never hit the big time. In his luckiest week as an actor or musician, he might have earned forty or fifty dollars. In some of his worst showbiz depths when the cast split the take, his share might be fifteen cents to a dollar or so.

The leading lady for whom he had cast aside Ione McBride was now his wife. Doris Berkeley got his ring and gave him a second child, a daughter named Jacqueline. The toddler was usually stashed in a nursery school while they traveled.

His ex-wife and son in Salt Lake City were in desperate straits. Alice, utterly sympathetic to Ione, from time to time dribbled them a few dollars. Ione thanked her January 7, 1926 for a $10 check and said "I'm surviving only because I surrendered to Jesus." Ione suffered a nervous breakdown and couldn't work, she wrote Alice October 2, 1929: "Thanks for the money." She needed an operation in February 1930, but couldn't afford it, explaining, "The rent is past due." Alice sent $10. By that June Ione got a traveling sales job—and a check for $25 from her mother-in-law. The job ended December 30 and Ione asked Alice if Jack could help her. The letters continued between Wewoka and Utah. Ione proudly informed Jack Junior's grandmother that the boy was a good student, "usually making 100 on exams." Through Ione's ordeal, her ex-husband never made any significant effort to help her. Ione's desperation is clearly shown in her June 27, 1934 letter to Alice:

> I don't know where to get in touch with Jack and I thought I would write him to see if he would help Jack Junior out. I have been ill and Jackie is too young to join the CCC (Civilian Conservation Corp, federal made-work Depression relief), and also too young for the work they are giving the men.
>
> He hasn't a thing to wear but one pair of overalls and one shirt. It makes me sick that Jack doesn't think enough of his own little boy to help him out. You have done you best but it is awful the way Jack has done. I do not want to weary you with my problems.

The terrible consequence of this father's neglect of his first-born was never known to Alice. It happened after her death. On September 6, 1935, Andrew Jackson Davis Junior, seventeen years old, climbed a telephone pole on a street in Salt Lake City. Passersby saw him stare into the clouds for several minutes, and then fling out his arms and dive onto the pavement, smashing his brain. [22]

SHOW BIZ took a hard hit during the Depression; meager family purses were opened for food instead of entertainment. Jack, unfortunately was induced to buy a tent show—canvas, stage, scenery, seats, the works for $600. He begged Alice for help; she couldn't come up with any money. By a complicated deal, he took possession of the show and started touring Nebraska and Kansas in early 1930.

"What an albatross!" he moaned at end of the first week. [23]

Doris wrote Alice: "We are having a hard time. It is terrible to have only six people in the house, three on passes. Your check got us out of town. John is here, trying to help. Sweet of you to suggest keeping baby for a while. She is spry as a cricket and would be a burden." [24]

On July 23, 1930, from Broadwater, Nebraska, Doris sent thanks for another check, adding:

We are taking in $10 to $20 a night and our expenses run from $90 to $100 a night. We are hoping to hang on till the fair starts and then we have a chance to make a little money. We are flat broke and no way to pay for the haul out of town. And the car payment is overdue. We paid the room rent and used the rest for food. The Depression is felt all over. Other shows, too, are having hard times.

The tent show folded. On December 15, 1930 Jack and Doris were in California looking for acting jobs. Their marriage broke up, but in the fall of 1931, Doris and their nine-year-old daughter Jackie rejoined Jack in Big Spring, Texas where he was with a tent show. But if Doris Berkeley Davis thought her thirty-four-year-old husband had reformed, had closed his roving eye, and was ready to settle down with one woman, she was a fool.

Their reunion lasted barely a month. It climaxed tragically at Weimar, Texas on November 20, 1931 in an exciting series of explosive scenes that contained more dramatic action than probably any script they had ever performed on a tent show stage. Doris told all in a long but interesting letter to Alice:

Dear Mother:

I hate to do this but since I know Denny (Jack's stage name was Denny Thornton) is going to try to paint me in a black light, in justification to myself I want you to know the absolute truth. The members of the company and the Weimar city marshal will verify what I say.

First, after rejoining Denny I was with him only two days when without any provocation, he returned to his old ways and openly began chasing other women. Going on drunken sprees with them, and because of his lack of principles, Denny was given his notice to close by the Sadler show.

Then this awful thing... He forced me to sit in the same car with him and the woman he had been with, and Jackie was there and saw him openly make love to this other woman in the back seat. Mr. Nichols had no one else to take our places and he couldn't show if Denny didn't come back.

Then I gave Denny another chance for I did so want us to try to make a home for baby, and I tried to forget my humiliation and hurt.

288

Then a woman named Charlotte called from Waco and told him to come 200 miles and get her. He was gone all night and came back in time for the show, bringing the woman with him and said he was going to keep her.

It was too much. I told Denny if he didn't get this drunken woman away from me I would knock her down. Denny said if I did he would kill me. Well, he protected her and he also jumped on every member of the show, the manager as well, calling them vile names, and started a fight with Mr. Nichols.

Mr. Nichols called the marshal and had Denny put in jail. I had nothing to do with that for when the manager called the law I was outside the tent talking to Denny and his drunken woman. Despite all Denny has done to me, I was sorry to think he was jailed, although I got satisfaction out of the fact that Charlotte couldn't take him back to Waco. She demanded to know what business it was of mine if she was sleeping with my husband, and she'd come around as much and as often as she liked with any man, married or single.

I went down to the jail as soon as we finished the show to try to get Denny out. He was very hateful and vindictive toward me. I passed everything off and got him out early next morning. He'd given me a gun as a safeguard, but I thought I'd better sell it, and buy shoes for baby, than have him use it in anger and spend the rest of his life in the penitentiary.

I would have you spared all this, God knows, but I knew you'd hear about it. I have omitted a number of unpleasant details needless to bring up. I do not know how you feel toward me, but I have done my very best and can go no further. You will still love your boy regardless. I have been a good and faithful wife to Denny. I wouldn't give up until I couldn't bear it any more. I have no money, nor has he given me any, except $2 and $1 he won gambling. I know this will be the last time I will worry you. I have no idea what Denny contemplates doing.[25]

Doris stayed in touch with Alice, telling her from Victoria, Texas where she was performing, it was her worst ever Christmas. On January 5, 1932 she wrote from Refugio, Texas: "It was hard to cash your $4 check, made out to A. Jack Davis. Sometimes it feels I can't go on..."

If she did, it would be without Jack. Cupid already was dealing from his stacked deck. A new love had lighted up Jack's life. In

289

Wewoka on February 4, 1932, he got from Canyon, Texas a letter from Helen Wood: "Darling Sweetheart: Sunshine and bright, just the kind of day for a picnic. Wish you were here for me to love. . ."

Jack asked for a divorce. Sadly, Doris surrendered, writing Alice: "I am deeply hurt. My dreams are shattered. If he has met someone, there is no reason not to give him a divorce. I said I wouldn't ask alimony, but it is hard to make a living for Jackie and me. This week we divided the show's proceeds; I got $4.85. I dare not leave the show. As bad as it is, it is better than nothing."[26]

Of course, Jack let her keep their daughter.

This is the only known photograph of the Davis family's residence at Arbeka and the Bar-X-Bar ranch. Taken in 1882, Alice (*center*) is flanked by (*from left*) R. H. Melot, Maye, Bess, Irene, Myrtle and Jim Webber.

Photograph of George Lytle Davis, Alice's doomed son. This photograph was taken in Leroy, Kansas while apparently visiting his paternal grandparents.

Jesse Edwin Davis on the old Bar-X-Bar ranch property where he spent virtually all of his forty-two years.

Photos courtesy THE SEMINOLE NATION MUSEUM
and Gene and Martha Aldridge

291

Letterhead dated May 22, 1892 from Alice's general store in Arbeka in the northern-most part of the Seminole Nation. Note the Indian motif and the panther image - possibly relating the idea that the children of *Kúnu Hvt'kē* were of the ruling Panther clan of the Florida Seminole.

When Alice accompanied missionaries organized by Jackson Brown to Florida in 1909. (*Back row, standing, left to right*) Dan Long, Andrew Jackson Brown, George Scott (interpreter), John Wesley, Sissy Long; (*seated*) Mrs. Andrew Jackson Brown, Mrs. Alice B. Davis, Lizzie Bruner, Irene Davis (later Mrs. W. S. Key), Lucy Brown (later Mrs. Barney McKellop), Mrs. George Scott.

In the center of this photograph in a thronged federal courtroom in Muskogee, Alice (*in dark hat, with hand upraised*) is sworn in as Principal Chief by Judge F. W. Farver, of the Choctaw Nation. Looking on (*center*) is Major Victor M. Locke, Jr., Superintendent of the Five Civilized Tribes.

After being sworn in as Principal Chief of the Seminole Nation, Alice (*center, first row*) poses with five daughters and three granddaughters on the steps of the U.S. Courthouse in Muskogee. On Alice's left is granddaughter Joycette Jones and on her right is Aleece Locke. Her first grandaughter, Pearl Davis Dovell, is on the left in the top row with (*left to right*) Maye, Maude, Irene, Bess, and Kitt.

Ladies of fashion were Alice's daughters. They were all attractive and most married well. In photo [*Right*] are (*back row*) Bess, Myrtle, Irene and Kitt. Seated are Maude and Maye.

[*Lower photo, left to right*] Kitt, Myrtle, Maye, Maude, Bess and Irene.

The drilling crew and townspeople gather jubilantly on the derrick floor of Wewoka's oil discovery well—the Betsy Foster No. 1. The well came in on St. Patrick's Day, March 17, 1923.

During the oil boom of the 1920s and 1930s, rigs sprouted over much of the Seminole Nation and royalties made millionaires of a large number of tribesmen. [*Above*] part of the Wewoka field.

The Emahaka Academy took on the unlikely characteristics of European castles.

Governor Brown and others had cotton gins. This one was located in Wewoka.

With portable boilers, sawmills were able around the turn of the century to move from place to place in the Seminole Nation.

Two contrasting views of the "mansion" built in Wewoka by Jackson Brown--the photos taken almost three-quarters of a century apart. [*Above*] The verandahed house when it was new, and [*below*] decaying and almost a total ruin in 2005. Belatedly an effort was started to restore the historic structure.

Lucy Crain, Alice's sister, died in an Indian mental hospital.

Alice with grandson Gerald "Jerry" Aldridge (*left*) in Montrose, Colorado on August 17, 1923 to visit Indian rancher William G. Glover (*right*).

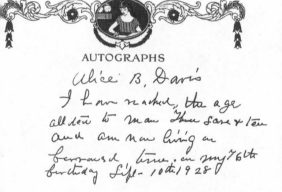

AUTOGRAPHS

Autograph book in which Alice wrote: *"I have reached the age all due to man, three score and ten and am living on borrowed time on my 76th birthday on Sept. 10th 1928."*

Maye on entering Kidd-Key College at age sixteen.

On the Bar-X-Bar ranch, Alice's first granddaughter, Pearl Davis, rides side-saddle with the grace of a sixteen-year-old equestrienne.

At Keokuk Falls, Alice's daughter Kitt (*left*) and her friend Mrs. Kim Seran in 1912 ford the Canadian River near the old grist mill.

[*Left*] Alice in the late 1920s.

[*Below*] Alice (*center*) with
daughter Maude (*right*) and an unidentified friend.

303

When occasion demanded, Alice dressed in fashion and looked somewhat regal. These photos probably were taken when the Davis and Brown families went to St. Louis for the 1904 World Fair.

Alice Brown Davis. Photographed in profile at a Tulsa, Oklahoma studio in 1929.

Four generations of the Davis family, photographed around Christmas 1934. Alice (*far left*) with her daughter Myrtle Davis Aldridge, and Myrtle's son, J. Bart Aldridge, holding his son, Gene C. Aldridge, Alice's great-grandchild.

Despite the ravages of time which have made the images distant and washed out, this 1880's photograph highlights the drama, atmosphere, and excitement of the long-ago Indian Territory frontier. The horsemen are galloping past Governor Brown's Sasakwa trading post.

Photos courtesy Gene and Martha Aldridge
and THE SEMINOLE NATION MUSEUM

17

Pierce Arrows and *Osofkey*

A T THE HEIGHT of the oil boom, perhaps as many as one-half of the Seminole Indians could slap down cash to buy Pierce Arrow luxury sedans and over-priced brick houses and squander recklessly on frivolity and luxury. In amazing contrast, most of the others led tattered lives. Some of these were still in log huts, subsisting mainly on corn they grew and pounded and boiled into a gritty mush called *osofkey,* cooked with rabbits killed on their farm or with an occasional chicken—or eaten plain.

The difference between feast and famine depended on which Indians were lucky enough to get oil royalties, and which did not.

Before statehood, the hills and prairies constituting their nation had been carved up into homesteads, and distributed equally and fairly to the Seminoles. But how could *que será será* be avoided? Liquid gold hidden a mile deep was the surprise jackpot; and it was owned exclusively by the individual who had been allotted that piece of land, not communal income to be shared by all members of the tribe.

This totally new and unexpected oil money created two classes of Indians—the *nouveau riche* and the starvelings. Just by chance, one Seminole might have become a Midas while his brother remained virtually a pauper.

Harmony in the tribe already was at low ebb. Thousands in oil money came to some, while Depression hardship rubbed their neighbors raw. Other "normal" conflicts split the fourteen clans; no longer did they have a strong leader to unite behind. They missed Governor Brown. As individuals, most had run into a nasty encounter with imperious federal Indian agents. Unsually, the Indian recoiled, and retreated empty-handed, irritated and confused, feeling demeaned by the autocratic and arbitrary instructions coming from his Great Father's minions.

This long-simmering unhappiness finally boiled over and a flood of gripes swept up to Washington, and caused political concern on Capitol Hill.

The United States Senate decided to send an Indian Affairs sub-committee to Oklahoma. Its mission was to hold public hearings and get on-the-scene facts about trouble in all the tribes.

On Wednesday, November 12, 1930, Senator Lynn J. Frazier of North Dakota led Oklahoma's two Senators, along with three Indian Affairs Committee staff aides, and two stenographers into a crowded courtroom in the Seminole County courthouse at Wewoka. [1]

They were a distinguished and impressive group. Frazier was a suave and experienced politician, three times North Dakota's governor, in the Senate since 1922. His Senate colleagues from Oklahoma, Elmer Thomas and William B. Pine, were respected and known as keen students of Indian affairs.

Their entrance interrupted and halted an excited buzz rising in two languages from the spectator benches. At least 100 locals had come to talk, or look and listen. A number of Indians, typically shy and timid, stood out in the hallway.

The Senate group dragged chairs beside the courtroom's witness box and positioned the secretaries with shorthand books.

Among the first witnesses sworn was Alice. When her name was called, she came slowly forward, looking her years. Her hair, black as coal, was coiled on her head, ending in a fist-sized bun that tilted to the left. Age spots dotted her face; the skin of her cheeks and jowls sagged noticeably. Her mouth turned down at the corners, making her countenance stern. Her eyes, deep-set and dark, had a sad glint. Her attire was not very attractive, a long black dress of heavy material, a baggy jacket, and scuffed shoes.[2]

The North Dakota Senator got out of his chair and courteously escorted Alice to the witness chair. He got right down to business, launching a long interrogation. Senator Frazier was anxious to tap this highly regarded Indian matriarch's keen knowledge across a broad spectrum—from education and health to tribal politics and economics.

Frazier's questioning quickly opened up some old wounds, particularly the historic and still lingering animosity between the Creeks and the Seminoles. And also the high-handedness of "them"—Government field agents, probate clerks, and others who ran offices to supervise and "assist" the Indians.

"These Indians who are coming into wealth," Alice informed the Senate committee, "have been taken from this nation into other nations; homes bought for them in the Creek Nation. Over in Hughes County they have built them fine homes. They buy wonderful furniture; they buy automobiles."

She was referring to how Indian agents doled out oil royalties that they were empowered to collect and hold for Seminoles who had oil wells on their land.

"Why have they been transferred or moved into other counties?" asked Frazier.

"That is what I do not know."

"Do these people know?" persisted Frazier. "Have you talked to any of the people who have been moved over there?"

"I never talked very much with any of these people that have come into wealth," Alice answered, "because seemingly I was interfering with the officials' rights out there. And I did not have anything to do with it. But there is a wrong being done to these people, to move them from their own nation. I talked with one out there and I said, 'Why did you go to the Creek Nation?' He said: 'Because the white folks told me to. They said we are going to build you homes there.' That is the only time I talked to them."

In further questioning, Alice made clear where the blame should lay. "We would like to have it so these field clerks would not have so much authority as they have because they are just like you or anybody else; they really do not know the wants and needs of these people. I think they act in good faith, but when a field clerk comes in here and recommends buying three automobiles for one family, and buy these fine homes—they will not buy farms, something they can make money out of—it looks to me like they have too much authority."

Senator Thomas interjected: "When these automobiles and homes are bought, they are bought on request of the head of that family, are they not?"

Alice responded, "They tell these people they have so much money—if they want a home or a lot of furniture. (Testimony later by field clerks revealed that some Indians had as much as $400,000 to $600,000 in their accounts, being doled out to them at up to $1,200 a month.) Some of that stuff is going to sit out in the rain. That is why we need a field matron here to tell them what to do with these things. I do not mean to say all our people are ignorant, but there are some who are, just like among the white people or any other race."

Senator Pine asked, "Do they sometimes sell this furniture to get a little cash?"

"I cannot say. I heard they did that, but I do not know."

"Do you think," asked Senator Thomas, "the Government should exercise more supervision over the Indians or less supervision?"

"I think," Alice answered, "they should send someone out here other than the field clerks to see what the field clerks are doing."

"So, they are not the right kind of people. They do not know what the Indians need or what they want. Is that it?"

"I am not blaming them," said Alice, "because they really do some of these things in ignorance, like you or I might."

"Well, that is natural of course."

"But," Alice said, "they should not have just one man. There is a little fellow who runs around here going into different Indian homes asking how many children they have of school age. These Indians do not know what the purpose is. They tell him how many children they have of school age and maybe not one of those children are in school. They are afraid of a Government man. They

311

stand in awe. Our Indian people stand in awe of a Government person."

"Why?" said Frazier. "From past experience have your children learned to be afraid of these Government officials?"

"From what I hear them say, I would think so. I do not come in contact with any of them. They would think I was interfering with their private affairs. I do not go around there, and I am just glad that you people are here and will listen to a few things I have to say."

"How many," said Thomas, "take the same attitude as you do toward the officials?"

"There may be all of them, but they would not come out and say it as I do."

"Your attitude," said Thomas, "is a result of a loss of confidence in the ability and the integrity of the service?"

"It might cover all of those."

Senator Thomas's face showed puzzlement. "We have complaint that the Federal Government is taking too much authority and telling the Indians what they can and what they can not do. Then we have other complaints that they do not do enough. We are trying to get the facts and, of course, we will have to judge for ourselves as to what we think about the matter. We are glad to have any circumstances of facts which any Indian will give us in regard to any matter in which they are interested."

"The most that we need now," said Alice, "is a field matron to go out among not only those who have riches but those who have none, and see conditions. I do not know whether there are any funds that could be used for this, but the tribe should have some money in the Government's hands."

Frazier asked: "You think there should be a hospital here for your Indian people in this county?"

"I do."

"Including a tubercular sanitarium?"

"Well," said Alice, "as to a tubercular sanitarium I do not know. They claim that this climate is not the best for tuberculosis, so I could not say as to that. But we do need a hospital for the older people who have no homes or who have no way of caring for their sick."

"From your experience and observation of the Indian children who have gone to school," continued Frazier, "do you think they get better results from attending the public schools or from attending the Indian Government schools?"

"The Indian Government schools, their own schools, because they will not go to these public schools."

"Why not?"

"For several reasons. They go. The white children are unkind to them. They fight on the way, and they fight on the way back. They go home and stay there. In different homes where I know they have children of school age there are families that have children who have grown up without knowing how to write their names. They will not go to a public school. And I am glad you mentioned this."

"Do you think," Frazier asked, "there is a prejudice against the Indian children attending public school?"

"Yes, sir. To these Indians, there is a prejudice."

In another series of questions, Alice brought up the need to teach the Seminoles better sanitation in their homes.

"I spoke about where there was a large gathering. They have a bucket. They all drink out of the same bucket, as I think you and Mr. Pine saw. Those things should not be, but we, as Indian people, we cannot ourselves go out and tell the people not to do that because they have been accustomed to doing those things. If you had a field matron, someone that would come in here, and say that through an interpreter and they would listen to them more than they would to us. I guess I am the oldest one among the Seminoles. My brother used to gather these people together and talk to them; but there is no one who has done that since his death. We have no leaders. We can never get together in a mass and do these things."

"Why can you not do that?" asked Thomas.

"Well, there are several reasons why we can not do that."

"Enumerate them."

"Well, one of them is that we do not have the conveniences to get together in council. When we used to have the council we would be called together to get our ideas, but we can not do those things now."

"The testimony is here that some 800 of the Seminoles are in rather good circumstances."

"There may be that many. I do not know that there is. I guess the field clerks can tell you how many."

"That was the field clerk's statement?" Frazier put in.

Senator Thomas asked: "What other reason exists for your not being able to get together."

"We are not of the same mind."

"In other words you are divided?"

"Well," Alice replied, "some one has his idea about it and another idea. It is not as if we had a regular council and had the power to act; say like we would elect a judge and we have to listen to him. If our people had any authority to put in some one as a spokesman for the people, for the mass meeting, we would have to listen to them and in that way might get in touch with the Government to show them our grievances."

Alice paused, her eyes hardening a bit, and then ran her gaze across the faces of the lawmakers who had come from Washington.

"It would not take one day," she said, "but one month to enumerate all those grievances."

"Do you care to make any other statement?" asked Frazier.

"No."

"Mrs. Davis," said Frazier, with a friendly smile, "how old are you?"

"I am seventy-eight years old."

The North Dakota Senator quickly rose and came to the witness stand, seized Alice's hand and shook it vigorously. He beamed at her again.

"You mean you are seventy-eight years young! And still able to account for yourself!"

He helped her down. Returning to a front bench, Alice looked around the courtroom wearily. She commended the Great Father for trying to look into the Seminoles' general discomfort. The Senators seemed to have a genuine interest in seeing that the native Americans were given a better chance to continue making progress in the white man's world. In fact she understood they intended to conduct public hearings in each of the Five Civilized Tribes. They wanted to have the whole picture—everything that was bad and whatever there was that might be good. It was a giant task for them. But these officials

314

seemed to understand and appreciate Indian heritage and customs, even though not many others in Washington did. She was hopeful they would enact legislation that would make the Seminole life better. [3] But she was enough of a realist to know that the beneficial effect, if any, might not come to the Seminole Nation for many, many moons. The Great Father did not take action with the swiftness of an arrow.

In the afternoon session, joined by Senator Burton K. Wheeler of Montana, a string of witnesses confirmed the plight of the tribal have-nots, and the erratic and sometimes astounding spending of the Seminoles' oil royalties.

Thomas asked Glenn L. Kivett, the U.S. field clerk for the Seminoles, to describe his duties.

"Our instructions are very vague. We go to take leases, supervise the leasing of land, make investigations requested by the general office in Muskogee, pass upon applications for removal of restrictions, see land is appraised, settle family quarrels."

"Is that done in an effort to keep the Indians out of court?"

"Yes, sir. It was done in this case yesterday to keep the husband and wife together as they have four or five little children."

"How many of these Seminoles," asked Thomas, "are what you would call independently rich? Who are solvent, and getting along all right."

"There are about 1,600 Seminoles in this jurisdiction," said the clerk. "I would say about half of them."

"Now tell us about the others. What about their condition?"

"The other 800 are the ones that are unfortunate in that their lands have no value for farming or oil either. They cannot get anything out of the soil. They are just scratching about the best they can."

Thomas asked: "What kind of houses have they?"

"There is no hard and fast rule about that. There might be an Indian out here who three or four years ago sold a lease and got a house built. Maybe the next one is living in a log house that has been there twelve or fifteen years. I will tell you how they live. They generally can raise enough side hill corn to make the dish that they live on—*osofkey*."

"What is there besides corn?"

315

"Corn and water. They take parched corn—"

Thomas interrupted. "And make coffee out of that?"

"Yes. They call it *abuske.*"

"Has there been much money spent providing homes to the Seminoles?"

"A lot of money. About $140,000."

They discussed an Indian named Frank Harjoche who had $130,000 in royalties on deposit, but complained he couldn't get his house repaired.

"In what conditions are the homes that have been built by the Government?"

"I will tell you," said Kivett. "You can build a house but you can not make a home of it. You can build a man a new house, but you can hardly sit there and see that he keeps it clean and sanitary. Plenty of them go into a new house and in a year it is unsanitary."

"You know Frank Harjoche?"

"Yes. He is a very irresponsible person. He will apply for things and then forget them."

D.D. Bronson, an attorney, presented two complaints. Indian agents supervised the repair and re-papering of the home of an Indian named John Burgess at a cost of $5,000. "That job wasn't worth $500," said the lawyer. Walter Wise, another Indian, was charged $6,000 to run an electric high line three miles to his home, and his monthly bill was double an ordinary user's. An outrage, said Bronson, inviting the senators to go look at the house.

Bronson told about two Indians on whose lands restrictions were removed without their knowledge, and the property was leased in secret. Frazier said: "Congress has given the Secretary of the Interior almost unlimited power. I think this is an abuse, but it had been done."

Another Indian, Johnson Porter, inherited land worth about $18,000, Bronson said. He had bought 135 gallons of bootleg whiskey. While he was on a long drunk, a woman paid him $350 to deed her the property. Porter hired Bronson to sue for recovery.

"Porter would get drunk every time he could get a dime or 15 cents to get some canned heat," said Bronson. "He was rather pestiferous. He wanted whatever they would give him, and settled the lawsuit. I think they paid him only about $1,200."

Jeanetta Tiger Burgess, the Pierce Arrow lady from Konawa, gave the senators a bushel of complaints. First, the Muskogee office had deducted her $95 gasoline bill from her $1,000 a month allowance. When she asked how much money she had, she was told it was none of her business. She was denied money to build her son a house. She wanted a new Pierce Arrow sedan—"I am tired of cranking the one I have."

Senator Wheeler interrogated H. B. McMillan, a Muskogee office superintendent. "In there any reason why your office could not give these Indians a statement showing how much money they have on hand?"

"That would be a danger," said McMillan. "People who have merchandise to sell would come to the field clerk and argue with him that the Indian has money and is able to buy his merchandise."

"Is not the money restricted so they can use it only in certain ways?"

"It is."

"It seems to me preposterous to keep these Indians in ignorance about their money," Wheeler said, briskly. "You would not think of doing business with a white man that way, would you? What is this witness's estate estimated to be worth?"

Two or three hundred thousand dollars, said the Government man.

Wheeler asked Jeanetta Burgess: "How much family have you got?"

She responded through interpreter Wesley Barnett: "Eleven children. Only five now—six died."

"Do you have an education at all?"

"I do not know a thing about it; I never did go to school."

"What," Wheeler asked, "do you do with your money?"

"For living expenses," through the interpreter. "There is big repair bills. She says she lives on it and the children lives on it—the children, her husband, and herself."

"How many automobiles have you got?"

"Three. One sedan and two one-seated affairs."

"What make?"

"Pierce Arrow."

"Pierce Arrow?"

"That is the one Mr. McMillan bought for her."

"Did she want a Pierce Arrow?"

"She says that is the kind of car she wanted. So she still got that car."

"What other kinds of cars?"

"A Chrysler and a Ford. And also a Chevrolet truck."

"Is that all the automobiles you have got?"

"There is a tractor."

Senator Wheeler lifted his eyebrows. "What else have they unloaded on you?"

"That is about all."

The questioning also brought out that the Pierce Arrow lady lives in an eleven-room brick house that just had $5,200 in repair. She wanted to trade in the Pierce Arrow on a new car, but McMillan wouldn't approve it.

Wheeler said: "She has two other cars. Tell her that is plenty for her. You tell her she will not have any money left at all unless she is more careful with the money she is getting now."

The interpreter relayed that to the Indian witness and then told the Senators: "She says she is not the only one that is using that money. People overcharge her and she is paying for these—"

Wheeler interrupted. "If she keeps on buying automobiles and drawing down as much money as she has, she will not have as much money as she has now."

"She says," responded the interpreter, "while she has a little money she likes to enjoy life like anybody else. Hereafter she says she could not use that money."

Senator Frazier inquired about her $29.18 electric bill. "What did you use the electricity for?"

"Used it for electric light, the electric radio, electric ironing, electric washing machine, electric vacuum cleaner."

"You tell her," said Wheeler, "that if she does not save her money she will not have an electric washer and electric heater and electric lights. She will be going back to the teepee if she does not take better care of her money."

The interpreter chatted with the witness a minute or two. "She says she has been in a tent all her life. That is the way her mother and father lived. If she had to go back like that, it would not be anything new for her. She says she was brought up on Indian food and don't know anything about the white man's food. *Osofkey* and things like that were common in her tent. She says she was brought up on plenty of wild animals, wild turkey, and prairie chicken, and squirrels. Now there is not any such thing as that, not even rabbits."

The senators got a grim view of Seminole life in this fall of 1930—during the presidency of Herbert Hoover—from an Indian named Sampson B. Harjo. He came to inquire about finding a job.

Senator Thomas: "I have just a question or two. You visit the homes of a great number of Indians, do you not?"

"Yes, sir."

"Will you tell the committee what condition the poor Indians are in at this time as to food?"

"Well," responded Harjo, "I am one of that class of people. The only way I can get food is to borrow from my good friends, the Seminoles, people that can trust me."

"Do you own land?"

"Yes, sir."

"Is it rented?"

"No. I am living on the place myself."

"And farming it?"

"Well, I got a renter; he works the place."

"How much money have you collected this year from your land?"

"At least about $25, I guess."

"Do you work at laboring by the day's wage?"

"I can not get any job," replied Harjo. "That is it. If I can get a job somewhere it would be all right; but then I can not get a job."

Frazier said: "Now, tell the committee just what bill of fare the Indians have; what food do you have to live on now?"

Thomas threw in: "What do you have to eat for your meals every day? Tell us what you have for breakfast and what for dinner and what for supper."

"Most of it's eggs and cornbread; in the wintertime we usually live on rabbits."

"Do you have coffee?" asked Frazier.

"Yes, sir, and sometimes a thing what is known as *osofkey.*"

"Is this the same bill of fare," inquired Thomas, "you people have been living on for many years back?"

"Absolutely; yes, sir."

"Your food is no better than it was a long time ago before the white men moved in among you?"

"No, sir."

"Is it any worse?"

"I believe it is worse, because a long time ago there was open spaces, and we can go out and hunt and all that; but nowadays you have got to buy a license to go hunting and we people are not able to buy licenses, and there we are."

The afternoon waned, and Senator said the hearing would have to end so the committee could drive on to Okmulgee for a Creek Nation hearing next day. Anyone who didn't get to testify could submit a statement. Senator Thomas said, "I have a statement signed by an Indian named Amos setting forth some matters he wants put in the record."

"So ordered," said Frazier, the chairman.

If he had testified as a live witness, Amos undoubtedly would have given the spectators a good show. Here is his story summarized from his statement:

Forty years old, Amos Joshua was a full blood Seminole (roll number 1469) living seven miles west of Holdenville on 120 acres on which were 16 pumping oil wells that produced a large amount of royalties held for him by the Interior Department. He didn't know how much money he had. He went to Washington and inquired. The Interior Department told him he spent $67,000 in the year 1929. He didn't know where it went, "but I did agree several times to donate to churches and other good causes."

He bought $5,000 worth of gravel; the county put it on his road free. Rain washed it away. The Jarrett Motor Company in Wetumka, Oklahoma presented a bill for $8,000 for Ford cars "they claimed I bought for certain girls." A Dr. Blair came from the Interior Department and approved the bill to be paid.

Amos was disturbed that the district court rendered a $20,040 judgment against him in March 1930. He attached a newspaper clipping explaining it. "I can't read nor write; I can't speak English language. I have been allowed to draw $750 per month, and my wife $375. I don't think I am half as bad Indian as I am branded. I would like these things looked into by this honorable body."

The attached newspaper clipping:

INDIAN GIRL GETS $20,040 FOR LOVE—SAYS WEALTHY
INDIAN BETRAYED HER; COURT TRIAL IS CONTESTED

WEWOKA, March 1 (Special)—Alleging that she had been seduced by Amos Joshua, one of the wealthiest members of the Seminole tribe; that he was the father of her child; and that he had promised to marry her, Jennie Naroomey, young Indian girl of Wewoka, was awarded $20,040 damages by a jury in Judge George C. Crump's court at Holdenville.

The Indian girl says that Amos Joshua, who lives on a modern well-equipped farm near Holdenville, had pleaded with her to marry him when she filed her petition in the damage suit, had taken her to Muskogee, promising her fine clothes, jewels, and other luxuries. She further alleged that he had represented to his friends that they were man and wife.

Heatedly contested, the lawsuit resolved itself into a legal battle as the trial continued for several days, and ended with the jury's verdict of $40 actual damages and $20,000 exemplary damages.

Alice was correct in predicting that there would be no arrow swiftness in whatever corrective action was inspired by the Senate hearings in Oklahoma. Co-authored by Senator Wheeler, the Indian Reorganization Act of 1934, was passed by Congress, lifting a few burdens on the Indians. But not enough to make daily life any more noble for the Seminoles. If they were better off, it somehow escaped their notice.

IN OKLAHOMA CITY, Alice with daughters Irene Key and Maye Locke, shielded by umbrellas, walked through misting rain and up marble steps into the new $500,000 building of the Oklahoma Historical Society.

"I don't know just why I am here," Alice whispered to the girls.[4]

It was the evening of Saturday, November 15, 1930, just three days after the Senate hearing in Wewoka. Alice was being given prestigious recognition.

With six other Oklahomans, she was introduced and honored for "an outstanding and meritorious contribution to the history and development of Oklahoma." It was the inaugural of the Oklahoma Hall of Fame sponsored by Governor W.J. Holloway.

C. Guy Cutlip, the Wewoka lawyer and her close friend, introduced her to the gathering of 500 and spoke at length about her character, accomplishments, and devotion to her tribe.

The others similarly honored were E. K. Gaylord, publisher of the *Daily Oklahoman*; Frank Phillips, the pioneer oilman; Col. Graves Leeper, lumberman and 1901 Oklahoma secretary of state; Dr. David W. Boyd, a founder of the University of Oklahoma; Dr. Joseph W. Scroggs, minister and author; and Mrs. Charles R. Hume, renowned historical photographer.

Alice remained overnight in Oklahoma City at Irene's home. The gala had left her exhausted but happy.

18

Into the Purple Twilight

IN THE BACK of the speeding ambulance, Alice hunched over, shivering and frightened. It was dark and cold and the ride bouncy. She laid her hand tenderly on the patient strapped to the gurney; the woman stirred and moaned. Alice whispered hoarsely in her ear. "Maude, Maude! We're going to the City. . .to the hospital. . . Dr. Van Sandt is with you!"[1]

The physician listened to Maude's fitful breathing. She was semi-conscious. Alice studied Dr. Van Sandt's face; it was pinched with worry, his eyes inordinately sad.

Abruptly the motor coughed and died. The ambulance was out of gas. It was Wednesday night, March 9, 1932. They got help and reached Oklahoma General Hospital a little before midnight. [2] Maude had been mysteriously ill since mid-February. She had been residing in Wewoka since breaking up with husband Madison Jones. She first went to the Wewoka hospital and when a crisis developed Dr. Van Sandt decided to take her to specialists at the Oklahoma City hospital.

Alice waited in Oklahoma City while physicians stabilized her daughter and undertook to identify her puzzling illness. On Saturday, March 12, she returned home because both John and Jack had come to visit briefly.

She recorded the ambulance trip in her diary, noting, "I almost froze." For several days she wrote: "Maude no better." Then on Saturday, March 17, her diary acknowledged that Wewoka was celebrating the St. Patrick's Day 1923 discovery of oil. The big parade offended her because people were yelling and laughing while she was sad and in tears about Maude being desperately ill. "I may be unfair, but I can't help it." [3]

Finally the Oklahoma City physicians discerned that Maude had been stricken with encephalitis lethargica, epidemic sleeping sickness. On Saturday, March 19, surgeons decided to open her left parotid gland and remove an infectious blood clot. The operating room was not quite ready when at 10 A.M. she died. [4]

It was well known that Maude desired to be buried in the hilltop cemetery at Arbeka next to her brother Jesse. Both English and Indian funeral services were to be on Sunday, March 20. Alice held back tears and helped make arrangements. "Maude would want Reverend Frank Tingo for the Seminole funeral. She has known him since childhood."

In the Saturday night gloom, Alice sifted through her little treasure chest of Maude memories. On mementoes from Emahaka days, and clippings of newspaper and magazine articles Maude had written concerning customs and affairs of her tribe, her tears fell. The silence may have reminded Alice of hearing Maude's powerful and beautiful soprano voice crooning classical and Indian songs she had cherished. Alice noticed a typed copy of one poem Maude was exceptionally proud of writing:

MY INDIAN BLANKET

'Tis only an Indian blanket
Frayed and worn and old
Yet in its folds are tales untold
Of deserts bleak and mountains high
Of winds and seasons cold and dry.
Just an old Indian blanket
Filled with Indian love.
An old tattered blanket
Only that and nothing more.

The brilliant rainbow colors
Taken from Nature's heart
Reflect the rare strange beauty
Of the noble Red Man's art.

Throw it about you gently,
The old blanket warms you thru and thru
Imparting in its gentle warmth
Things you never knew.

'Tis only an Indian blanket
But precious as rare fine gold
Treasured for memories golden
And tales it could unfold.

At the lonely Arbeka cemetery, Alice stood silently with other sad-faced family members. They were waiting for the sun to set on Maude's grave, alongside Jesse's. Bittersweet memories inundated Alice. Her mind's eye undoubtedly could picture a carefree and energetic Maude joining her sisters and brothers as they grew up in innocent fun and frolic at Arbeka. If she reminisced further . . . the Bar X Bar cowboys. . .the trading post and the Indians who came . . . the visiting drummers and the preachers. . . and—and—and—

There always came, her daughters had noticed, the point at which Alice must stop and throw up a barrier before her memory reached dark heart-ripping scenes too painful to stir out of the cobwebs of time.

HEALTH PROBLEMS of her own commanded Alice's attention. Optometrist W. I. Davis excitedly passed on to Alice new information he felt would retard her budding cataracts. A scientific bulletin he received as a member of the New York and Brooklyn Optometric Society recommended drinking six extra glasses of water daily, and removing pterygiums from the eye. "And," he wrote to her on May 30, 1932, "there are three doctors in Wewoka who are trained to do that."

The aches and pains of old age bothered Alice so much she again went to the warm water spas at Sulphur. While walking in the hallway at Bess's house, she stumbled over something. She fell, cutting her face and banging her knees severely enough to cause a limp; the baths also eased those injuries.

At times she felt very weak. She learned to be careful about standing up too quickly, or making sudden moves. It became too easy to lose her balance. Dr. Van Sandt examined her carefully, listening to her lungs, checking her reflexes, taking her blood pressure.

"Doctor, what is your opinion?"

"Well, Mrs. Davis..." The physician paused, turning cautious. "I don't find anything that really surprises me. Living to be eighty, or even close, that's remarkable." He again was hesitant. "The simple truth is your heart... It has been stout through so many, many years of struggle. . ." He paused. " Now it's wearing out." [5]

Dr. Van Sandt didn't find it necessary to write any prescription. "Just slow down and relax as much as possible. Don't worry about little things. Eat sensibly. Keep your mind active. You've got some good years left."

Escaping worry was not all that easy. John and Jack continued to cause her concern. John wrote and cashed a $25 check on her Wewoka bank account. That astonished and angered her; that was forgery! By mail he begged forgiveness, and promised to never again pull such a dastardly trick. [6] But then just months later he forged a second check on her. Of course, she made the checks good; she couldn't set the law on her own child.

Did he honestly appreciate the many extra, and usually difficult, steps she had taken to enhance his life? Or her many gifts—such as sending a wedding ring because he couldn't buy one when he married Mae Good in 1922. It felt sad to recall that John did not reciprocate Mae's love and goodness. The boy would not—perhaps could not—change. [7] He still roamed. To Colorado Springs she sent $10, to Kansas City $4, to Cushing $3, to Oklahoma City frequent amounts, sometimes as little as a dollar, and to Denver $12 in care of General Delivery, but John responded: "I have my suit and overcoat in pawn for $10. Will try to catch a ride home. I know I have done wrong and I am sorry. Will make it up to you and never leave you again."

When she had expended virtually all the money she had earned from little fees, Alice took a startling surprise step. It was so uncharacteristic that later she must have been stunned to realize her own lapse of sensitivity. Granddaughter Pearl's husband, Gordon Dovell, was killed in an automobile wreck near Paden. A little later Pearl mentioned collecting his life insurance. Alice asked to borrow $1,000 of it. Pearl replied that she needed it, and turned down the grandmother who had always been generous to her.

Kitt knew her mother was hard up. She sent $1. "Pay it on your light bill. I wish it were more." [8] Later Kitt sent another dollar "for stamps."

Life on the tent show circuit continued to be a struggle for Jack. His first child with new wife Helen Wood was born September 16, 1932 and was named Frank Rollin. On December 16, 1933 came their second son, Gerald Eugene. Helen kept up a lively correspondence with her Wewoka mother-in-law. On January 3, 1933, on rejoining Jack after their first son was born:

> Believe me I am happy to have our little family back together again. My folks didn't think I was strong enough to travel. We have been cooking and eating in our room. We are trying to live cheaply. Baby is real pretty. Quite a lot of hair and blue eyes. Was skinny but is beginning to fill out now. Good baby. Surely do thank you for the two dollars.

On January 10, 1934 Helen wrote from Anson, Texas that her mother was now traveling with them to care for the two boys and do the laundry. They were eating in the room; for their breakfast coffee they borrowed tin cups and a percolator from one of the girls in the show.

About six weeks later suddenly came a new episode in Jack's real life soap opera. He stumbled across his ex, Doris. Their trails crossed February 25, 1934 when Jack's show opened in Waco, Texas. On the street he met Doris and her new husband, Dick Marino. They resided in Waco. What could have been an embarrassing or awkward encounter turned out well.

Jack wanted to see his daughter Jacqueline. Doris objected at first. Finally she relented, let Jackie see her father's show, visit his room and meet Helen and their two children. "Jackie was wild about Frankie," Helen wrote Alice on February 27. "Wanted to take him home with her." The new and old wives, the old and new husbands had a pleasant dinner together.

Helen relayed other exciting news: Brunk's Shows had hired them at $45 a week for a long tour in Colorado. Jack worked a side deal to also sell candy to the audience and keep 10 per cent of his sales.

At the end of the year, Helen wrote on December 6 from Ranger, Texas: "Today is Jerry's birthday. Good business last week in Cisco. Have a tree for the kids, candy, fruit, a few things on it. We won't give each other presents, but will try to have a good dinner."

Helen was already pregnant with their third child, a boy, who would be born April 8, 1935. He would be named Bill King Davis. (They would have a daughter, Diane Delores, born September 19, 1939. Helen would suffer a fatal heart attack two years later. Jack would marry for the fourth time, Mignon Poteet, an actress who would be a caring stepmother, and outlive Jack.)

Before his career as a western movie actor failed, Jack had written scenarios for one-reelers. Later he turned to songwriting, and one ballad he sent his mother obviously sprang from nostalgia of his boyhood in rustic Oklahoma. Titled "Just a Little Old Log Hut," marked to be played legato (smooth, even style):

> *Songs have been written about castles in Spain*
> *But not about my little log cabin at the end of a lane*
> *that holds my story of happiness.*
> *I never worry with life's care and woe*
> *for I can pack up and hurry to a place that I know*
> *in all its glory—my last address.*
> *And when I reach the end of the trail*
> *and for life I beseech to no avail,*
> *I'll close my eyes and sleep content*
> *for I realize this blessing's Heaven sent.*

> CHORUS:
> *Just a log hut, you-all see*
> *Beneath an old oaken tree.*
> *But I'm satisfied because I tried wand'ring away*

328

Just like a stray from the fold.
A port in life's storm, a fireplace warm,
an old rockin' chair a-waitin' there
with wide-open arm, a shield from all harm
when you're old.
In a sandy dell hear old Bossy's bell ring,
and at dusk, so still, thrush and whipperwill sing.
Now I'm on my way back to this little shack
with memories to me so Heavenly,
and no more I'll roam from my childhood home.
Evermore content I'll be.

Romance had also come again into John's life. He was quiet about it until "Rita" in Oklahoma City wrote him in Wewoka expressing her hope that his mother's illness wasn't bad and wishing "Daddy" would come back soon.

DESPITE HER TRAVAILS, Alice never abandoned her role as always-available counselor, confessor, and advisor to her people, many of whom remained baffled on how to get along in the white man's world.

One rainy summer day unexpected visitors repeatedly interrupted Columnist Cora Miley as she interviewed Alice in her modest little house for Oklahoma's *Harlow's Weekly*. [9]

"I had thought," the journalist wrote, "the weather being what it was, I would have the lady chief to myself, but I was to learn that the weather was never too bad for the Indians to come in and ask her counsel."

Alice was telling the writer a colorful story when she caught sight of "a comely Indian woman standing in the edge of the verandah waiting patiently in the rain until Mrs. Davis could come out and see what she wanted."

Noticing the visitor, Alice promptly arose and went outside and dealt with the Indian's problem.

"She was resuming the story," Mrs. Miley's article continued, "when an Indian man came with a load of wood as a present for her. He was a friendly fellow who insisted in talking to me in Seminole even though I could not understand him."

Next another Seminole woman appeared, and Alice welcomed her at the kitchen door. Cora Miley could hear them talking. "The Seminole speech on the tongue of its women is like sighing leaves and cooing doves and running water. Presently, I heard her laugh and the merriment was full of the sound of bird trills, up and down notes, which were delightful."

So it went all day, "this one and that one came to see the chief."

WEAKENING GRADUALLY, Alice in early 1935 frequently had to stay abed. Nobody, it seemed, could be immediately found to come in and attend her. Irene drove down to Wewoka and took her mother back to Oklahoma City where the Keys had built a stately residence in keeping with Colonel Key's rise to prominence in Oklahoma business, politics and the military.

Missing familiar surroundings, Alice begged after several days to return to Wewoka. Back in her modest little house, she acquired good caretakers, and many visitors. Frequently came her nephew, the Rev. Louis C. Brown from Sasakwa, Governor Brown's son.

"Tob," she would say, taking his hand, "pray with me." [10]

She smiled when her great grandchild, Eugene Aldridge, three and a half, came with his parents, J. Bart and Marjory Aldridge, and gave her a "recital." The child said the Lord's Prayer and sang "America."

"Give him some Jell-O," Alice suggested. "Little Gene likes Jell-O." [11]

Alice suffered a series of "sinking spells." The second week in June Dr. Van Sandt decided to move her to the Wewoka hospital. Visitors who took her weak hand found it noticeably limp. Tob came every day to pray with her.

"I am ready, Tob," she said, quietly. "The Maker has forgiven my sins. I am prepared to go to Jesus."

When the family pressed him, Dr. Van Sandt sadly said her heart might last only a few more days. They began planning her funeral. Tob would preach. Alice wanted only a simple burial service at Wewoka's municipal Oakwood Cemetery, and without delay.

On Friday, June 21, 1935, Alice lay awake under a starchy white sheet and through her hospital window watched the break of dawn.

It was her last time to see the sun rise.

About 1:45 in the afternoon, one hand fluttered briefly. She gave a sigh, and closed her eyes forever.

GRASS WAS GREEN over Alice's grave when Mrs. C. Guy Cutlip rolled a clean sheet of paper into her husband's Underwood No. 5. Amo Cutlip didn't need to look at any notes. She had been asked to write a eulogy for Alice. Amo knew her friend's life story, first-hand. As well as the whole saga of Indian Territory. She had lived part of it, and had done extensive historical research. How many newspaper and magazine articles Amo had watched Guy hammer out on this typewriter, she could only guess—certainly more than a thousand.

This was a speech to be delivered in Wewoka at the Historical Building the night of November 16, 1935. Amo Cutlip got comfortable in her chair and began typing:

> I have been asked to pronounce a eulogy upon my good friend Alice Brown Davis, a distinguished woman of my town and county who has passed on to her reward. To do so is a simple task; it is but to recount the events of her life, and the task is accomplished.
>
> There is something tenderly appropriate about the serene death of the aged. Nothing is more touching than the death of the young, the strong, the vigorous. But when the duties of life have all been nobly done, when the sun of life touches the horizon and the purple twilight falls upon the past, the present and the future; when memory, with dim eyes, can scarcely spell the blurred and faded records of yesterday; then surrounded by kindred and friends, death comes like a strain of sweet music. The days have been long, the road weary, and the traveler gladly hastens to the waiting inn.
>
> So it was with Mrs. Davis.
>
> It has been said that a good deed is the best prayer; then, that be true Mrs. Davis's life was a continuous prayer for hers was a life of sacrifice for others.

The life of this good woman was set aside within itself for generous deeds, for good will, and for gladness. A life where shadows were forgotten, where the rains and storms of life were ignored and the sunshine and happiness welcomed. It was natural for her to forget the briars and thorns of life's winding path and there gather the fruits and the flowers. Hers was a life of giving to the hungry, a cheer to the poor and lonely and the unfortunate. Hers was a life wherein was felt and lived the fellowship and brotherhood of man. Hers was a life wherein was remembered the widows and children, the old, the unfortunate and the imprisoned.

She forgot herself in thinking lovingly of others and administering to the wants of the needy.

(Amo Cutlip then sketches Alice's biography and heritage, at some length.)

She was a great woman, a kind woman. She was a benefactor to all in need who came within the scope, the active scope, of her life.

She died after almost eighty-four years of active service to her fellow man. Her life was a benediction; and now she has passed on; passed from the trials of her day, passed from the accounts on lawsuits, the deeds and the shops and the papers, the banks and the debts and the affairs of her people. All of these have been cast aside, put away in death, together with her kindly deeds and loving actions. All have been locked up in death and the weary heart and brain have been given a voyage to perfect peace.

The telling is but a sham; the knowing the woman was the eulogy.[12]

THE END

Afterword

The march of time has not been generous in leaving monuments to the Browns and Davises. There were in 2005 progeny aplenty. Grandchildren of both Alice and Governor Brown, scattered across America, remained active in business, a few successful and wealthy in finance, oil, and real estate; and many accomplished great-grand-children, one of whom earned her Ph.D. writing a biography of the blood-thirsty Seminole warrior Wild Cat; as well as several hundred descendants of the Brown siblings who largely have faded into non-entity.

The Sasakwa mansion fell to rack and ruin and vanished. The Governor's only monument is the stone slab covering his grave in the rural family cemetery, which often is weed-riddled and nested with rattlesnakes. (Gone also is even the highway historical marker that alerted travelers approaching his home site.)

Alice, though far less important as a chief, fared better. Her bronze portrait bust was unveiled at the 1964 New York World's Fair and later installed at the National Hall of Fame for American Indians at Anadarko, Oklahoma. In an outdoor garden there, her sculpture stands beside 33 other noted Indians such as Osceola, Quanah Parker, Cochise, Will Rogers, Jim Thorpe, Sequoyah, Hiawatha, and Pocahontas. She was inducted into the Oklahoma Hall of Fame in 1930, and in 1950 the "Davis House" at the University of Oklahoma was named for her.

Only one significant residence remains, Jackson Brown's "junior" mansion in Wewoka, an abandoned, gaunt, decaying wreck, on the verge of caving in, but undergoing a chancy restoration. Wind, rain, rust, fire or rot have taken Dr. Brown's "honeymoon" cabin in Park Hill, the old Agency building on Greenhead Prairie where he

333

died, the Governor's stores, buildings and cotton gins in Sasakwa, as well as the Wewoka Trading Post, lost in 1925 to fire that also destroyed many Seminole tribal records.

Dr. Brown's grave is in a bramble patch in Pottawatomie County; his wife Lucy lies in an unmarked "lost" grave somewhere just north of Wewoka; Alice is buried in the Wewoka municipal cemetery, Oakwood. Other kinsmen are in widely scattered graves.

Although Longfellow asserted that great lives leave behind "footprints in the sands of time," that wise maxim may not hold for Governor Brown & Chief Alice. They left footprints in Oklahoma's red dirt perhaps too lightly to long survive the devilish prairie wind and the whirligig of time.

Notes

CHAPTER 1: Red Threads of Destiny

1. Dr. Brown readily shared with his children in later years details of significant episodes in his life, beginning with his arrival in New Orleans, Some early aspects, such as his Scottish heritage and interest in literature, he freely discussed. But he kept murky and vague the Charleston chapters. Three of his granddaughters became dauntless investigative genealogists, collecting and preserving several thousand documents dealing with family legends and memoirs. The most useful source of intimate knowledge of the lives of the Browns is the private collection of Dr. Brown's great-grandson, Gene Aldridge of Richardson, Texas. He and Martha, his wife and research colleague, opened the collection to the author, providing many specifics, such as Dr. Brown's recollection of his New Orleans arrival. Subsequent citations are identified as from the Aldridge Files

2. *Loc., cit.*

3. Waring Historical Library, Medical University of South Carolina

4. Aldridge Files

5. *Loc., cit.*

6. Standard clause in employment contract with Dr. Brown and other acting assistant surgeons in U.S. Army Medical Department. Records of Adjutant General's Office, Medical Officers and Physicians of All Classes, 1836-57.

7. Edwin C. McReynolds, *The Seminoles* (Norman, 1957) p 164

8. Aldridge Files

9. *Loc., cit.*

10. Dr. John Frippo Brown, "Therapeutics," unpublished ms., 1031 CH, Brown-Locke-Davis Family Papers

11. *Loc., cit.*

12. *Loc., cit.*

13. *Loc., cit.*

14. Data on Dr. Physick and Dr. Rush provided by Billie Broaddus, M.S.L.S.,director, Academic Information Technology and Libraries, University of Cincinnati Medical Center

15. Aldridge Files

16. Dr. C.S. Tripler, Assistant Surgeon, Fort Brooke, to Thomas Lawson, Surgeon General, U.S. Army, Washington City, June 1, 1837

17. McReynolds, *The Seminoles,* pp 200-203

18. *Loc., cit.*

19. Aldridge Files

20. McReynolds, *The Seminoles,* p 201-202

21. Aldridge Files

22. Aldridge files

23. Patrica R. Wickman, *Osceola's Legacy* (Tuscaloosa, 1991) p 100

24. *Ibid.,* pp 144-145

25. Aldridge Files

26. Dr. R.S. Satterlee, Surgeon, Fort Cass, to Gen. Thomas Lawson, Surgeon General, USA, Washington City, June 22, 1838

27. Aldridge Files

28. *Loc., cit.*

29. *Loc., cit.*

30. *Loc., cit.*

31. *Loc., cit.*

32. Elizabeth Ross, *Indian-Pioneer Papers 7596,* Sept. 17, 1937, Oklahoma Historical Society

33. Aldridge Files

34. How the chance encounter triggered by a blue norther catapulted him into marriage so struck Dr. Brown as inexplicable that in later years he would detail the episode more than once to his children, which resulted in the "frozen eyeballs" legend being handed down to present great grandchildren.

CHAPTER 2: Facing the Firing Squad

1. Aldridge Files

2. *Loc., cit.*

3. *Loc., cit.*

4. *Loc., cit.*

5. *Loc., cit.*

6. Grant Foreman, *The Five Civilized Tribes* (Norman, 1934), pp 224, 267

7. Mc Reynolds, *The Seminoles,* p 251

8. Carolyn Thomas Foreman, "Journal of a Tour in the Indian Territory," *Chronicles of Oklahoma* (Vol 10, No. 2), p 235

9. Aldridge Files

10. *Loc., cit.*

11. Mary C. Gillett, *The Army Medical Department 1818-1865* (Government Printing Office, 1987) pp 138-139

12. Aldridge Files

13. Foreman, *Five Civilized Tribes,* p 135

14. Brown to Lawson, August 26, 1850, National Archives, Office of Indian Affairs, Record Group 75

15. Gillett, *The Army Medical Department 1818-1865,* pp 128-129

16. Foreman, *Five Civilized Tribes,* p 138

17. Brown to Lawson, May 26, 1851, National Archives, Office of Indian Affairs, Record Group 75

18. Ibid., July 4, 1851

19. Ibid., April 2, 1852

20. Aldridge Files.

21. Page from Dr. Brown's journal now in Shirley Pettengill Library Collection, George Murrell House, Park Hill

22. Aldridge Files

23. Bess Howard, *A Frivolous History of Fort Gibson,* unpublished ms., n. d., Box 777 No. 8, Archives John Vaughn Library, Northeastern State University, Tahlequah, contains further entries by Dr. Hitchcock including, "Wednesday, Sept. 10. Little Johnny Ross who has been sick several days is in a very critical condition. Dr. Brown was sent for today. I am happy to resign the case in advance."

24. *Ibid.,* Jan. 6, 1857

25. Foreman, *Five Civilized Tribes,* p 270

26. *Ibid.,* p 271

27. McReynolds, *The Seminoles,* p 276

28. Aldridge Files

29. Aldridge Files

30. *Loc., cit.*

31. *Loc., cit.*

32. *Loc., cit.*

33. *Loc., cit.*

34. *Loc., cit.*

CHAPTER 3: 'The Wolf Has Come'

1. Dean Trickett, "The Civil War in the Indian Territory 1861 (continued)" *Chronicles of Oklahoma* (Vol 18 No. 3) pp 271-275; John Bartlett Meserve, "Chief Opothleyahola" *Chronicles of Oklahoma* (Vol 9 No. 4), p 449

2. Aldridge Files

3. McReynolds, *The Seminoles,* pp 302-303

4. Trickett, "The Civil War in the Indian Territory 1861 (continued)," p 151; William H. Graves, "Indian Soldiers for The Gray Army," *Chronicles of Oklahoma,* (Vol. 69, No. 2), p 143 (* Historians have spelled the chief's name several ways.)

5. "Chief Opothleyahola" p 444

6. *Ibid.,* p 451

7. McReynolds, *The Seminoles,* pp 293-294

8. *Ibid.,* 297. In some instances McReynolds refers to Chupco as "Long John," a misnomer as the Seminole word "capke" means "long." This sobriquet may have arisen from the fact that John Chupco, identified as the "greatest Seminole tall walker," is said to have on foot gone from Wewoka to Fort Gibson between sunup and sundown, at least 80 miles.

9. *Ibid.,* p 299

10. Trickett, "The Civil War in the Indian Territory 1861 (continued)," pp 272-273

11. *Ibid.,* p 275

12. *Ibid.,* p 276

13. *Ibid.,* p 277

14. McReynolds, *The Seminoles,* p 302

15. *Ibid.,* pp 304-305

16. *Ibid.,* pp 307-312

17. Ohland Morton, "Confederate Relations With The Five Civilized Tribes," *Chronicles of Oklahoma,* (Vol. 31, No. 2), p 310

18. Brown to Major Sanford B. Hunt, U.S.A., surgeon in charge, Fort Smith, Sept. 30, 1864, National Archives, Office of Indian Affairs, Record Group 75

19. Order signed by Colonel Van E. Young, provost marshal general, and George S. Kimble, surgeon U.S.A., medical director, Department of Mississippi at Vicksburg, May 15, 1865, National Archives, Office of Indian Affairs, Record Group 75

20. Brown to James R. Smith, surgeon U.S.A., medical director, Department of Arkansas, June 30, 1865, National Archives, Office of Indian Affairs, Record Group 75

21. Aldridge Files

22. Grant Foreman, *A History of Oklahoma,* (Norman, 1942) p 113

23. Angie Debo, *The Road to Disappearance* (Norman: University of Oklahoma Press, 1941), pp 279-282

24. Aldridge Files

25. *Loc., cit.*

26. *Loc., cit.*

27. Elijah Sells to D. N. Cooley, October 16, 1865, *Report of the Commissioner of Indian Affairs for 1865,* pp 436-437

28. Michael Welsh, "The Missionary Spirit," *Chronicles of Oklahoma* (Vol.61, No. 1), p 31

29. Aldridge Files

30. John Frippo Brown, M.D., "Therapeutics," unpublished ms., Brown-Locke-Davis Family Papers. (Copy of ms. has been donated to Oklahoma Historical Society.)

31. *Loc., cit.*

32. *Loc., cit.*

33. Aldridge Files

34. *Loc., cit.*

35. *Loc., cit.*

36. John Franklin Brown also heard this story from his father and related it to the editor of the *South McAlester Capital,* which newspaper published it on December 1, 1904

37. *Loc., cit.*

CHAPTER 4: Hark! The Dark Angel

1. McReynolds, *The Seminoles,* p 316; Harry Henslick, "The Seminole Treaty of 1866," *Chronicles of Oklahoma (*Vol 48, No. 3) p 280

2. *Loc., cit;* Aldridge Files

3. *Loc., cit.*

4. Aldridge Files

5. McReynoles, *The Seminoles,* pp 316-317

6. Aldridge Files

7. *Report of the Commissioner of Indian Affairs for 1866*

8. Aldridge Files

9. *Loc., cit.*

10. *Loc., cit.*

11. Stan Hoig, "Jesse Chisholm: Peace-maker, Trader, Forgotten Frontiersman," *Chronicles of Oklahoma,* (Vol.66, No.4) p 361

12. Aldridge Files

13. Hoig, "Jesse Chisholm," pp 368-369

14. Aldridge Files

15. *Loc., cit.*

16. *Loc., cit.*

17. *Loc., cit.*

18. *Loc., cit.*

19. *Loc., cit.*

20. *Loc., cit.*

21. *Loc., cit.*

22. In 1990, Eugene and Martha Aldridge made a field trip searching for Dr. Brown's grave. He writes: "After much research and effort, we did find it. Took photographs and video. It is on private property but no one was home so we went in anyway. The lady there was most upset that we not only found and photographed it, but made a map for others to find it." The headstone was almost obscured in a tangle of brush.

23. Aldridge Files

CHAPTER 5: Falling in Love in Sasakwa

1. Hoig, "Jesse Chisholm," p 370

2. Aldridge Files

3. C. Guy Cutlip (1881-1938) manuscripts, n.d., Western History Collection

4. *Loc., cit.*

5. *Loc., cit.*

6. Aldridge Files

7. *Loc., cit.*

8. Grant Foreman, *A History of Oklahoma,* pp 60-61

9. *Ibid.,* p 62

10. Aldridge Files

11. *Loc., cit.*

12. *Loc., cit.*

13. *Loc., cit.*

14. *Loc., cit.*

15. *Cherokee Advocate,* March 2, 1872

16. *Loc., cit.*

17. *Loc., cit.*

18. Aldridge Files

19. Debo, *The Rise and Fall of the Choctaw Republic,* p 193, quoting Indian Office Files, Choctaw, 1873, p 112

20. Aldridge Files

21. *Loc., cit.*

22. *Loc., cit.*

23. *Loc., cit.* For an extensive study of tribal medical lore and customs see James H. Howard in Collaboration with Willie Lena, *Oklahoma Seminoles: Medicines, Magic, and Religion* (Norman, 1984).

24. Aldridge Files

25. *Loc., cit.*

CHAPTER 6: 'She's a Witch! Kill Her!'

1. Interviews given by Antoinette C. Snow Constant at age 81, *Tulsa World,* April 8, 1923 and *The Daily Oklahoman,* June 17, 1923; For further details of the episode and her life among the Seminoles see *Wewoka Capital-Democrat,* November 20, 1924; Michael Welsh, "The Missionary Spirit," *Chronicles of Oklahoma,* (Vol. 61, No. 1), pp 40-43; Antoinette S. Constant, "A Sketch of Mr. Constant's Work Among the Seminoles," Oklahoma Indian Archives, Section X: Missions and Missionaries

2. *Tulsa World,* April 8, 1923

3. *Loc., cit.*

4. *Loc., cit.*

5. *Loc., cit.*

6. *Loc., cit.*

7. *Loc., cit.*

8. *Loc., cit.*

9. Margaret Berry Blair with R. Palmer Howard M. D., *Scalpel in a Saddlebag* (Oklahoma City, 1979), pp 73-74

10. Memoir of Pearl Marie Simpson, Brown-Davis Family Miscellany, collection of uncatalogued documents and photos, SEMINOLE NATION MUSEUM

11. Blair, *Scalpel in a Saddlebag,* p 73

12. Compilation of Seminole Laws, as furnished by the U.S. Indian Inspector for Indian Territory, and translated by G. T. Grayson, July 1904, certified by Winfred M. Clark at Muskogee, August 13, 1937, Oklahoma Historical Society, Press Book No. 1 Department, Decisions and Instructions, pp 379-500

13. Howard, *Oklahoma Seminoles*, p 210

14. C. Guy Cutlip in *The Oklahoman,* October 9, 1921

15. *Loc., cit.*

16. *Loc., cit.*

17. Howard, *Oklahoma Seminoles,* pp 21-23

18. C. Guy Cutlip in *The Oklahoman,* October 9, 1921

19. *Loc., cit.*

CHAPTER 7: Chupco to Jumper to Brown

1. Carolyn Thomas Foreman, "Billy Bowlegs," *Chronicles of Oklahoma* (Vol 33, No. 4) p 529, describes burying horse with Billy Bowlegs in Florida

2. McReynolds, *The Seminoles,* p 327

3. Foreman, *A History of Oklahoma,* p 177

4. Joseph F. Murphy, *Tenacious Monks* (Shawnee, 1974), p 133

5. J. Stanley Clark, *Open Wider, Please—The Story of Dentistry in Oklahoma* (Norman, 1955) p 44

6. *Ibid.,* p 24

7. Blair, *Scalpel in a Saddlebag,* p 73

8. Aldridge Files

9. *Loc., cit.*

10. *Loc., cit.*

11. *Loc., cit.*

12. Courtland L. Long memoir, n. d., Brown-Davis Family Miscellany

13. *Loc., cit.*

CHAPTER 8: Saying 'No' to Senator Dawes

1. Loren N. Brown, "The Dawes Commission," *Chronicles of Oklahoma* (Nol. 9, No. 1) pp 72-76

2. *Purcell (I.T.) Register,* November 16, 1893, reporting the incident in full; Aldridge Files

3. *Loc., cit.*

4. Dee Brown, *Bury My Heart at Wounded Knee,* (New York, 1970) p 170. Attributed to General Phil Sheridan and also General Nelson Miles, the discriminatory quote apparently had already permeated American culture by 1886 when Theodore Roosevelt in a New York speech said: "I don't go so far as to think that the only good Indians are dead Indians, but I believe nine out of ten are, and I shouldn't like to inquire too closely into the case of the tenth."

5. Aldridge Files

6. Brown, "The Dawes Commission," p 77

7. *Ibid.,* p 78

8. *Loc., cit.*

9. *Loc., cit.*

10. *Ibid.,* p 75, quoting first annual report of Commission to Five Civilized Tribes—Nov. 1894, p 18

11. Full text of letter in *Muskogee Phoenix,* May 31, 1894

12. Robert E. Trevathan, "School Days at Emahaka," *Chronicles of Oklahoma* (Vol. 38, No.3) p 267

13. *Muskogee Phoenix,* July 26, 1894

14. *Loc., cit.*

15. *Loc., cit.*

16. C. Guy Cutlip papers, n.d. article on Seminoles, Box 2, File 18, Western History Collection

17. Juliet L. Gallonska, "The Role of Women in the Federal Court for the Western District of Arkansas," National Park Service, Fort Smith National Historic Site

18. *Loc. cit.;* Most famous woman in Judge Parker's court was Belle Starr, the so-called "Bandit Queen," who was found guilty of horse theft in 1883 and sentenced to one year in Detroit House of Corrections.

19. *Indian Chieftain,* November 15, 1894

20. Aldridge Files

CHAPTER 9: Magic in a Child's Heart

1. Memoir of Eleanor Maye Davis Locke, January 8, 1958, Brown-Locke-Davis Family Papers

2. *Loc., cit.*

3. *Loc., cit.*

4. *Loc., cit.*

5. *Loc., cit.*

6. Memoir of Laura Myrtle Davis Aldridge, n. d., Brown-Locke-Davis Family Papers

7. Aldridge Files

8. *Loc., cit.*

9. Eleanor Maye Davis Locke memoir, Brown-Locke-Davis Family Papers

10. Aldridge Files

11. Glenn Shirley, *West of Hell's Fringe,* (Norman, 1978), p 389

12. *Ibid.,* pp 422-427

13. Aldridge Files

14. Eleanor Maye Davis Locke memoir, Brown-Locke-Davis Family Papers

15. Aldridge Files

16. *Loc., cit.*

17. Eleanor Maye Davis Locke memoir, Brown-Locke-Davis Family Papers

18. Aldridge Files

19. *Loc., cit.*

20. *Loc., cit.*

21. *Loc., cit.*

22. *Loc., cit.*

23. *Loc., cit.*

24. *Loc., cit.*

25. *Loc., cit.*

26. Marriage of George R. Davis and Victoria Banash shown in Pottawatomie County Marriage Record Book 2B, page 308, on December 27, 1897, performed in Tecumseh by F.R. Clasah, justice of the peace. Edward Earl Davis is listed in 1900 Census of Seminole Nation, Indian Territory as son of George R. and Victoria and as four years old.

CHAPTER 10: Whiskey and Human Torches

1. John W. Morris, *Ghost Towns of Oklahoma,* (Norman, 1977), p lll

2. Blake Gumprecht, "A Saloon on Every Corner: Whiskey Towns of Oklahoma Territory, 1889-1907," *Chronicles of Oklahoma* (Vol. 74, No. 2) pp 155-157

3. *Loc., cit.*

4. *Loc., cit.*

5. Morris, *Ghost Towns of Oklahoma,* p 111

6. Aldridge Files

7. Unidentified newspaper clipping, Brown-Davis Family Miscellany

8. Unidentified Wewoka newspaper clipping, circa 1949, Brown-Davis Family Miscellany

9. *Loc., cit.*

10. *Loc., cit.*

11. Brown, "The Dawes Commission," p 87

12. *Ibid.*, p 94, quoting Report of Dawes Commission of 1896, p 98

13. Ibid., p 81, quoting Report of Drew M. Wilson—Union Agency (1895), page 180

14. McReynolds, *The Seminoles,* p 343

15. Aldridge Files

16. Brown, "The Dawes Commission," p 101 [McReynolds, p 343, incorrectly lists the date as December 16.]

17. McReynolds, *The Seminoles,* p 343, quoting Commissioner of Indian Affairs, *Annual Report* (1898), 448-51; (1899), 197; (1900), 14, 28, 56, 85-86; (1902). 164; (1904), 231; (1905), Part I, 516

18. Brown, "The Dawes Commission," p 101, quoting 55th Congr. 2nd Sess.—Senate Doc. Vol 4, No. 105, p 4

19. *Tulsa World,* November 12, 2001, detailed history of Dawes Commission.

20. McReynolds, *The Seminoles,* p 347

21. Daniel F. Littlefield, Jr., *Seminole Burning: A Story of Racial Vengeance* (Jackson, 1996), p 33. In this work, Dr. Littlefield, a distinguished and prolific writer of Indian Territory history, has corrected numerous errors that seriously flawed previous published accounts of this grotesque tragedy. Dr. Littlefield told the author his accuracy was due to fortunate discovery of a trove of unexplored court documents.

22. *Loc., cit.*

23. *Loc., cit.*

24. *Ibid.,* p 34

25. *Ibid.,* p 35

26. *Ibid.,* p 38

27. *Ibid.,* p 49

28. *Ibid.,* p 50

29. *Ibid.,* pp 52-53

30. *Ibid.,* p 54

31. *Ibid.,* p 60

32. *Ibid.,* p 80

33. *Ibid.,* p 83

34. *Ibid.,* p 157

35. *Mangum Star,* May 17, 1906

36. McReynolds, *The Seminoles,* p 341

37. *Ibid.,* p 342

38. *Ibid.,* p 340

39. *Claremore Progress,* March 5, 1898

40. Margaret Berry Blair with R. Palmer Howard, MD, *Scalpel in a Saddlebag: The Story of a Physician in Indian Territory: Virgil Berry, MD* (Western Heritage Books, Inc., Oklahoma City, 1979), p 72

41. *Loc., cit.*

42. *South McAlester Capital,* August 11, 1895

43. *Loc., cit.*

CHAPTER 11: Stringing Up a Horse Thief

1. *Weleetka American,* January 6, 1907

2. *Eufaula Indian Journal,* May 5, 1887

3. *Holdenville Tribune,* February 2, 1905

4. McReynolds, *The Seminoles,* p 347

5. *Ibid.,* p 349

6. *Ibid.,* p 351

7. *Ibid., p 352*

8. *Ibid.,* pp 348-349, quoting Oklahoma Indian Archives, Seminole Miscellaneous Documents (39518-H, "Opinion of Frank L. Campbell," March 19, 1904

9. *Ibid.,* p 350

10. The booklet, with a bison on the cover, in Brown-Davis Family Miscellany

11. *Loc., cit.*

12. Aldridge Files

13. *Loc., cit.*

14. Junius B. Moore, "The Survey of Indian Territory 1894-1907," *Chronicles of Oklahoma* (Vol.28), pp 446-448

15. *Loc.,* cit.

16. Aldridge Files

17. Pearl Davis Dovell memoir, dated 1970, Oklahoma Historical Society; Brown-Davis Family Miscellany

18. Aldridge Files

19. *Loc., cit.*

20. Kitt to Alice, December 7, 1899, Brown-Davis Family Miscellany

21. Aldridge Files

22. *Loc., cit.*

23. *Loc., cit.*

24. *Loc., cit.*

25. *Holdenville (I.T.) Times,* June 10, 1902

26. Aldridge Files

27. Alice diaries, Brown-Locke-Davis Family Papers

28. C.C. Patten, former secretary to Governor Brown, writing in *The Oklahoman,* January 16, 1921

29. *Loc., cit.*

30. *Loc., cit.*

31. Brown-Davis Family Miscellany

32. Interview with A. M. Seran, May 18, 1937, Indian-Pioneer Papers, No. 5987, Oklahoma Historical Society

33. *Holdenville Times,* June 3, 1904, quoting *St. Louis Republic*
34. Brown-Davis Family Miscellany, n. d.

CHAPTER 12: Feuding Over Emahaka

1. Milligan, *The Choctaw of Oklahoma,* (Durant, The Choctaw Nation) p 174

2. Foreman, *A History of Oklahoma,* p 312.

3. *Indian Citizen,* Atoka, I. T., September 26, 1907

4. *The Seminole Capital,* Wewoka, I. T., March 7, 1907, quoting *Washington Herald*

5. Aldridge Files

6. McReynolds, *The Seminoles,* pp 355-356

7. *Ibid.,* 356

8. *Ibid., 357*

9. *Loc., cit.*

10. *Purcell Register,* October 4, 1906

11. *Seminole Capital,* April 5, 1906, quoting *Indian Citizen*

12. *Indian Citizen,* Atoka., I. T., August 22, 1907, reporting the trip under a Muskogee dateline

13. McReynolds, *The Seminoles,* p 357

14. Aldridge Files

15. McReynolds, *The Seminoles,* p 358, quoting Seminole Miscellaneous Documents, Oklahoma State Archives, Document 39543

16. Aldridge Files

17. Alice diaries, Brown-Locke-Davis Family Papers

18. Aldridge Files

19. Mrs. Kidd-Key to Alice, July 3, 1911 and October 16, 1911

20. Alice diary, Jan 31, 1925: "made on eggs 75c," Brown-Davis Family Miscellany

21. Sacred Heart College to Alice, March 1, 1913

22. Alice diaries, Brown-Locke-Davis Family Papers

CHAPTER 13: Heartbreak in Love and War

1. Alice to Maude, October 20, 1909.

2. *Loc., cit.*

3. *Loc., cit.* The accuracy of Alice's letter is challenged by one Indian scholar, who says (1) Seminoles in Florida usually slept on platforms about three feet high, not on the ground; (2) It is most unlikely she could have found beads 200 years old; (3) Florida Seminole women rarely wore buckskin, and Alice may have acquired a man's buckskin shirt.

4. Joe Bowers to Alice, November 3, 1909

5. Joe Bowers to Alice, October 28, 1910

6. Stanton to Alice, November 29, 1909

7. Julia to Alice, May 10, 1910

8. Julia to Alice, May 25, 1910

9. Aldridge Files

10. Inez Womack to Alice, Feb. 3, 1913

11. Maye to Alice, May 19, 1914

12. Jack to Alice, December 1, 1915

13. Records in District Court Clerk's office at Wewoka show Vernon L. Kiker was indicted for embezzlement on February 12, 1916, pleaded guilty on March 21, 1917, and was sentenced to three years in the Oklahoma penitentiary on May 21, 1917

14. Aldridge Files

15. *Wewoka Capital-Democrat,* January 11, 1917

16. John to Alice, February 13, 1917

17. Jack to Alice, September 12, 1917

18. Nigel Sellars, "With Folded Arms? or With Squirrel Guns?: The IWW and The Green Corn Rebellion," *Chronicles of Oklahoma,* (Vol.77, No. 2), p 163

19. *Loc., cit.*

20. *The Oklahoman,* August 4, 1917

21. *Loc., cit.*

22. *Loc., cit.*

23. Sellars, "With Folded Arms? or With Squirrel Guns?" pp 158-159

24. *Loc., cit.*

25. *Loc., cit.*

26. *Wewoka Capital-Democrat,* August 9, 1917; Aldridge Files

27. Aldridge Files

28. *The Oklahoman,* August 5, 1917

29. *Loc., cit.*

30. John to Alice, May 6, 1918

31. Gertie Dobson to Alice, n. d., circa 1918

32. *Aldridge Files*

CHAPTER 14: The Indian Rope of Love

1. Aldridge Files

2. Maye to Alice, November 11, 1918, Brown-Davis Family Miscellany

3. Ione to Alice, November 17, 1918, *Ibid.*

4. Alice Diaries, Brown-Locke-Davis Family Papers, Garrard Ardeneum

5. Kitt to Alice, March 17, 1919, Brown-Davis Family Miscellany

6. Aldridge Files

7. *Loc., cit.*

8. *Loc., cit.*

9. *Wewoka Capital-Democrat,* October 9, 1919

10. Aldridge Files

11. *Loc., cit.*

12. Memoir by Rev. Louis C. (Tob) Brown, n. d., Brown-Davis Family Miscellany

13. *Loc., cit.*

14. *Loc., cit.*

15. Aldridge Files

16. *Loc., cit.*

17. Alice to Maude, January 3, 1920, Brown-Davis Family Miscellany

18. Bess to Alice, January 14, 1920, *Ibid.*

19. Maude to Alice, January 15, 1920, *Ibid.*

20. Jack to Alice, February 13, 1920, *Ibid.*

21. Joe Bowers to Alice, n. d., *Ibid.*

22. Mae Good to Alice, July 14, 1920, *Ibid.*

23. Aldridge Files

24. On August 26, 1920, from Paden, Julia Davis returns to Alice $6 check rejected by Farmers National Bank, Wewoka for "insufficient funds." Brown-Davis Family Miscellany

25. John to Alice, July 12, 1920, *Ibid.*

26. Kitt to Alice, February 17, 1921, *Ibid.*

27. Mae to Alice, March 17, 1921, *Ibid.*

28. Aldridge Files

29. *Loc., cit.*

30. *Loc., cit.*

31. *Loc., cit.*

CHAPTER 15: An Indian 'First' in the West

1. *The Oklahoman,* August 20, 1922

2. *The Oklahoman,* July 2, 1922

3. Grant Foreman, "The Hon. Alice M. Robertson," *Chronicles of Oklahoma,* (Vol. 10 No. 1), pp 13-17

4. *The Oklahoman,* August 20, 1922

5. Aldridge Files

6. Original typescript, n.d., *Brown-Locke-Davis Family Papers,* file 648 CH, in the Manuscript Collection of Garrard Ardeneum at McAlester, Oklahoma.

7. *Loc., cit.*

8. *Loc., cit.*

9. *The Oklahoman,* Sunday, Aug. 20, 1922, pp 49-50

10. Aldridge Files

11. *Brown-Locke-Davis Family Papers*

12. *Muskogee Daily Phoenix,* Aug. 17, 1922

13. *Tulsa World,* March 7, 1943

14. *Brown-Locke-Davis Family Papers.*

15. *Ibid.;* Aldridge Files

16. Aldridge Files

17. *Muskogee Phoenix,* June 23, 1923

18. *Harlow's Weekly,* June 30, 1923

19. Aldridge Files

20. *Loc., cit.*

21. *Loc., cit.*

22. Glen Cornelius to author, April 16, 2004

23. The attempts to get George Jones to sign these documents were detailed in testimony by Jones and Alice before a Senate subcommittee in Wewoka on November 12, 1930. See Survey of Conditions of The Indians in the United States: Hearings Before a Subcommittee of the Committee on Indian Affairs—United States Senate 72 Congress, Second Session, printed 1931. [Full hearing testimony appears in Chapter Seventeen.]

24. *Tulsa World,* March 7, 1943

CHAPTER 16: Oil Wells, Death, and Romance

1. Aldridge Files

2. Ira Rinehart in the *Tulsa World,* December 1, 1923, who writes that Smith eventually sold his well to Dixie Oil, a subsidiary of Standard Oil of Indiana, for $3,000,000.

3. Jack to Alice, March 28, 1922, Brown-Davis Miscellany

4. Louise Welsh, Willa Mae Townes, John W. Morris, *A History of the Greater Seminole Oil Field* (Oklahoma Heritage Association, 1981) p 7

5. *Ibid.,* p 19

6. *Ibid., p 25*

7. *Ibid., p 100*

8. Alice Diaries, January 27, 1929, Brown-Locke-Davis Family Papers

9. Maye to Alice, November 22, 1922, Brown-Davis Family Miscellany

10. Alice diary, Oct. 27, 1923, Brown-Locke-Davis Family Papers

11. Kitt to Alice, November 18, 1925, Brown-Davis Family Miscellany

12. Alice diary, December 30, 1923, Brown.Locke-Davis Family Papers

13. Maye to Alice, May 24, 1924, *Ibid.*

14. Maye to Alice, February 10, 1922, Brown-Davis Miscellany

15. *Loc., cit.*

16. Muriel H. Wright, "William Shaffer Key: Oklahoma Patriot," *Chronicles of Oklahoma,* (Vol. 37, No. 2), p 142

17. Aldridge Files

18. *Loc., cit.*

19. Glover to Alice, February 23, 1923, Brown-Davis Family Miscellany

20. Glover to Alice, October 9, 1923, Brown-Davis Family Miscellany

21. Glover to Alice, Feb. 3, 1928, Brown-Davis Family Miscellany

22. Aldridge Files

23. Aldridge Files

24. Doris to Alice, April 7, 1930, Brown-Davis Family Miscellany

25. Doris to Alice, November 22, 1931, Brown-Davis Family Miscellany

26. Doris to Alice, February 14, 1932, Brown-Davis Family Miscellany

CHAPTER 17: Pierce Arrows and *Osofkey*

1. The dialog between senators, Alice and other witnesses included in this chapter is reproduced verbatim from the official transcript of the hearing, published in 1931 as "Survey of Conditions of The Indians in the United States: Hearings before a Subcommittee of the Committee on Indian Affairs—United States Senate 72 Congress, Second Session." (Government Printing Office. 1931)"

2. Aldridge Files

3. *Loc., cit.*

4. *Loc., cit.*

CHAPTER 18: Into The Purple Twilight

1. Aldridge Files

2. *Wewoka Times-Democrat,* March 20, 1932

3. Sequence of diary entries, Alice diaries, Brown-Locke-Davis Family Papers

4. *Wewoka Times-Democrat,* March 20, 1932

5. Aldridge Files

6. John to Alice, January 6, 1933, Brown-Davis Family Miscellany

7. Aldridge Files

8. Kitt to Alice, November 29, 1932, Brown-Davis Family Miscellany

9. *Harlow's Weekly,* July 2, 1932, Cora Miley column, "The Great and the Near Great"

10. Memoir by Rev. Louis C. (Tob) Brown, n.d., Brown-Davis Family Miscellany

11. Aldridge Files

12. Copy of Mrs. Cutlip's eulogy is included in Brown-Davis Family Miscellany

Bibliography

BOOKS

Blair, Margaret Berry with R. Palmer Howard, M. D., Scalpel in a Saddlebag: The Story of a Physician in the Indian Territory: Virgil Berry MD (Oklahoma City 1979)

Brown, Dee, Bury My Heart at Wounded Knee (New York 1970)

Clark, J. Stanley, Open Wider, Please—The Story of Dentistry in Oklahoma (Norman 1955)

Cummings, Joe, Northern Mexico Handbook (Chico, CA 1994)

Dale, Edward Everett, Cow Country (Norman 1942)

Debo, Angie, The Road to Disappearance (Norman 1941)

———, The Rise and Fall of the Choctaw Republic (Norman 1934)

———, And Still The Waters Run (Princeton 1940)

Foreman, Grant, The Five Civilized Tribes (Norman 1934)

———, Advancing the Frontier (Norman 1933)

———, Indians and Pioneers (New Haven 1930)

———, A History of Oklahoma (Norman 1942)

———, Indian Removal (Norman 1932)

Gillett, Mary C., The Army Medical Department 1818-1865 (Government Printing Office 1987)

Howard, James H., with Willie Lena, Oklahoma Seminoles: Medicines, Magic, and Religion (Norman 1984)

Littlefield, Daniel F., Jr., Seminole Burning: A Story of Racial Vengeance in Oklahoma (Jackson 1996)

Marcy, Capt. R. B., Thirty Years of Army Life of the Border (New York 1866)

Miller, Susan Allison, Coacoochee's Bones: A Seminole Saga (Lawrence, Kansas 2003)

Milligan, James C., The Choctaw of Oklahoma (Durant 2003)

Morris, John W., Ghost Towns of Oklahoma (Norman 1977)

————,Charles R. Goins, and Edwin C. McReynolds, Historical Atlas of Oklahoma (Norman 1976)

Murphy, Joseph F.,Tenacious Monks (Shawnee 1974)

Shirley, Glenn, West of Hell's Fringe (Norman 1978)

Thoburn, Joseph B. and Muriel H. Wright, Oklahoma: A History of the State and Its People (New York 1929)

Welsh, Louise, Willa Mae Towns, John W. Morris, A History of the Greater Seminole Oil Field (Oklahoma Heritage Association 1981)

Wickman, Patricia R., Osceola's Legacy (Tuscaloosa 1991)

Wright, Muriel H., A Guide to the Indian Tribes of Oklahoma (Norman 1951)

NEWSPAPERS AND JOURNALS

Claremore Progress

Eufaula Indian Journal

Holdenville Tribune

Holdenville Times

Indian Chieftain

Mangum Star

The Oklahoman

Purcell (I.T.) Register

Muskogee Daily Phoenix

Seminole Producer

Seminole Capital, Wewoka

South McAlester Capital

Tulsa World

Cherokee Advocate

Weleetka American

Wewoka Capital-Democrat

Wewoka Times-Democrat

Harlow's Weekly

⌐ne Dawes Commission," Vol, 9, No. 1

⌐arolyn Thomas, "A Journal of a Tour in the Indian Territory," Vol. ⌐o. 2

————, "Billy Bowlegs," Vol. 33, No. 4

Graves, William H., "Indian Soldiers in the Gray Army," Vol. 69, No. 2

Gumprecht, Blake, "A Saloon on Every Corner: Whiskey Towns of Oklahoma Territory, 1889-1907," Vol. 74, No.2

Foreman, Grant, "The Hon. Alice Robertson," Vol. 10, No. 1

Henslick, Harry, "The Seminole Treaty of 1866," Vol. 48, No. 2

Hoig, Stan, "Jesse Chisholm" Peace-maker, Trader, Forgotten Frontiersman," Vol. 66, No. 4

Johnson, Walter A., "Brief History of the Missouri-Kansas-Texas Railroad Lines," Vol. 23, Autuumn

Maxwell, Amos, "The Sequoyah Convention," Vol. 28, Sum mer

Meserve, John Bartlett, "Chief Opothleyahola," Vol. 9, No. 4

Moore, Junius B., "The Survey of Indian Territory 1894-1907," Vol. 28

Morton, Ohland, "Confederate Relations With the Five Civilized Tribes," Vol. 31, No. 2

Sellars, Nigel, "With Folded Arms? Or Squirrel Guns?: The IWW and the Green Corn Rebellion," Vol. 77, No. 2

Trevathan, Robert E., "School Days at Emahaka," Vol. 38, No. 3

Trickett, Dean, "The Civil War in Indian Territory 1861 (Continued)," Vol. 18, No. 3

Welsh, Michael, "The Missionary Spirit," Vol. 61, No. 1

Wright, Muriel H., "William Shaffer Key: Oklahoma Patriot," Vol. 37, No. 2

OTHER SOURCES

Aldridge, Laura Myrtle Davis, memoir, Brown-Locke-Davis Family Papers

Broaddus, Billie, M.S.L.S.,University of Cincinnati Medical Center

Brown, John Frippo, M.D., "Therapeutics," unpublished ms, Brown-Locke-Davis Family Papers and Oklahoma Historical Society

Brown, Rev. Louis C. (Tob), memoir, Briown-Davis Family Miscellan

District Court Records, Wewoka

Dovell, Pearl Davis, memoir, Oklahoma Historical Society

Gallonska, Juliet L., "The Role of Women in the Federal Court for the Western District of Arkansas," National Park Service, Fort Smith National Historic Site

Howard, Bess, A Frivolous History of Fort Gibson, unpublished ms, John Vaughn Library, Northeastern State University, Tahlequah

Indian-Pioneer Papers, Oklahoma Historical Society

Locke, Eleanor Maye Davis, memoir, Brown-Locke-Davis Family Papers

Long, Courtland L., memoir, SEMINOLE NATION MUSEUM

Oklahoma Indian Archives

Pottawatomie County Marriage Record

Reports of the Commissioner of Indian Affairs

Report of Drew M. Wilson—Union Agency, 1895

Reports of Commission to the Five Civilized Tribes

Seminoles Laws, compilation by U.S. Inspector for Indian Territory, Oklahoma Historical Society, Press Book No. 1

Simpson, Pearl Marie, memoir, SEMINOLE NATION MUSEUM

Shirley Pettengill Library Collection, George Murrell House, Park Hill

Survey of Conditions of the Indians in the United States; Hearings Before a Subcommittee of the Committee on Indian Affairs—United States Senate, 72 Congress, second session (Government Printing Office 1931)

Waring Historical Library, Medical University of South Carolina

U.S. Army Medical Department, Records of Adjutant General's office

National Archives and Records Administration, Record Group 75